W9-CFO-044

BARBRA STREISAND

Barbra Streisand

Redefining Beauty, Femininity, and Power

NEAL GABLER

Yale
UNIVERSITY
PRESS
New Haven and London

Yale University Press books may be purchased in quantity for educational, business, or promotional use. For information, please e-mail sales.press@yale.edu (US office) or sales@yaleup.co.uk (UK office).

Set in Janson type by Integrated Publishing Solutions, Grand Rapids, Michigan.
Printed in the United States of America.

frontispiece: Photo by Lawrence Schiller. © Polaris Communications, Inc.,
All Rights Reserved.

Library of Congress Control Number: 2015957531
ISBN 978-0-300-21091-0

A catalogue record for this book is available from the British Library.

This paper meets the requirements of ANSI/NISO Z39.48–1992
(Permanence of Paper).

10 9 8 7 6 5 4 3 2 1

For my beloved daughters, Laurel and Tänne,
and my beloved son-in-law, Braden,
And for all those who have ever been told they could
not succeed

You never quit, do you?
—Hubbell Gardner, *The Way We Were*

CONTENTS

An Introduction: Shaynkeit

It is one of the seminal moments in American film and, quite possibly, American culture generally. The camera dollies in toward a woman in a leopard-skin coat and matching hat, her back to the camera, then veers slightly to the left to reveal an ornate, gold-framed, full-length mirror in which we see the woman's image, though her face is obscured by the coat's collar. She pulls down the collar just enough to reveal that inimitable Streisand visage, arches her brows, and assesses herself—coolly. Then she purrs, "Hello, gorgeous." There is a cut to a close-up, and Streisand emits the tiniest, almost inaudible laugh/snort, as if it were a joke, though she acts as if the joke is on us. It is. But then her expression turns dark, wistful, as if to tell us how far she has had to come to utter those words.

This is how Barbra Streisand introduced herself to the film audience in *Funny Girl* in 1968, and what an introduction it was! First, there is her look—a kind of exoticism, half Afghan hound,

I

half Jewess. And then there is the manner—the secretiveness, the cool, diva elegance only slightly betrayed by those arched brows, the self-scrutiny that gives way to self-consciousness that gives way to self-confidence that gives way to self-doubt. And then there is the voice—that unmistakable Brooklyn accent, the "gorgeous" elongated to "gaaaaw-jus," an accent that just didn't comport with the regal bearing, the expensive coat, the sense of control. And then there is that laugh, as if to say . . . well, it said a lot. And then that sadness, which said even more.

One of the things it said is that Streisand wasn't making fun of herself or being ironic—she *was* gorgeous—even though no one who looked like Streisand or had Streisand's obvious ethnicity, that double whammy of Judaism and Brooklyn, or had that strange self-regard Streisand had, had ever become an American movie star, certainly not a dramatic star, and Streisand would become the biggest. When Streisand addressed her image in that mirror, she was asserting her beauty and validating a new kind of glamour, a new kind of star, a new kind of power. "Hello, gorgeous" was Streisand's way of ushering in a new era, and just about everybody seemed to recognize it. Although there had never been anyone on movie screens like Streisand, there were millions of Streisands, tens of millions, watching those screens, as Streisand herself had before she became a star. Now they had someone of their own—someone whom they didn't have to dream of becoming, which was the general vicarious transaction for movie audiences, but someone they felt they already *were*. Barbra Streisand had that effect. She wasn't Hollywood. She was Brooklyn. She wasn't them. She was us.

It may seem peculiar to freight an entertainer with that much psychological and cultural weight, but Streisand isn't just an entertainer. She has long been a cultural force—the kind of personality who inspires effusions, poems (Wayne Koestenbaum's "Streisand Sings Stravinsky"), stage plays (*Buyer and*

Cellar by Jonathan Tolins), art (*Four Barbras* by Deborah Kass), songs ("Barbra Streisand," by Duck Sauce, in which her name is the only lyric), even a viciously hostile *South Park* episode. After fifty years in our eyes and our ears, she is part of the American consciousness as few entertainers have been.

Obviously none of this would have happened without her enormous talent. She was the "most successful, and perhaps talented, performer of her generation," Michael Shnayerson wrote in *Vanity Fair*.[1] Almost from the moment she first sang publicly, at the age of seventeen, she elicited adulation. The classical pianist Glenn Gould called her voice "one of the natural wonders of the age," and composer Quincy Jones called it a "Stradivarius of a voice."[2] Most music critics regard her as the greatest popular female vocalist, and the only singer to stand comparison to Frank Sinatra. Like Sinatra, she changed the dynamics of American popular singing, and she spawned a generation of imitators. Every time you hear a female vocalist trilling in the highest registers or stretching a vowel or shaping the air with her hands or putting on the Bernhardt, you can rest assured that Streisand was there first.

But talent alone, even talent as abundant as Streisand's, doesn't make a cultural icon. It may not even be a prerequisite. What makes an entertainer into a cultural icon is the way in which he or she strums our psychic chords and comes to serve as an embodiment of our own deep impulses. He or she seems not only to understand us but to express us. The lives of such rare entertainers, or at least the lives they express through their work, comprise a theme about us.

Usually this appeal is subtext, a whisper under the performance: Marlon Brando's brooding iconoclasm, Sinatra's cool, the Beatles' irreverence. In Streisand's case, it was all text—a shout rather than a whisper. Streisand, whose mother discouraged her from pursuing show business because she felt her daughter was too unattractive to succeed; Streisand, who never

3

even got the solo in her own high school chorus because a classmate sang more operatically; Streisand, who was immediately dismissed when she auditioned for parts because of her looks; Streisand, who seemed to be an afterthought in everything she attempted—Streisand stood for every plain girl who had ever been rejected.

She sang songs of loneliness and despair and longing. "People who need people . . . ." "What's too painful to remember, we simply choose to forget . . . ." "You don't bring me flowers anymore . . . ." In her plaintive voice, one could hear and feel every slight, every insult, every wound. Tennessee Williams said of that voice that it was "pure and sweet but bolstered by so much rage, all of which had been invested in the pursuit of artistic excellence."[3] Only Streisand could take Franklin Roosevelt's cheery campaign song, "Happy Days Are Here Again," and turn it into a dirge. Streisand seemed to understand in the very depths of her soul how arduous life was. And her fans responded—responded because they knew she knew. One artist said of her, "To be an adolescent coming across Barbra Streisand was the most exhilarating moment of identification."[4] Streisand was the girl who beat the odds, not by assimilating or changing but by not assimilating and not changing. As she herself put it, "You know, maybe not being a beauty explains my success. Maybe being the girl that guys never look at twice, and when I sing about that—about being like an invisible woman—people feel like protecting me."[5]

And hers was a *Jewish* American success story, too. Her sense of marginalization in a culture increasingly devoted to homogenization was a Jewish alienation. "I am deeply Jewish," she once said, "but in a place I don't even know where it is."[6] She was not religiously Jewish—at least not until she made *Yentl* and studied Judaism. She did, however, have a Jewish sensibility, especially that Jewish sense of being the other. She was tormented as a girl for her Semitic looks. She was called "Big

Beak" because of her nose. When she entered show business, she was told repeatedly that she would have to get a nose job if she were to have any hope of succeeding. Of course, she refused, in large part because, she said, she did not want to betray herself, which also meant betraying her Jewishness. As she once put it, "No nose job. Because most of all I want to be true to myself. Really, people should be left to themselves, instead of everyone trying to change everyone else."[7] The fact that she indulged her Jewishness, even seemed to luxuriate in it, became one of her trademarks. "What was amazing about Streisand," the cultural critic Camille Paglia would write, "was her aggressive ethnicity. The Nose, which she refused to have changed, was so defiantly ethnic. It was a truly revolutionary persona."[8] Indeed, Streisand seemed to understand that it was her look and her flaunting of her Jewishness that made her so distinctive and that connected her to the audience. It has been said of her that she was the first star who succeeded because of her Jewishness and not in spite of it.

Of course, there had been other Jewish stars before Streisand, but Jewish entertainers were typically comedians who played their Jewishness for laughs, or they were actors who camouflaged their Jewishness, either masking it in makeup, as Paul Muni did, or ignoring it, as John Garfield did. Streisand could be funny, but she was no comic, and she never ignored her Jewishness or sought to hide it. On the contrary, by insisting on her Jewishness, she transformed it into a metaphor— arguably the commanding metaphor of her career. One observer called her the "Jackie Robinson of female Jewish performers."[9] But Streisand the Jewess became not just the touchstone for all those plain girls but for *everyone* who had ever been dismissed and then had to fight for empowerment. The novelist Bernard Malamud once said, "All men are Jews except they don't know it."[10] With Streisand, they knew it. They knew it because they knew the humiliations she had endured in the process of assert-

5

ing herself. Her Jewishness was both her social burden and her triumph. She was the entertainer of the marginal, the disenfranchised, the disadvantaged, the disaffected, the put-upon, and, not least of all, the different. Only Streisand, among all Hollywood's blond gentile beauties with their pert little noses, or its sexy bombshells, could really understand them.

And not only understand them but win for them. If in her songs, she conveyed the pangs of lost love, she also conveyed the defiance to soldier on. Just listen to her rendition of "Cry Me a River" and you hear the anguish turn into strength. And if, in her films, she always portrayed the ugly duckling, she also made that duckling into someone indomitable and self-confident. She was neither sultry nor sweet, neither a siren nor the girl next door—unless you happened to live in one of America's urban enclaves. She played a woman who was loud, uninhibited, smart, brassy, sassy, and kooky (a word frequently used to describe the young Streisand)—the point being that if she didn't look like any female star, she didn't act like one either. She was a force of nature. No one could subjugate her.

And that is where the persona interfaced with the person. Fans have no idea about the real-life experiences of most entertainers or the forces that defined them. Where does Brad Pitt or George Clooney or Julia Roberts come from? What struggles did they endure on the road to stardom? For Streisand, we know the experiences; we know the struggles. There may be no other entertainer whose own life conflates with her work as much as Streisand's does. That life, which traced an arc from mieskeit to beauty, from a poor, awkward, neglected Brooklyn girl to a self-possessed woman, from an outsider to a guiding light, was also the story she repeatedly told in her films. In effect, she was the most postmodern of entertainers, simultaneously living her story and telling her story in her work, basically performing her life. She became popular by demonstrating how someone like her, someone with her seeming disadvantages, could become popular.

While this forged an iron bond between performer and audience that has lasted decades, it also turned Streisand into a cultural trailblazer—again, in a way that no other entertainer was or is. Streisand arrived at the beginning of the feminist movement, and her gutsy, unsinkable, indomitable persona resonated with women. "Today you cannot imagine what it was like when Streisand burst on the scene in the 1960s," Camille Paglia wrote. "There was nothing like her. . . . Barbra Streisand broke the mold, she revolutionized gender roles."[11] It wasn't only that she was tough and tough-minded. It was that Streisand never let herself be defined by a man, which is why her untraditional looks didn't seem to cause her the anguish women had always suffered under the withering judgment of men. She found a lure beyond conventional attractiveness—something deeper. It was the critic Pauline Kael who identified it and made what may be the most astute appraisal of this psychological legacy of Streisand's: Streisand was proof that "talent is beauty."[12]

Almost singlehandedly in the world of entertainment, Streisand demonstrated that for a woman looks weren't everything. She had this uncanny confidence that her talent was what counted, that it would trump everything else, and that embracing who she was became instrumental to that talent as it became instrumental to her admirers. This is how Tennessee Williams, a huge Streisand fan, put it to a friend: "She makes me believe in my talent because she so passionately believes in and shares her own. She makes me believe in all the talents in all of the world."[13]

As odd as it may seem now, this idea that women were more than the sum of their looks was so original and empowering that Streisand changed or, at the very least, signified the change in how women came to think of themselves. It is not too much to say that she helped redefine femininity and beauty. And she did more. She became an example of empowerment—first as a star who made her own decisions; then as a producer who controlled her own films; and then as a director who bulled her way into Hollywood's creative sanctum sanctorum where women had never been welcome. With Streisand, Hollywood had no choice. She was a force with whom everyone in the film industry had to reckon. No woman in film had ever had that kind of power, save possibly for Mary Pickford at her peak.

Still, though her talent catapulted her, it does a disservice to Streisand to say that her talent was her beauty. One of the most remarkable things about her, and one of the central elements in the Streisand appeal, is the transformation she underwent as her stardom blossomed in which her beauty was her beauty. Streisand herself often cited it. She called herself "Brooklyn's ugly duckling and Broadway's beautiful swan."[14] And what was even more remarkable is that she was the one who effected the transformation, practically willed it. As the director Arthur Laurents observed, "Changing fashion wasn't all that made her more attractive; what she thought of her face played an equal part."[15] The more Streisand believed in herself, not only the more powerful she became but also the more beautiful, so that if talent was beauty, so was self-confidence. She even turned into something of a sex symbol. In doing so, Streisand proved the cliché that everyone was beautiful inside, everyone powerful, and that society often missed what was right before its eyes.

All of these qualities made Streisand arguably the most important entertainer of her time—as Paglia wrote, a revolutionary. Just how much she challenged the prevailing moral, social, sexual, and cultural order may be seen in even greater focus by those who detested her. Streisand was a threat to every verity of traditional America—to conventional ideas of beauty, conventional ideas of female roles and femininity, conventional ideas of decorum, conventional ideas of the exercise of power, conventional ideas of what it meant to be American. To her detractors, Streisand was always "too much," whatever that meant exactly. In part, it seemed to mean too Jewish, which was the name of an exhibition at New York's Jewish Museum, for which a triptych of Streisand served as the cover image of the exhibition's brochure. It was only a short distance from "too Jewish" to "too forceful"—someone who didn't know her place. A vicious *Mad* magazine parody called her "Bubbly Strident." An even more vicious *South Park* episode depicted her as, in the words of a cartoon by Leonard Maltin, an "evil, egotistical, diabolical bitch," so much so that in a transmogrification of the Superman trope, Streisand morphs into a monster out of a Japanese horror movie, Mecha-Streisand, who is only prevented from destroying South Park when she is punched in her nose—her Achilles' proboscis.

Admittedly, some of this hostility may have arisen less from Streisand's performances or from her no-holds-barred persona or from her Jewishness than from her reputation as a diva with ever-intensifying demands—not only a powerful Jewish woman but a narcissist and megalomaniac to boot. But it testifies to her iconic position in the culture that she could *be* a diva, which, for a poor, plain Jewish girl from Brooklyn, may be the greatest transformation of all. Streisand isn't just a brilliant singer and actress, not even just a significant cultural figure. She has ascended into the American pantheon, where—ironically, for someone who made it by seeming ordinary—the normal rules no longer apply. She has undergone a kind of apotheosis.

This volume doesn't purport to be a biography of Barbra Streisand. There are already plenty of those—another indication of her status. Instead, it is a book-length biographical essay that explores who Streisand is and how she became what she became, and examines her position in our cultural cosmos. It recounts her life for those who don't know the details, but it places them in a larger context than personal history. In effect, it is as much a biography of the metaphor that we have come to know as "Streisand" as of the woman herself, which necessarily means that it is a look at the relationship between Jewishness and popular culture. Streisand is so much more than Streisand. The aim of this book is to understand how and why that happened, how and why she changed our world.

1

Mieskeit

THE ROSEBUD in Barbra Streisand's life came early and it came hard. She was born, the second child of Emanuel and Diana Streisand, on April 24, 1942, in Israel Zion Hospital in the Borough Park section of Brooklyn, just months after the Japanese raid on Pearl Harbor and America's entrance into World War II. It was said that there was an air-raid drill during the delivery, which meant she was, appropriately enough, born into din, though that would have been true of any day in Brooklyn.[1] Brooklyn was not exactly sedate, which was something that would be said of Streisand. At the time, it was more than a geographical borough of New York City. It was a wild ethos that arose from one of the great ethnic enclaves of America where the Irish abutted the Italians who abutted the Poles who abutted the African Americans, and everyone abutted the Jews, since of the nearly three million people in Brooklyn, one-third were Jews like the Streisands. It was the largest concentration of Jews in America.

Brooklyn was where Jewishness and America converged. It was a dialect, streetwise and blunt; a behavior, loose, unself-conscious, and occasionally vulgar; an attitude, bold and even arrogant—and the dialect, the behavior, and the attitude all drew from Jewishness. In part that attitude, like the attitude of so many Jews, was one of grievance. Brooklynites knew they were condescended to—the sad sacks of life. They saw it in their baseball team, the beloved but hapless Dodgers (named by Manhattanites after Brooklynites dodging trolley cars), Dem Bums, who always fell to the august, and aptly named, Yankees, not to mention—and you didn't want to mention it in Brooklyn—the detested Giants, who, in a 1951 playoff, came from thirteen games back in August to win the National League pennant when Bobby Thompson homered off Ralph Branca in the ninth. "Wait 'til next year" was the Brooklynites' stoic refrain. And then, two years after the Bums finally won a championship, by vanquishing their haughty Yankee adversaries no less in the 1955 World Series, the team was gone to California. That is the way it seemed to go for Brooklyn.

But though Brooklyn was caricatured as comically intrepid, Truman Capote thought it a much darker place—"a sad brutal provincial lonesome human silent sprawling raucous lost passionate subtle bitter immature innocent perverse tender mysterious place."[2] The intrepidness, a kind of stubborn pride, was the antidote to the hurt and despair and bitterness—a form of superiority wrung from seeming inferiority. Unlike Manhattan across the East River, Brooklyn was real, unaffected. It had no airs. Essayist Philip Lopate said that "American popular culture celebrated the Brooklynite as Everyman bittersweetly contented, in the end, to stay in that grubby lower-middle-class environment, with the El train rattling the windows, because somehow it was still 'the greatest spot on oith.'"[3] In the World

War II movies where the platoon was a polyglot, the obligatory Brooklynite, often Jewish, was either the guy who was salt of the earth or the savvy urbanite who knew what's what or both. He was what he was and didn't pretend to be anything else.

Last, Brooklyn was resilience and resistance—a place where you looked the boredom, the poverty, and the condescension in the eye and spit. Brooklynites didn't recede. They exulted. Lopate thought there must be "some mercury in the water that promotes a need to recount, show off or intimidate," to which he attributed the borough's knack for turning out writers, gangsters, and entertainers.[4] Norman Mailer, Bernard Malamud, S. J. Perelman, Arthur Miller, Joseph Heller, Woody Allen, Eddie Cantor, Mel Brooks, George Gershwin, Harry Houdini, Danny Kaye, the Three Stooges, the Ritz Brothers—all were from Brooklyn and, more important, of Brooklyn, with that Brooklyn ethos. And those were just the Jews.

Streisand had certainly drunk those waters, and drunk deeply, though she was once quoted—and then endlessly requoted—as having said that Brooklyn to her was "baseball, boredom and bad breath."[5] She would later vehemently deny having said it, and she was no doubt being honest in her denial. Brooklyn born and bred, Streisand had nothing against Brooklyn. If anything, she was Brooklyn personified, in its grievance, its pride, its resilience, and its self-regard. One could almost say that Barbra Streisand was to entertainers what Brooklyn was to cities. "Brooklyn likes a beautiful loser," wrote Lopate.[6] That was Streisand in incubation before, like the Dodgers, she decamped to Los Angeles and became a beautiful winner.

So when Streisand said, "From the day I was born, I was trying to get out. I've never been nostalgic about my past," she wasn't necessarily talking about getting out of Brooklyn.[7] She was talking about escaping the deprivations and denigrations of her life—especially one big deprivation that led to many of the littler denigrations: that Rosebud. "I always felt there was a gaping hole somewhere," she would later say, "something missing."[8] It wasn't hard to figure out what it was. That hole was the loss of Emanuel Streisand.

Emanuel was the first child of Jewish immigrants from Galicia who met in the United States. His father, Isaac Streisand, emigrated in 1898 at the age of seventeen, married Anna Kessler in 1907, worked as a tailor, sold his sewing machine, and opened a fish market on the Lower East Side and then another in Williamsburg in Brooklyn, where young Emanuel grew up wrapping fish. But Emanuel Streisand was no fishmonger. He had aspirations—large ones. An exceptional student, he entered City College at the age of sixteen on a partial scholarship that he supplemented by driving a Good Humor ice cream truck. His college yearbook described him as "one of those fortunate few who can graduate and say that college work has been easy."[9] He earned a Phi Beta Kappa key and hoped to become a professor. But first he took a job teaching elementary school to underwrite a master's degree in education at City College, which he received in 1930. It was that December he married Diana Rosen, also the child of Jewish immigrants, in her case from Russia. They had met, the story goes, at the apartment of a girlfriend of hers, and on seeing him, Diana swooned. They dated for a year, had a lovers' spat and parted, and then, a year later, ran into each other on the elevated train. Diana called it "an act of God."[10]

The memory of Manny Streisand has obviously been burnished, especially by his daughter, who had no actual recollection of him. He was described, by her and others, as intelligent, good-looking, gregarious, self-confident, and adventuresome—in short, the father of a Jewish girl's dreams, which is literally what he was: a dream father. And he was indefatigable, too. To ride out the Depression, he took a job teaching at a reformatory in Elmira in Upstate New York, then left that job to teach English to truants and delinquents at the Brooklyn High School for Specialty Trades. He earned additional money teaching off-hours at a yeshiva, and at night, he began studying for his PhD in education at Columbia Teachers' College. When he approached his Flatbush apartment after work, Diana would instruct infant Barbra to stand in her crib and look out the window, and Emanuel would enter and sweep the baby into his arms. This was the Streisand paradise.[11]

And it was to be a paradise lost. Stories vary on exactly what had happened to Manny. By one account, it was the night of his wedding to Diana, and they had gone to celebrate at a restaurant in Manhattan when he got into a car accident and hit his head on the windshield, which triggered severe headaches and dizzy spells. He may have also suffered from epilepsy, either as a result of the accident or not, and it was after having a seizure while working at Elmira that Manny decided to leave for Brooklyn to be nearer his family should something happen to him and the family need support.

Something did. He had taken a job as a counselor at a Catskills summer camp run by a teaching colleague. The camp was understaffed, and Manny worked himself ragged. By one account, he had taken campers on a hike the morning of August 4, 1943, fell, and hit his head.[12] That afternoon, he supervised a swimming race, then retired to his cabin, complaining of fatigue. When, an hour later, Diana couldn't rouse him, she called for an ambulance. He was taken to nearby Fleischmanns Hospital, named, like the town in which it stood, after the yeast-making family. He never revived. He died that afternoon at 2:45. He was thirty-five years old. Barbra was a toddler of fifteen months.

The cause of death would always remain vague, which had its effect on Barbra. She assumed he had suffered a cerebral hemorrhage. She also assumed that she would inherit the condition, so she spent much of her youth with the apprehension that her life would be cut short like his. Many years later, she learned that he had likely died from improper hospital treatment after a seizure, possibly an overdose of administered morphine, than anything congenital.[13] But by then she was already thinking of her life as beclouded.

And if the death would later adumbrate her life as a kind of ticking clock of mortality, it had a deeper, more immediate, and more enduring impact. It created an ongoing emptiness. Diana would describe how young Barbra would wait for her father, as she always had, looking out the window for his arrival. But he would not arrive. Barbra would tell a friend that she longed for her father "in her bones" and that she had the feeling that she was "missing something" inside her that she had to fill.[14] In one interview, she attributed her restlessness, dissatisfaction and drive to not having had a father. "I know if I had a father," she said, "I would probably be happily married and have two or three children."[15] As a girl, she came to identify herself as the child without a father. The loss worsened because her father was also, in her mind, her real progenitor—the source of who she was and of what she would become. "I must have gotten my detailed, obsessive streak from my father," she would say, "because my mother wasn't like me at all."[16] And she attributed to him her intellectual curiosity, boasting that he had written *two* dissertations, presumably his master's thesis and the doctoral dissertation that was near completion at the time of his death, and that one was a study of Shakespeare, Dante, and other classical writers—*her* favorite writers, which she took to illustrate the almost mystical connection between father and daughter.[17]

Yet the real impact of Emanuel Streisand's death on his daughter, deeper even than the emptiness or the almost mystical sense of communion, was the feeling of Dickensian anguish into which young Barbra was thrust. This was the life she would talk of leaving behind—a life full of awful memories that she would recount for interviewers again and again, with new nightmarish twists, prompting one of them to quip, "No madeleines are recollected without hunting down the damn recipe for updating in today's test kitchen."[18] These are the stories of her mother crying endlessly after her father's death, virtually incapacitated for months; of going to live with her maternal grandparents on Pulaski Street in a cramped, three-room apartment where her brother, Sheldon, slept on a cot and she and Diana shared a bed, and where she and Sheldon would crawl under the table to avoid beatings from their grandfather; of the apartment being so Spartan that she would later say, "Couches to me were what rich people had"; of her testy grandmother calling her *farbrent*, Yiddish for fire, because Barbra was so restless and rebellious; of a childhood so bereft of toys that Barbra took a hot water bottle and treated it as a doll.[19] Sheldon later said that "there was no love in that house."[20]

And when Diana finally gathered herself from her depression and mourning and took a job, out of necessity, as a bookkeeper, Barbra felt abandoned again—in her recollection, basically left to fend for herself. There were caretakers, some relatives who minded her, and a woman upstairs, Toby Borokow, the mother of a friend, to whose apartment Barbra would retreat each afternoon, sitting in front of their new seven-inch television set and watching old Laurel and Hardy movies, making Mrs. Borokow laugh by imitating the comedians. When Diana sent Barbra to a Hebrew health camp in Upstate New York, which she detested, Mrs. Borokow knit her a burgundy sweater, and Barbra would fondly recall years later how that sweater distinguished her from the other girls in their drab blue uniforms.[21] But even those afternoon idylls with their kindnesses ended each day when Mr. Borokow would come home from work and send Barbra back to her grandparents. "That really set me back years," she would later say.[22]

And there was worse to come, much worse. On a parental visit during one of Barbra's summers at the health camp, Diana arrived with a man in tow. His name was Louis Kind, and if ever there were a misnomer, this was it. Barbra had never been happy with her mother dating to begin with. "I hated those men," she said. "I once saw a man kissing my mother. I thought he was killing her. Except she was laughing."[23] But of all these suitors, Kind would earn special opprobrium.

From the beginning, their relationship was tense. During that camp visit, Barbra insisted on returning to Brooklyn with her mother, and Diana reluctantly agreed. But the Brooklyn to which she returned now included Kind—a man in the midst of a divorce with three children and a lackluster work ethic as well as a gambling habit. "I would wait for her in the living room," Kind would say of his dating Diana, "and then when she was ready to go out with me, I would take her arm and lead her to the door. Barbara, sensing that her life was to undergo some terrifying change, would hold on to her mother's skirts, pulling her back, fearfully, that this strange man was taking her mother away from her. 'Don't go, Mommy, stay with me,' she would plead."[24]

The real catastrophe came when Diana discovered she was pregnant, even though Kind's divorce had yet to be finalized. The Rosens were scandalized, ordering their daughter out of the house. Kind rented an apartment on Newkirk Avenue in Flatbush, and he and Diana were married on December 23, 1950. The new baby, Rosalind (later Roslyn), was born seventeen days later—and would become yet another curse in Barbra's life.

"He lavished all his attention on [Rosalind]," Kind's son would tell biographer James Spada. "His feelings for her were *huge*."[25] And his love for Rosalind was a zero-sum game with Barbra, who craved his attention and affection. "So one day I decided I'd call him Dad and crawl on my stomach underneath the TV so I wouldn't interfere with his boxing when I passed," she recalled to Kevin Sessums in a *Vanity Fair* interview. "I groveled at his fucking feet and called him Dad and brought him his slippers for two days! There was no change. He didn't treat me any better. He didn't ask me how I was. He didn't talk to me. He didn't see me. He didn't recognize me. He didn't like me."[26]

Then, beyond the neglect, came the verbal abuse. He called Rosalind "beauty" and Barbra "the beast." He once refused Barbra money for ice cream, saying, "No, you're not pretty enough." "He taunted her continually," her brother Sheldon said. And Sheldon bucked up her spirits, telling her with obvious allusion to their late father, "You're different, that's all, different, and you're smarter than most kids your age. And being smart is what counts."[27]

Diana fared little better. Kind verbally abused her, too, using, she would later tell a court, "vile, obscene and scurrilous language" to her. In time, he began staying away for days, taking up with other women, "scandalously flaunting" his affairs, according to Diana, and leaving the family in financial distress.[28] "Why do you take his side?" Barbra would ask her. "He doesn't need you. I do. He doesn't even love you. If he did, he'd be nicer."[29]

In time, Diana agreed and filed for a legal separation. In court, Kind protested that he was forced to work two jobs to meet her needs and that when he came home, she refused to cook for him. But the judge concluded that Kind was a "pathological liar" who "testifies in any manner which he thinks will best fit his needs on a particular occasion, and that he would say anything if he felt that it would aid his cause."[30] Eventually Diana sought and received a divorce. She and Kind had been married seven years, and Barbra would say, "I don't think this man asked me how I was in the seven years we lived together."[31]

Yet if Kind was abusive, Diana was not the prototypically overprotective mother either. Though she hustled Barbra off to that health camp and though she fretted endlessly about her daughter's scrawniness right up to the time when Barbra was making her show business debut, she was, in her daughter's account at least, self-absorbed, cold, and implacable—a maternal brute. "Subconsciously, I was always trying to please my mother, which it happens I can never do," Barbra confessed to Nora Ephron in an interview.[32] Diana seldom displayed affection to her daughter. "When I wanted love from my mother," Barbra said, "she gave me food."[33] Nor did she give praise. "Never give your kids too much praise," she told a reporter after Barbra's success. "In fact, I try to tone them down if I see they have an exaggerated opinion of themselves. I just kind of make a remark that calms them down."[34] Barbra would tell Chaim Potok that of her father's two dissertations, the second was a study of a "mother's behavior toward her son," referring to Diana and Barbra's older brother, Sheldon. "After every chapter there's an analysis of everything that was wrong, the mixed messages my mother was giving my brother. I always had these books, but I could never look through them."[35] Thus did Emmanuel become Barbra's ally against her mother.

Diana would later defend herself, declaring that Barbra had scared her because "she was so smart" that she had "an answer for most things," and that she was so "complex" that she never shared her emotions with her mother.[36] "She bottled everything up inside her," Diana would say. "Perhaps if she could have voiced to me how she was feeling, things might have been easier, but she didn't." And then Diana added another source of friction between them—not Barbra's opacity but her independence: "She had her own way of looking at life and that that was the way she liked things to be. Barbra always saw everything depending on how it affected her."[37]

This may have been projection, since Barbra would tell Oprah Winfrey that the mother-daughter disagreements were not so much a matter of two conflicting iron wills as of the mother's jealousy of her daughter—a jealousy born of Diana's own thwarted teenage ambitions to be a singer when she had actually auditioned for roles. "I remember one Christmas when

I was doing *Funny Girl*, she went nuts," Streisand told Winfrey. "With tears running down her face, she closed her eyes and said, 'Why is Barbra getting all the presents? Where are my presents?' That's when I realized that she wanted to be famous too."[38] So the iciness, the withholding of approval, the ongoing criticisms that continued well into Streisand's career were, to Barbra, finally retribution against a daughter who would have similar aspirations to those her mother once had and who would fulfill those aspirations as fully as anyone ever had.

And it wasn't just her stepfather and her mother who targeted Barbra. Her playmates would ridicule her, too. She was painfully thin and slightly cross-eyed and had that large nose, which drew taunts of "Big Beak." She called herself a "real ugly kid, the kind who looks ridiculous with a ribbon in her hair."[39] More, she was tormented. "When I was nine years old," she once recounted, "sometimes the girls would gang up on me in my neighborhood, make a circle around me, make fun of me, and I'd start to cry."[40] (She reenacts this treatment in a segment in her first television special where children call her "Crazy Barbra.") As a defense, according to one of her biographers, she developed an attitude—a standoffishness that only served to fuel the hostility against her.[41]

What all the abuse, ridicule, and hostility also fueled was a growing hunger, almost a desperation, for recognition—a desperation she herself hinted was compensation for not having had a "normal childhood with a living father" and for being ignored by everyone else.[42] She loved attention. Attending a yeshiva on Willoughby Street, she would yell "Christmas!" when the rabbi left the classroom just to stun her classmates.[43] When the Kinds got their first television set, she would sit there riveted, then retreat to the bathroom and act out the commercials in front of the mirror.[44] And every Saturday afternoon, she would go to Loew's Kings Theatre on Flatbush Avenue and imagine herself on the screen: "It was *me* up there and those attractive men were pursuing *me!*[45] And she would remember walking back home from the theater because she didn't have enough money to take the bus and being struck by the "grim reality of a hot New York summer" and determined to escape. "From the age of seven," Diana would later recall of Barbra, "she wanted to be in films. I couldn't fathom why she wanted to be famous [of course she could], but she did. I was worried that she wouldn't succeed and that she would be hurt, so I tried not to encourage her. But I couldn't break up her ideas and her thinking."[46] Even as a girl, Barbra would go to the photo booth at the arcade and take pictures of herself in a variety of poses.[47] "I always wanted to get out of Brooklyn and be someone," she would later say.[48]

But if she dreamed of the movies, it was singing even then that would provide her ticket out of her misery. "Growing up, I used to wonder: What did I have to do to get attention?" she would say. Early on, she found out. "When I started to sing, I got attention."[49] Of course, many children sing for attention. Streisand was different. Her voice was different. "I remember when I was five living on Pulaski Street in Brooklyn," she would recall, "the hallway of our building had a brass banister and a great sound, a great echo system. I used to sing in the hallway. I was known as the girl on the street with the good voice. No father, good voice. That was my identity."[50] Even her stepfather would remember Barbra on the stoop of the apartment building. "I can see her now," he said, "singing songs she had heard on the radio in her little girl voice, which even then was remarkably true and delivered with great feeling. The neighbors would stick their heads out of the window, clap loudly, and yell, 'More, Barbara, give us more!' She was only too happy to oblige. Then, as a final encore—double-jointed as she was— she would roll down on the pavement, take both of her feet, wrap them around her neck, and roll like a human ball."[51]

But it was not just her voice that was different, better, than most children's. It was her interpretation, which is not something you expect from a child. She would later say that the way she delivered songs was a product of being raised on the streets in "hot, steamy Brooklyn, with stifled air," and that it infused her singing with, "I don't want to say 'pain,'" but "words meant something to me. So I think it somehow unconsciously influenced whatever I do."[52] In effect, she was saying that she sang with feeling—with the anguish of her childhood.

This was still stoop singing, but the idea of a show business career was not all wishful thinking. At the age of seven, she gave her first public performance in the Willoughby yeshiva, later describing herself as a "weird-looking kid standing pigeon-toed and very skinny with bows in her hair." She said she ran off the stage afterward to get her mother's verdict, which was that she was too thin.[53] But she was not deterred. She was never deterred. She formed an impromptu singing group with two classmates, the twin Bernstein sisters: Bobbie and the Bernsteins.[54] She attended Miss Marsh's ballet school—Diana said, "She spent hours getting up on her toes and walking around the apartment."—until Miss Marsh moved out of Brooklyn.[55] She began attending Star Time, a school for child performers on Church Avenue in Brooklyn who were training for a Star Time show, until Diane couldn't afford it. She sang at talent shows at the Coronet Hotel in Glen Wild, New York, where the family spent a few weeks in the summer and was good enough to be asked to perform at two weddings there.[56] And at PS 89, where she attended grammar school after the yeshiva, she tried out for a role in the school's folk dance festival, though her teacher, Seymour Lebenger, told her, "You can't sing a note or dance a step. You just don't have the talent."[57]

But if her mother could not discourage her, neither could her teacher. There was something in her that needed not only attention but success. When she attended Erasmus Hall High School, she auditioned for the Choral Club—and was rejected again. "I never knew her to have any particular or outstanding talent," the club's director would tell her biographer James Spada in what certainly ranks among the greatest misevaluations in show business history.[58] Still, she kept singing—kept singing even though she was eventually shoved into the chorus's back row, kept signing even though the solos went to a fellow student with a more operatic voice, kept singing even though she received no encouragement or recognition. And not only kept singing but kept striking out into the world to realize her show business dreams. It wasn't a matter of talent, though she obviously had plenty of that. It was a matter of determination.

Erasmus Hall, set on a campus on Flatbush Avenue, was not an especially propitious place for an outcast and iconoclast like Streisand to be. Erasmus thought of itself as the Harvard of Brooklyn high schools. Erected as a private academy in 1787 with funds from Alexander Hamilton and Aaron Burr, among others, it even looked Ivy League, with the original colonial-style building sitting on a quadrangle rimmed by three collegiate gothic structures. And Erasmus had a formality that befitted the architecture. One former student recalled, "My biology teacher wore spats, my Spanish teacher made us stand to do verb conjugations, and my social studies teacher addressed his students by their surnames, preceded by Miss or Mister."[59] At Erasmus, students didn't go to study hall. They went to "chapel."

Streisand arrived in September 1955, no doubt choosing Erasmus because she was an excellent student and still saw herself as her father's daughter, an intellectual, and because among the school's esteemed alumni were Bernard Malamud, Nobel laureates Eric Kandel and Barbara McClintock, and historian Herbert Aptheker. (Alumni also included a who's who of show business from Mae West to Barbara Stanwyck to Beverly Sills to Neil Diamond.) Whether in the sciences or in the arts, it was a place where the outstanding could be recognized.

But not Streisand. The word she frequently used to describe herself during her high school years was "loner." "I never took part in any school activities or anything," she told *Time* magazine. "I was never asked out to any of the proms, and I never had a date for New Year's Eve. I was pretty much of a loner."[60] In another interview, she described herself as an ugly duckling. "Like the duckling, I was teased," she said, "because I was 'different.' I was a loner—not *lonely*, understand, but just alone. I wasn't like the others, and I suppose it bothered me a bit then."[61] No one paid her any attention, she would say. She was befriended by a quirky classmate named Susan Dworkowitz, "who looked like a pixie with white make-up," and Barbra remembered taking a subway with her. "I saw all the people looking at her, not at me. I never felt anyone was looking at me."[62] This wasn't just Barbra's retrospective self-pity. A classmate told biographer James Spada, "The strongest memory I have of her is her standing and waiting by herself, holding her books."[63]

She would, of course, attribute the lack of attention primarily to her looks—that skinniness and her slightly crossed eyes and a severe case of acne that she tried to hide with thick make-up, and her oversized nose. But high school classmates would dispute that Barbra was ugly or that her nose was a source of ridicule. "We all had Jewish noses," one told biographer Christopher Andersen, adding, "All of us thought she was good looking."[64] Still, she felt disaffected. She envied the rich girls "who always wore the latest clothes and had money to spend on whatever they wanted."[65] And she envied their ease and their camaraderie. Barbra couldn't mingle.

But however much rejection she suffered, Streisand was not one to concede or shrink. On the contrary, she fought her ostracism by embracing it. As *Time* would put it in a cover story after her debut in *Funny Girl:* "Barbra has never striven to be inconspicuous."[66] So the girl who wasn't noticed began a campaign to demand notice. "I didn't sulk because I wasn't gorgeous," she would tell Gloria Steinem in an early *Ladies' Home Journal* interview. "I dressed wild to show I didn't care."[67] Part of this display was simple contrarianism—the desire to be different. "If we wore shorter skirts," a classmate recalled, "Barbara wore them long. When we wore sweaters, she wore a baggy blouse. She always did the opposite of everyone else."[68] And part of it was outrageousness. She wore purple lipstick and blue eye shadow. She dyed her hair platinum blond. She wore her nails very long—"so I wouldn't have to type," she once said in defiance of her mother's pressure for her to be a secretary—though one biographer noted that it also had the effect of keeping people at bay and avoiding intimacy.[69] To perfect her image, she even began dating a black boy, which, for a young white girl in the 1950s, was scandalous.[70]

By her senior year, when she had begun to make regular forays into Manhattan to take acting lessons, she was dressing in black head to toe—"like a real beatnik," she said.[71] On her graduation day, according to a classmate, she bleached her hair and dyed it red, blue, and green and wore her purple lipstick. "I wanted attention so I made myself uglier than I was," she would later admit. "I was outrageous. I never spoke softly. I was always loud, even in my thoughts. Of course, I got attention, the wrong kind of attention, but at least I was noticed."[72]

And yet she aspired to something beyond this kind of shallow attention. She held on to her childhood dreams of stardom. At night in her loneliness, she would lock herself in the bathroom, glue on false eyelashes, drag on a cigarette, pose in front of the mirror, and see herself as a star—a Great, Great Star. "I hadda be great," she would tell Shana Alexander of *Life* magazine. "I couldn't be medium. My mouth was too big."[73] Stardom would be her way to get the attention "I missed as a child," she would say.[74] And stardom would be her revenge:

"I wanted to prove to the world that they shouldn't make fun of me."[75]

This is the great mystery of Streisand. While just about anyone else, after all the abuse and neglect and criticism and discouragement and alienation, and in the face of unrelenting negativity, would have surrendered, she never abandoned her ambitions or lost faith in herself. As much as her voice and her acting, this was her gift: fortitude. It had been that way from the time she was little. "I always knew I wanted to be famous," she would say. "I was always trying to be something I wasn't."[76] But just about everyone *wants* to be famous. Streisand didn't just want it. She willed herself to achieve it. "Perception creates reality," she would later say, explaining her determination to succeed, and citing George Bernard Shaw, "Thought transcends matter."[77]

Where did that fortitude come from? Certainly, it came from her dead father, that great hole in her life, and from the need she felt to complete him. (Successful children often cite an obligation to repay parental sacrifices, and what greater sacrifice than death?) And no doubt it came from her mother's lack of confidence in her and even her stepfather's cruelty, which drove her to show them how wrong they were. It may have come from that Brooklyn swagger that Brooklynites had assumed to show up everyone who condescended to them. And finally it may have come from her Jewishness, which prompted her to believe in her special status and which legitimized her feeling of difference, turning what could have been a liability into an asset. It was *good* to be different. (Another Brooklyn-born Jew, Bella Abzug, later Congresswoman Bella Abzug, had the same sense of fortitude and attributed it, in part, to her Jewishness.) Indeed, studies of success have shown that a combination of superiority, which Streisand certainly had, and a sense of inferiority, which she also had, is a potent motivator.[78]

And Streisand seemed to recognize this seeming contradiction. She would later say, "With a strong sense of self, there is also deep insecurity. Don't get fooled."[79]

Young Barbra was motivated. She had always had drive. Her high school counselor described her as "hard driving," something for which Jews had often been denigrated.[80] Detractors said they were pushy. But Barbra had more than drive. She thought of herself as different—not just different in the sense of being odd, but different in the sense of being special. She thought of herself as "chosen"—a Jewish endowment?—and said that she felt she could "see the truth."[81] So when she decided to become a star, she was not just pursuing a goal; she was fulfilling a destiny. Barbra Streisand was going to be a star, no matter what. It was written.

This was not, of course, her mother's idea of Barbra's destiny. "She was not a good looking girl," Diana would later say. "In show business at that time, there were very pretty girls around."[82] She wanted her daughter to find something secure, a steady paycheck, which is why she pushed her toward a secretarial career. For their part, Barbra's school counselors insisted that she go to college. She was a bright student, in the top 3 percent of her class, and she had been invited to take honors classes. But Barbra had no interest in being a secretary or in going to college. She was fixated on stardom. Even before Erasmus Hall, when Barbra was eleven, she cajoled her mother into taking her for a singing audition in Manhattan at MGM, which offered her a spot in its training program. Diana said no. When she was thirteen, Barbra wheedled Diana again to let her cut a demo record at the NOLA Studios in Steinway Hall on Fifty-Seventh Street, and this time Diana agreed, no doubt because she was going to record a song, too. So Barbra sang "Zing! Went the Strings of My Heart" and "You'll Never Know," and Diana sang "One Kiss."[83] And Barbra did something that afternoon: She extended the ending of "You'll Never

Know." "Where did that come from?" she would say after she had achieved stardom. "It was like *The Exorcist*, you know? . . . I guess you could call that inspiration."[84]

Inspiration or not, nothing came of it, and in any case, singing was not her goal. Acting was. But the next year, on her fourteenth birthday, April 22, 1956, Barbra and a friend went to see the Broadway production of *The Diary of Anne Frank* with Susan Strasberg in the title role. As she sat in the very last row, Barbra had an epiphany. She identified with Frank, a young Jew who had her own aspirations, and Barbra could see herself onstage, imagining herself as the star just as she had imagined herself on-screen in the movies she saw as a child. *She really could do this.* She was so smitten, and so confident, that when she read that director Otto Preminger was holding auditions for his new film, *Joan of Arc*, she went to the call. She was turned down, but it only seemed to steel her determination.

That summer she convinced her mother to let her join a small theater company in Malden Bridge, New York, not far from Albany, using $150 from her late grandfather's bequest for her college education to defray the fee the company charged to let novices learn stagecraft. She appeared as a Japanese child in *Teahouse of the August Moon*, a comedy about the American occupation of Japan, and as a rambunctious secretary in *Desk Set*, for which she received her first review—a favorable one that remarked on her character's flirtatiousness. But, again, it was not so much her talent as her ambition that was striking. A fellow intern described her as "determined" but self-centered: "Me first. I'm gonna get where I'm going no matter what. And nobody's gonna get in my way."[85] She was a bulldozer.

Barbra returned to New York and her junior year at Erasmus Hall intoxicated with the theater. It was her intoxication that impressed a young actress named Anita Miller whom Barbra met, depending on the source, either when she visited a fellow Malden alum at the Cherry Lane Theater in Greenwich

Village or when she was granted an internship at the theater. Anita was married to an acting teacher, Alan Miller, and she pestered him to let Barbra into his classes. When he demurred, she invited Barbra to dinner at their apartment. Alan said she was a "misbegotten, misshapen, skinny little nudnik," but he also said that he detected "something special," so he let her audition.[86] Alan would call it "the worst audition I think I've seen in my entire life," but like his wife, he was taken by her hunger to succeed and let her into his class, which she paid for, in part, by babysitting the Miller children.[87] This was when Barbra began her black phase.

She was so hungry that by the time she started her senior year of high school, after a summer performing at another theater company, she had decided to take a double load of classes so that she could graduate six months early to pursue acting full time. She left Erasmus on January 26, 1959, fourth in her class of 136. And she determined to leave Brooklyn where, she said, "I always felt like a character out of Paddy Chayefsky."[88] Over Diana's objections, she immediately debarked to Manhattan and an eighty dollar–a-month apartment that she shared with her fashionable friend Susan Dworkowitz, the girl whom everyone had noticed on that subway ride.

Now it was time for them to notice the *mieskeit*. Now it was time to notice Barbra.

2

Chutzpah

THE BULLDOZER bulldozed her way into Manhattan. She possessed none of the usual niceties, none of the novice's modesty, none of the traditional humble working-one's-way-up-the-ladder sentiments. "I had to go right to the top or nowhere at all," she later said. "I could never be in the chorus, know what I mean? I had to be a star. . . . I'm too whatever-I-am to end up in the middle."[1] She had no doubts—or at least she didn't show any. When her mother attended a workshop at Alan Miller's class, a friend of Barbra's said, "She told Barbra she was a fool, she was only kidding herself. She had no talent, and no one would ever pay good money to see her on a stage." Barbra listened coolly, then replied, "You're wrong, Mama. Wait. You'll see."[2]

Casting directors told her the same thing as her mother. After she auditioned for one theater company, an owner said, "She's very talented, but God, she's so ugly. What are we going to do with her?"[3] Despite her confidence, it hurt. "I cried in every office," she recalled. "I was humiliated—people looked at me like I was crazy." She said she could only summon the energy to go to two auditions a week.[4] Unable to land an acting job, she took other jobs to support herself—as a clerk at a business firm, where she annoyed her bosses by humming; as an usher at the Lunt-Fontanne Theatre, where she watched *The Sound of Music* again and again; later as a switchboard operator at the advertising agency where her brother, Sheldon, worked. But she knew she was just killing time until her break. "The most thrilling time was when I was eighteen," she said. "I knew then I'd be famous, but no one else did. It was my secret, and I always had something to look forward to. Excitement came in the proving."[5]

And she worked at acting, worked hard, not only in Alan Miller's classes at the Theatre Studio on Forty-Eighth Street, but in classes conducted by other acting teachers—Eli Rill, Herbert Berghof, Curt Conway—to which she was admitted through Miller's intercession. It was acting that captivated her, not singing. Singing was too easy. "It's only wind and noise," she said. "I open my mouth and the sound comes out."[6] Acting was different. It demanded training, discipline, and seriousness, and could reward them with the stardom for which she so desperately strove. And it was not just acting. She wanted to be a *dramatic* actress, like Duse, she said, even though she had never actually seen Eleanora Duse act and even though her acting classmates couldn't stifle their giggles when she would emote in her broad Brooklyn accent. Yet again undeterred, Barbra challenged Rill: "If you're such a good teacher, make it so that they'll stop laughing."[7]

Everyone who knew her then saw something naked about young Streisand, something desperate and hungry. Dustin Hoffman, a fellow acting student, compared her to a baby bird struggling more than the other birds to get the mother's worm, while Anita Miller said that Barbra acted "like someone who had been starved."[8] Sometimes she had so little money she literally was starving, and for a young woman whose mother was in constant fear that she was too thin and brittle and who constantly tried to force her to eat, when Barbra did eat, she ate greedily, her appetite for food a sign of her appetite for everything, especially love, since she had clearly conflated food with the attentions of her usually inattentive mother. "Food was love," she would admit, saying how important it was, when she finally began singing professionally, that the club owners feed her as a demonstration of their commitment to her.[9] "There's nothing that can make me stop eating," she would later say.[10] Another time she said, "I live to eat. Happiness is noshing."[11] A few years later, when he was helping her during *Funny Girl*'s pre-Broadway tryouts and trying to get a reaction from her, Alan Miller would have a stagehand eat a chunk of cake in the wings where she could see him. "She sobbed like a baby," Miller would say. "That's how powerfully she felt about food—and about someone enjoying something that she wanted."[12]

If she was voracious, she was wary, distrustful, self-interested. She didn't have time for civility and never expressed gratitude even when someone cast her in a play.[13] A friend at the time described her as "always rushing forward, as if afraid she'd be late for her life."[14] Another acquaintance said that she had an attitude, the same attitude she had cultivated as a little girl— "letting you know she thought she was better than you were, and that she'd be a big success and you wouldn't"—though no one at the time could really appreciate how much effort it took for her to project that superiority when everyone was telling her she was a failure.[15] She was so uninterested in anyone else that fellow students didn't like performing scenes with her. "Especially the guys," recalled one classmate. "They were intimidated by her. She was relentless in her desire to learn. She would focus so completely that it was like, 'All of you can just float away.'"[16]

Barbra wasn't entirely oblivious to the animosity she elicited, but she excused herself on the basis that she was a ragamuffin who really never had parents to teach her how to behave. "I didn't know the rules," she said on one occasion.[17] On another she said, "I used to sit at the table with my feet up. I didn't know you were supposed to put a napkin in your lap. My mother ate from a pot standing up at the kitchen stove."[18] (People would say the same thing about Jews generally: They didn't know how to behave.) But then she also cited this lack of decorum as a reason why she would be a great actress—because she didn't see the line between what she was supposed to do and what she wanted to do, and had no filter in her head to make her think about her behavior. Like her prescription for success generally, she would say of acting, "You feel it. You make it happen."[19] One could have said of her, as would sometimes be said of Jewish *luftmenshen*, men whose heads were in the clouds, that she lived in her dreams, which seemed a particularly Jewish affliction since Jews had often been driven into their dreams by the malice of the world, just as Streisand had been. She had no taste for the world.

At least the world of people. But as she was working, taking classes, and auditioning, seventeen-year-old Barbra Streisand, still her father's daughter, was also trying to educate herself. Often staying at the Millers' apartment, she began reading their books, looking at their art, listening to their music. (It was at this time that she discovered the affinity between her late father's taste in literature and her own.) "I read Russian plays, Russian novels, Greek tragedies. *Anna Karenina* changed my life," she told *Playboy* magazine. "I remember hearing Respighi's *Pines of Rome* that summer; *The Rite of Spring* by Stravinsky. Can you imagine what that's like? To hear that music for the first time?" She made a point of saying that most people assumed she grew up under the influence of artistic parents, but "it isn't true."[20] She was entirely self-taught. This self-education

34

was as close to college as Barbra would get, but it did spark a lifelong interest in the arts, and whatever detractors would say about Streisand—and they would say just about everything— no one seriously called her ignorant.

Still, in some ways the education was less important than that the Millers were taking the time to facilitate it. This was something striking about the gangly, desperate teenager— something that would continue throughout her life. Long before her talent was in evidence, long before anyone thought she would succeed, she attracted mentors—individuals, like the Millers, who wanted to take her under their wing, nurture her, instruct her, support her, even though people still didn't interest her much, and Barbra was not particularly gracious in return. What each mentor got from this is difficult to say. They couldn't explain it themselves. Terry Leong, a young golf-shirt designer who met Barbra when she was at the Theatre Studio and who taught her about fashion and thrift shops, recalled to biographer Christopher Andersen, "Everyone was very protective of her. We were willing to work for nothing because we all knew there was just something magical about Barbra even then. I don't know what it was. . . . It's impossible to explain, really."[21]

Part of the explanation may have been that three of her early mentors—Leong, a handsome young California-born actor named Barry Dennen, and an illustrator friend of Dennen's named Bob Schulenberg—were gay (Dennen a closeted gay), and that they seemed to be attracted to Barbra both for her sense of estrangement and for her willingness to be outré. In a way, Barbra became their Galatea: Leong for fashion, Schulenberg for makeup, and Dennen for general taste. She was a medium for them to mold—all the more appealing for being so malleable and so willing to try or do anything. The girl who grew up without rules had no rules to break.

But she was also, as she would later be for her audiences, a vicarious vessel for their challenge to society. Barbra was their "point girl"—the spear that kept attacking and that couldn't be blunted. This is what may have been so magical about Barbra: her invincibility. Anyone who met her knew she couldn't be stopped. That invincibility merged with something else. It was probably no coincidence that Dennen and Schulenberg, while gay, were also Jewish, as so many of Barbra's later mentors and acolytes would be. The Jews' relationship to America was fraught. Either they seemed to try to appease the prevailing order by assimilating, or they sneered at the prevailing order by going more deeply into their Jewishness. Barbra was obviously the latter kind of Jew. And for these early supporters, as for so many of her later fans, she became the Jews' Jew, the woman whose lack of shame over being Jewish, whose flagrant display of her Jewishness, was empowering. Even then, Barbra made people feel better about themselves because she seemed, overtly at least, to feel so good about herself.

But Barbra was unfinished. She was effectively undergoing three educations in 1959 and into 1960: an artistic education with help from the Millers, an education in style from her three gay mentors, and her acting education. It was a time of great tumult and excitement and challenge for her. As Dennen wrote about this period, "She was, in her speech as in her life, trying on ideas for size, turning things over and over, examining, questioning, searching, pushing forward, retreating, heatedly coming to conclusions at the same time she was skeptically doubting everything."[22] This was true of her acting as well. It is unclear exactly how good an actress she was at the time, though Miller would tell interviewers about assigning her a seduction scene in *The Rose Tattoo* and finding her having difficulty—she was unschooled in seduction—until she came up with the idea of playing the scene as if she were blind and had to *feel* her way into the intimacy, even mounting her male partner. Miller called it the sexiest scene he had ever seen.[23] Barbra would talk about the transformation she felt herself undergoing as an actress, a kind of spiritual awakening: "I could feel something that transcended the intellect take over and live its own life."[24]

This awakening did not, however, necessarily translate into roles. In May 1960, she landed a part in a production of a 1920 allegorical drama titled *The Insect Play*, in which she played a butterfly. It ran for all of three performances. During rehearsals she met Barry Dennen, who noted her immediate impact on him. "She had what my acting teacher called 'The Actor's Mask,'" he would write, "a face dramatically distinctive, sculptured, carved features that demanded, 'Look at me, look at me!' on the stage."[25] The problem was that those who cast shows didn't want to look at her. Back on the hustings, she kept hearing the same old complaints and kept meeting the same rejection she had always met. "Great talent but a dog!" said an agent at William Morris for whom she auditioned. "We'll never be able to sell her."[26] In Brooklyn, among her fellow Jews, she could be different. She could embrace her difference. But in the theater world, even when she was among Jews, she was not just different. She was the *other*. She was the person who didn't belong—in some cases, the reminder of who those casting agents and producers actually were and what they wanted to escape.

Here again there was an almost atavistic Jewish sense of oppression in Barbra. "People could use their power over me," she told Chaim Potok in an interview. "They had power to treat me like an animal. I had no dignity." She said she found it "demeaning" to ask for a job. "I couldn't do it."[27] She was hurt, but she was also resentful, and as detractors would later snarl, if Streisand were the queen of fortitude, she was also the queen of vengeance. Indeed, the fortitude seemed to arise from the resentment. When Anita Miller asked her if she would be an audition partner at the famous Actors Studio, where Brando had trained, and she didn't get invited to join the studio herself, she began penning furious letters to Actors Studio head

Lee Strasberg, fulminating against him: "I hear you're a star-fucker," she wrote. But she didn't mail them.[28] (Later she would write in her *Playbill* bio: "She is not a member of the Actors Studio.") She claimed to have launched similar tirades against those insulting casting directors, screaming at them, and a few years later she would upbraid producer David Susskind to his face on a television program for refusing to see her when she was out trolling for a job.[29] The vehemence was authentic, but she had the social gift of making her resentment seem odd, even funny, rather than embittered, as if they were the fools for not recognizing what they had in front of them in this outlandish and outlandishly talented teenager.

But embittered she was. And frustrated. "I gave up," she told Potok. She decided she would abandon acting to design clothes. Then she said a friend [Dennen] told her, "'There's a talent contest where you get free meals'—which always interested me."[30] So she said she entered as a singer, and she won. In fact, this moment, which would be a milestone, wasn't quite the way she described it. For one thing, as much as she may have disdained singing, it wasn't a default. She knew from her youth that she could sing, even if she kept that talent hidden from just about everybody else as she pursued acting. Singing was a kind of secret weapon. Cis Corman, a surrogate mother of hers at the time and later one of her closest friends, said she met Barbra in an acting class both were taking when the girl was fifteen or sixteen and Barbra began hanging out at Corman's house with Corman's husband and four children. They were sitting in the kitchen one day when Barbra said she was going to enter a singing contest. To which Corman said, "Why would you do that? You don't know how to sing." This from someone who had known her well for two years. Corman then asked her to sing, which Barbra agreed to do on the condition that she face the wall as she did so. "So she sat down and faced the wall," Corman recalled, "and sang Harold Arlen's 'A Sleepin' Bee.' She turned around when she got through, and we were drenched in tears. It is something I'll never forget."[31]

In fact, Barbra had been cultivating her singing with a fellow actor named Carl Esser, who played guitar.[32] But she hadn't any need for it until early 1960, when she was ushering at the Lunt-Fontanne Theatre during the run of *The Sound of Music*. The casting director, Eddie Blum, had put out a call for the touring company, and Barbra, with her typical chutzpah, submitted a résumé—an unmistakably Jewish girl vying for the role of the unmistakably gentile Von Trapp daughter Liesl. Blum would say that the only reason he even deigned to see her was because she had submitted a photo so outrageous, a photo in which Barbra was playing exotic with thick makeup and heavy jewels, that he felt he had to meet her. According to Barry Dennen, Barbra immediately rushed to his Greenwich Village apartment and asked if she could record a song on his tape machine. Like Corman, Dennen had no idea that Barbra could sing. But as he described it in his book on his relationship with Barbra, she began singing "Day by Day," and "as the first few cool phrases of the song floated out of the speakers, I remember I blinked. And then something like a cold electric shock ran right up my spine from my heels to my head." He said he thought he was going "crazy" and calls it "the exact moment when 'Barbara' first began to metamorphose into 'Barbra.'" He also says it was at that moment he suggested Barbra enter the talent contest at the Lion, a small club at West Ninth Street off Sixth Avenue directly across the street from Dennen's apartment. And then, in his account, Barbra returned to her own apartment, told her roommate that Dennen thought she should sing, and agreed to sing for the roommate so long as she didn't look at Barbra.[33] Meanwhile, Blum auditioned her, told her she wasn't right for the Liesl role ("You should see me with blonde hair," she told him, "I bleached it once and even my mother thought I was gentile"), but was entirely charmed by her audacity—and by her talent.[34] His advice: Look for work in a nightclub.[35]

Barbra was still resisting. She insisted on acting. "I hated singing," she later said. "I wanted to be an actress. But I don't think I would have made it any other way."[36] Dennen later claimed that he was the one who pushed her to sing and to enter the contest by telling her that singing was just another form of acting. Indeed, when she rehearsed Arlen's "A Sleepin' Bee," from the Broadway show *The Grass Harp*, Dennen told her to think of it as a three-act play—moving from a young girl experiencing love for the first time early in the song (act 1) to a middle-aged woman reminiscing to her daughter about that first love (act 2) to a grandmother sharing the secrets of love with her granddaughter (act 3). At one point, he even put what he said was a bee in her hand. (It was actually a house fly.) This way Dennen got Barbra to accept singing as worthy of her, but he also taught Barbra how to invest a song with emotion. He said the first time she sang the song this way it was "electrifying."[37]

In effect, Dennen says, Barbra was in training. It was not only how to act a song that he said he taught her. He claimed to have introduced her to Edith Piaf and Peggy Lee and Judy Garland and Billie Holiday, saying that Barbra had been musically naive, even ignorant, before he met her.[38] Dennen's and Barbra's mutual friend Bob Schulenberg corroborated Dennen's boast that he had been Barbra's real mentor. He would tell her biographer Christopher Andersen, "His contribution to what she became was just incalculable," and Dennen would be deeply aggrieved that Barbra would not acknowledge that contribution later on.[39] It became one of those criticisms that would follow her throughout her life—that she, as her first manager, Ted Rozar, would say, was "always a master of sucking up to anybody who could help her," but that "if you were of no value to her, that little switch went off in her head and she treated you like shit."[40] Dennen's version was that she had a habit of "cutting out of her life people who were not directly relevant to her success," even though in "her early years she had a lot of people to be grateful for."[41]

Whether she was ungrateful or not, Barbra seemed to understand from a fairly young age that she was not Galatea the way her mentors may have thought. Dennen no doubt helped her sell a song, Leong certainly helped her dress, and Schulenberg would help refine and define her style, but Barbra understood that none of this would have made a scintilla of difference if she hadn't been who she was, if she didn't have the native talent she had. If she had thought any other way, it is unlikely she would have succeeded. The photographer and designer Cecil Beaton, who worked with her on *On a Clear Day You Can See Forever*, called her a "self-willed creation," which is exactly how she thought of herself.[42] As her biographer William Mann wrote of her early PR: "That was the bottom-line message of all the publicity about Barbra: *It was her*."[43]

And it *was* her, no matter what others contributed. They had played off of her. They hadn't changed or shaped her. When she appeared on July 2, 1960, at the Lion for that Tuesday night's talent show, eighteen-year-old Barbra was already formed. She arrived in a purple ostrich-feathered boudoir jacket over a dress of lilac and purple that Leong had found in a thrift shop—a variation on the strangeness she had cultivated in high school. She looked like "a nightingale about to be set free from her cage," as Dennen would put it.[44] And she looked a little preposterous, which fit with the way that Barbra saw herself. By one account, some members of the audience thought she might be a comic put-on. It didn't hurt for an odd duck like Barbra that the Lion was what Dennen called "Fairy Heaven"— "wall-to-wall gay guys." It was the sort of audience that knew what it was like to be different, even knew what it was like to try to have to fit in. (Dennen said many of the club's clientele wore suits and ties so as not to attract the attention of the police.)[45]

And in a way, that first appearance would be a microcosm of Barbra's entire career. Her competitors in the contest that summer night were a light operatic singer, a comic, and, more daunting, Dawn Hampton, the beautiful niece of jazz xylophonist Lionel Hampton, who was herself a jazz vocalist. Hampton preceded Barbra and sang a hot number that roused the crowd. It was, as it was always to be, Barbra against the conventionally beautiful and sexy. Still, though some might have seen her as comical, Dennen thought that her outfit and her tentativeness, coming on the heels of an obvious charmer, seemed to elicit a mothering instinct.[46] She was nervous. Dennen calmed her by telling her, as he had told her in training, that this wasn't really singing; it was acting. Just act. Then she began. She began the song they had rehearsed endlessly, the Arlen song about the woman finding love and then passing her knowledge on, the sad, plaintive song that she had broken into three acts. Dennen would recall that when she finished there was "utter silence." A kind of stunned silence—as audiences would later be stunned by her. "And then suddenly the whole room crashed into applause, an eruption of yells and whistles, ear-shattering stomping and screaming."[47] They demanded another song, and she broke into "When Sunny Gets Blue." She won the contest that night, was asked back for an appearance on Saturday, won again the next week and for many weeks thereafter until she was forced to retire from the contests to give someone else a chance. By this time, by one account, she had become a legend. People lined up outside the club to see her.[48]

But after that first night, that first transformative night, she, Terry Leong, and Barry Dennen went to a restaurant called the Pam Pam with Barbra already flushed with a sense of her success. When a patron who had seen her at the club asked for her autograph, she told her companions that she was thinking of changing her name—not "Barbara" but "Barbra." "You look the same to me," Dennen said he told her. Taking a sip of her Cherry Coke, she told Dennen simply, "I'm not." Years later she would say, "My lack of an 'a' made me different."[49] But it wasn't the lack of an "a" that made her different. That was just a certification of what she had felt that evening when the audience loved her. That love is what made her different. She had been reborn, and nothing would ever be the same.

She knew. On her way to audition with Dennen, Schulenberg, and the Lion's manager, Burke McHugh, at another Greenwich Village club, the tonier Bon Soir, she said she thought to herself, "This is the beginning of something."[50] She had spent the summer of 1960 at a theater in Fishkill, New York, appearing in a number of plays, but as soon as she returned to Manhattan, she was thinking of singing. Yet despite her reputation, the owner of the Bon Soir, Ernie Sgroi, decided to sneak her into one of his shows to see how his audience would respond. She sang "A Sleepin' Bee," by now her signature, and a novelty song that she and Dennen had selected, "Who's Afraid of the Big Bad Wolf?" The crowd loved it, and Sgroi signed her up that September for two weeks that stretched into eight.

Still, Barbra played on her oddness. When she would rehearse with Dennen, she would take her gum out of her mouth and stick it to the mike. She did the same thing at the Bon Soir. (Dustin Hoffman, who saw her there, said of the gum gambit that he thought, "What a smart girl. It was a seemingly natural act but it has a method to its madness.")[51] And she acted as if it was all spontaneous, as if she had just shown up and begun singing. Apparently, she even convinced herself, because years later she would say that when she stepped on stage there for her opening, she couldn't remember her set. "I'd keep saying,

'What's the first note? When do I come in?' Things like that. They loved me. I don't know why."[52] But of course she knew why. They loved that she was so seemingly unstudied, so raw, so herself.

But the fact is that she was anything but unstudied. She and Dennen rehearsed endlessly before she debuted there. They had gone over every single one of her six songs and its spot in the set. He drilled her by studying those other singers to whom he had introduced her. They had even practiced what to do if the audience kept talking while she sang: stop and stare them down. So when she took the stage on September 9, on a bill with the comedians Tony and Eddie and Phyllis Diller, wearing a high-necked black velvet bodice and a black velvet skirt and antique shoes with black and silver buckles—shoes that she said would be burnt out that night from the heat of her feet—she had a pretty good sense of what impression she was making.[53] She was the forlorn girl—the "girl the guys never looked at twice," and the "invisible woman," as Marty Erlichman, who rushed backstage after he saw her there and offered to become her manager, would remember. He said she reminded him of Charlie Chaplin.[54] And she and Dennen had the perfect closer— the Rodgers and Hart song "Nobody's Heart," in which a girl laments that nobody's heart belongs to her, nobody's arms will surround her. It was a song so naked in its emotion, so clearly self-reflective, that the audience cheered. As one critic wrote, she had a "dynamic passion that tells the listener that this Plain Jane is holding up a vocal mirror to her own life."[55]

Even the band knew something was aborning. "First you looked at the nose," said Tiger Haynes, the band's leader. "Then you looked at the dress. Then you heard the voice—and that was it."[56] But it wasn't just the audience and the band. Barbra herself was emboldened. "In life I felt, you know, people paid no attention to me," she said later. "When I would talk, it came out so enthusiastically that they would disregard it. All of a sudden, singing, I could say what I felt, and I was listened to."[57] Singer Kaye Ballard said that after the Bon Soir appearance Barbra had a different demeanor. "Barbra believed she was beautiful. She was thoroughly convinced of the fact." Ballard said that she herself would never do ballads because she felt she was too ugly to make the sentiments convincing. But confident Barbra feasted on ballads.[58]

There were still some holdouts. At the *New Yorker*, the organ of urban sophistication, critic Roger Whittaker harrumphed: "At the Bon Soir, Barbra Streisand singer—file and forget."[59] Barbra wasn't a sophisticate. And Diana Streisand still was not a convert. After seeing Barbra perform, she told her, "Your voice is very thin. You need eggs in your milk to make your voice stronger." Barbra said that she used this criticism to further herself. "I had to go out into the world and prove I was something and I would be remembered in some way."[60]

But those voices were in the minority, or rather the minority voices were the majority. It is difficult to say whether Streisand would have succeeded had she not started out in New York, had she not had such a large gay following, and had she not drawn support from the Jewish and ethnic communities of the city. Hers was not a midwestern talent or, for that matter, even a California talent, and though she would eventually be welcomed there, it was only after she had made it in New York among her fellow oddballs and pariahs. Streisand would always appeal to the fringe—and to the tattered fringe in everyone's psyche. And in the beginning, it was the fringe that celebrated her, adored her, saw her as one of their own. It was the fringe, not the typical show biz promoters, that had actually discovered her.

In time, the others would come. After the Bon Soir engagement, she got her first agent—a man named Ted Rozar, of whom Barbra would say, "He's such a goy!"[61] (Later she replaced him with the Jewish Erlichman, who would remain her manager for the rest of her career, save for a very brief period.) But Rozar had problems getting bookings. The different girl was just too different outside New York. Still, she worked. She would go to bars with cabaret licenses and, one pianist friend remembered, "do the same thing at every one of them—just slide onto the bench next to the guy who was playing the piano."[62] She would listen to old records, and she would get sheet music by calling publishers and pretending to be the secretary of the crooner Vaughn Monroe. When she finally did get some gigs outside New York—in Detroit and Saint Louis—a pianist at the first said, "She worked harder than any girl I've ever met." People talked about how she used her hands, her long fingers shaping the lyric in the air. "A lot of it was instinct," the Detroit pianist said, "but I saw her work in front of a mirror four and five hours a day perfecting her gestures."[63]

But if she was working on her performance, she was also working on her persona since she was smart enough to realize how much her persona infused her performance. The girl who dropped an "a" from her name in order to be different wanted to look different, too. Since high school, of course, she had dressed offbeat with her black stockings and sweaters. Terry Leong had altered that style by introducing her to those thrift shops and clothing that was the opposite of severe. "Before anyone else in the world became aware of it," Dennen would write, "she appreciated that this rare, antique clothing was of a quality you simply couldn't find anywhere else."[64] This style became her uniform, which only added to her appeal as an alien. But it also turned her into a trendsetter. As Camille Paglia observed, "She was the first public figure to wear retro clothes from the 1930s. This 'thrift-shop look' became a hippie style later adopted by Janis Joplin."[65]

But while it may have been a trendsetting style, it was one that was decidedly contrarian to the prevailing idea of good taste. It wasn't just that the outfits were gaudy and even discordant.

46

It was that they—and Barbra—were seen as dirty, which was another criticism that trailed her. Even Dennen asked her if she sent her second-hand purchases to the dry cleaner before she wore them, to which Barbra huffed that she did, but that the clothes were all donated by rich women. "I mean, they're rich, they take baths, they gotta be clean, right?"[66] As for her personal hygiene, the manager of a rival club in Detroit told the manager of the Caucus Club where she was playing that she looked as if she needed a bath, and another club owner was appalled by her dirty slip and later fired her.[67]

And yet Dennen, who lived with Barbra for a time, insisted that she was "compulsively neat and immaculate about her appearance and dress," and Bob Schulenberg, who knew her well in this period, concurred that she was clean and meticulous.[68] In fact, though she was then something of a vagabond, moving from one friend's apartment to another because she had trouble affording an apartment of her own, carrying a cot and bags of clothes with her wherever she went, Schulenberg said she always left the premises spotless.

The idea that Barbra dressed in dirty clothes and didn't bathe was of a piece with the sort of derision hurled first at immigrants and then at beatniks in the 1950s and then at student rebels in the 1960s and 1970s. It was a form of cultural superiority and a put-down—triggered in Barbra's case because she threatened the middle-class sense of decorum. She didn't look the way an entertainer was supposed to look. Even Ernie Sgroi, the Bon Soir owner, worried that the female members of his audience would find Barbra's clothes distasteful, and he enlisted Phyllis Diller, who shared the bill with Barbra, to buy her a dress at S. Klein's. Diller chose a chic black Chanel, but Barbra wouldn't wear it, finally asking Diller if she could return it in exchange for fabric.[69]

Barbra's own explanation for why she dressed the way she did was convenience. "If I wore black tights it was to keep warm," and if she dressed in thrift-shop clothes it was because "the salespeople in department stores are so mean, a haughty bunch. In thrift shops, nobody's mean," which also played up the notion that if she were different, she was nonetheless down-to-earth.[70] She told *Life* a similar story: "I never was a beatnik. I bought that stuff because it was cheap."[71] But this attitude was part of the persona, too, like the insistence that she couldn't remember her songs or the seemingly impromptu gesture of placing her gum on the mike, which she repeated every night. She continued to cultivate the image of someone who was far outside the boundaries of ordinary deliberation, much less taste—the image of someone who never gave anything a second thought, who just acted in the moment. In a business where everything was planned down to the last detail, Barbra was the show business rebel.

But the clothes weren't the entirety of the "look." There was also the face itself—the face that, Barbra seemed to feel, had sunk a thousand ships. This was where Bob Schulenberg came in. Schulenberg, Dennen's college friend from UCLA, was an illustrator who happened to be intrigued by fashion and makeup. For him, Barbra's face was a canvas, and the painting he sought was something exotic, something dramatic, something that would transform the plain Jewish visage into one that was modern and daring. As he told it to Streisand biographer Anne Edwards, "What I did was make cheekbones where there was still baby fat, and I contoured the eyes and feathered some false eyelashes shorter than her own and extended the line at the corner of her eyes"—the last an effect that made her look like Nefertiti and that would also become a signature. Finally, he said he used heavy greasepaint—"to hide the scars of her skin condition."[72]

The one feature that Schulenberg could not change was her nose. And the nose was at the center of so much of Streisand's self-regard or lack thereof. Schulenberg said that she did consider getting a nose job. "We'd be in her apartment or at a restaurant and she'd stop everything to play with her nose. She'd push the tip of it up with her middle finger and say, 'See . . . this is how I want it to look. What do you think?'"[73] She discussed a nose job with Dennen, too—just a little nip, she said. And when Erlichman first approached Barbra to represent her, she asked him whether she should change her name or fix her nose. He told her neither, which, it was said, impressed her, and was one reason why she opted to sign with him.[74] Even so, she later told a reporter that she decided against getting a nose job, not because she preferred her nose the way it was, but because "I'm afraid of the pain."[75]

But the nose issue would not subside. When she appeared at the Blue Angel late in 1961, a step up from Bon Soir, Abel Greene in his *Variety* review said she needed to have a "schnoz bob" or be consigned to comedy.[76] Streisand was hurt and she was angry. Appearing shortly after on the late-night talk show *PM East*, she began riffing on her nose, Cyrano de Streisand, telling fellow guest Mickey Rooney that she would never be allowed on-screen because of her nose, which prompted Rooney to rhapsodize about it. But this wasn't just a case of vanity. It was a case of ambition. As David Kaufman would observe in his book *Jewhooing the Sixties*, the bias against Ashkenazic Jewish features "represents a subtle form of anti-Semitism in our culture." The emphasis on her nose, even by Jews like Greene, was to conflate Jewishness and ugliness.[77] This mattered to her. The only way to become a movie star, which remained Streisand's goal, was either to surrender and get that nose job or to challenge the idea that Jewishness was unattractive. That was not easy. Deciding not to get a nose job was an act of professional bravery—her greatest assertion both of her Jewishness (though there were occasions when, presumably as a joke, she called herself Turkish) and of her own idea that she was beautiful if she felt beautiful.

The refusal to get her nose fixed said something else about her: that if she was determined to be a star, she was also determined to be a star on her terms. In fact, rather than run from her Jewishness, she pushed it onstage, which in New York may have actually been an advantage, but was certainly not an advantage away from New York. Appearing in spring 1961 at a club in Saint Louis, not exactly a center of urban Judaism, she began vamping between songs, using Yiddishims, and pointing to her dress and asking the audience how they liked her *schmatta*. She claimed that she was bored, so she slipped into the role of the Brooklyn Jew, seemingly not caring whether the audience got it or would take offense.[78]

But Greene's prediction that she didn't look like a star wasn't far off. Though she had her club following in the Village for whom she was transcendent, as an actress the only role she was able to land was as a comedienne. In October 1961, Erlichman got her a part in a comic revue—actually a send-up of revues— called "Another Evening with Harry Stoones," where she sang some comic songs (in one of which, "Value," a song she would sing on occasion throughout her career, a girl weighed two suitors on the basis of their bank accounts) and performed in sketches. It closed after a single performance.

But by this time Barbra was in full rehearsal for another role that was to figure prominently in advancing her career: the role of kook. The figure of the kook was largely a product of late-night television talk shows, where there was a premium on animated, spacy, garrulous, and unpredictable guests who seemed to blurt out whatever was on their minds, the more outrageous the better. They made for good entertainment, allowing the host to serve as a flabbergasted straight man. (It was as a kook on an early TV quiz show that Zsa Zsa Gabor became a phenomenon.) Jack Paar, host of *The Tonight Show* in the late 1950s and early 1960s, was the connoisseur of kooks. Among his recurrent guests were a risqué author named Alexander King, a French chanteuse who mangled English named Geneviève, two ditzy character actresses, Peggy Cass and Dody Goodman, and the wry comedy writer Jack Douglas with a young Japanese wife named Reiko whose malapropisms, like Geneviève's, were a source of hilarity. These weren't entertainers in any conventional sense. They were personalities whose job was to be themselves or, at least, some bizarre, exaggerated version of themselves. They were "good TV."

You certainly don't think of Streisand now as a kook. She is a grande dame, a diva, a legend. But the Streisand of those early years, the teenage Streisand who was just starting out in clubs, was one of those characters who got attention not simply by looking outrageous but by saying outrageous things. "The best fried chicken I know comes with a TV dinner," she told the *New Yorker* in a stream-of-consciousness "Talk of the Town" interview. "I have a railroad flat in the East Sixties, but it's getting too small. It's getting too small because I just bought two marvelous Victorian cabinets with glass shelves. I got them in a shop at Eighty-third Street and Columbus Avenue, called Foyniture Limited. That's how it's spelled. I like to get shawls that I can wear instead of a coat, and that can also serve as bedcovers. I was bald until I was two. I think I'm some sort of Martian. I exist on my will power, being Taurus."[79]

This was how audiences first came to know Streisand. She was spontaneous and unmediated to begin with, even without the curation of her persona, so the persona wasn't entirely a confection. Still, she kept refining that persona and created herself as a "character," the sort of personality who would appeal to talk shows: talkative, often nonsensical, bizarrely dressed in those thrift-shop outfits, self-absorbed, oblivious, Jewish ethnic urban, and, oddly enough, given all that, seemingly unaffected. As David Kaufman observed in *Jewhooing the Sixties*, "Coming from Brooklyn in a literal sense, the actress drew upon her background to create a more figurative invented self, which only seemed 'authentic' due to the real-life referent. Building on her 'natural' Brooklyn Jewishness with all its idiosyncratic intonations and mannerisms, Streisand established an engagingly 'real' public image."[80] She became a kook.

But a kook without a venue is a street character. Streisand developed her persona for the media, especially television. Comedian-actor-host Orson Bean had caught her act at the Bon Soir and like almost everyone was captivated. So when he was asked to sub for Paar on *The Tonight Show* in April 1961, he asked for Streisand, and even got the network to fly her in from Detroit, where she was playing the Caucus Club. Arriving in a burgundy dress made for her out of furniture upholstery a friend had scored from a store, she was, Bean recalled, a "nervous wreck." She was also logorrheic and ditzy. But then she got up to sing her standard, "A Sleepin' Bee," and as Bean later described it, "It was like God singing through her. She got a standing ovation, which doesn't happen on TV. It was an incredible moment."[81]

And it was incredible not just because Streisand had that gorgeous voice. It was incredible because of how she had suddenly transformed herself from a nutty babbler into this astonishing singer. The dissonance was surprising, even discombobulating if you weren't familiar with Streisand, and of course, just about no one at the time was. It set a tone for her early appearances—the Jekyll-and-Hyde novelty of a silly girl who could suddenly turn the switch and become a serious, and seriously great, singer. "When I was on tour, I noticed the audience reaction in a dozen different cities," she wrote early in her career. "It was always the same. When I came on stage, people laughed. But when I begin to sing, the audience changes somehow. They're with me. It's as if they'd like to say they're sorry they laughed at me."[82] Of course, the audience couldn't have known that it was the stunt she had been playing since she was a little girl: Streisand didn't act like the kind of person who had that fund of talent until she decided to turn it on. It was her way of showing up all of those who had pigeonholed her as a comedienne.

That *Tonight Show* appearance was the beginning of a new vocation for Streisand as talk-show kook cum torch singer. Even as she continued to appear at the Bon Soir, the Blue Angel, and other clubs in the hinterlands, she was invited to chat and sing on *PM East*, hosted by Mike Wallace, who would later become famous as an acerbic reporter on *60 Minutes*. Jaundiced and worldly-wise, Wallace was not entirely charmed by her. He thought the kook persona—the persona that got her on the show—was an affectation, and he would goad her about it, showing that he hadn't fallen for the act. But precisely because it wasn't *all* an act, Barbra could best him, and did, sometimes leaving Wallace fumbling with her non sequiturs, telling him she wanted to be a fireman or an opera impresario, and intimidating him by showing that *she* would not be intimidated, even though she was a teenager. She was, said a *PM East* producer, the "essence of every confused, not-very-attractive girl who wanted extravagantly more out of life than birth circumstances could possibly give her."[83]And that's what the audience saw: a plain-looking girl with the chutzpah to say and do whatever she pleased.

But then, as on *The Tonight Show*, it also saw the transformation and heard the voice and felt the thrall. The persona may have gotten her on the show; the ever-recurring trick kept getting her invitations to come back until she became a regular. Or put another way: If you never knew what was going to come out of her mouth when she talked, you knew exactly what would come out of her mouth when she sang. It may have been difficult to square the two, but the kook and the torch singer were perfectly synchronized, perfectly strategized halves. It took both to make Streisand into a unique personality, and it took a unique personality to make her into a star.

This was the Streisand who first gained national attention. When Groucho Marx, substitute-hosting on *The Tonight Show* in July 1962, enthused that she was going to be a "great success," she snapped, "How can I be such a great success if he calls me Stree-sand," referring to announcer Hugh Downs, who had mispronounced her name. (She had actually connived her way on by telling the casting director that her mother was dying in Cleveland and TV was the only way the poor woman could see her daughter.)[84] When she appeared again with the show's new host Johnny Carson that October, he asked her point-blank if she were kooky, prompting one of her monologues about how she made the rounds of auditions during the winter: "I wore a big coat and a big hat because I can't stand the cold, but, um, so I walked into offices and they really thought I was nuts . . . like one woman said to me, 'When you go make rounds, when you meet people, you should wear stockings and high-heeled shoes and so forth.' I said, 'It's freezing out lady, y'know? It's so cold what difference does it make? If . . . if I'm an actress and if I'm talented or not talented, what difference does it make if I wear tights or not.' So kooky, kooky, people said I was kooky, but now they sort of look at me and say I'm a style-setter or something."[85] Then she sang, and Carson was enthralled, asking her back several times.

In time, of course, Streisand had to shed the persona in order not to remain a novelty. Kooks seldom graduated into stardom. As she would tell Nora Ephron some years later, "I was never that kooky. It was all very logical. When I first sang, I wore a brocade vest I'd bought in a thrift shop, and people looked at me like I was a nut. Was it really kooky? I never did it for effect [of course, she did]. I only did it because I got the most for my money in thrift shops. But when people started saying, 'You gotta go see this girl who sings in nutty clothes,' I immediately changed. I never wore those clothes again. I was a singer, and I wanted them to watch me sing."[86]

This was something of an exaggeration. She didn't change her style immediately. Nor did she drop the kookiness. But she did undergo another aesthetic transformation that actually began before her second *Tonight Show* appearance. As biographer William Mann tells it, that was when Bob Schulenberg, her volunteer style consultant, decided that she needed a more sophisticated look and handed her fashion magazines to peruse. Schulenberg wanted something Audrey Hepburnish. So he gave her a shorter, sleeker hair style, and he got her a simple Geoffrey Beene dress.[87] But if Streisand was now dressed for success, it was largely because she had achieved it, at least a measure of it, not on TV or in nightclubs, but on the place where she had had that inspiration on her fourteenth birthday: the Broadway stage.

Perhaps it was foreordained that Barbra Streisand would get her first big accolades in a Jewish show playing a neglected Jewish secretary whose lifelong lament was that she was a lonely heart. Streisand was made for the part—or almost made for it. She had been rehearsing for it her entire life. She auditioned for the minor role of Miss Marmelstein in *I Can Get It for You Wholesale*, an adaptation of Jerome Weidman's novel of the same name, on November 29, 1961, around the time she was making appearances on *PM East*, and like so much in her early career, it was memorable. Weidman recalled her arriving at the audition at the St. James Theatre in a wild fur coat—"a combination of tans browns, yellows and whites, all swirling about in great shapeless splotches, like a child's painting of the hide of a piebald pony" with a hem of "great fat rolls of not quite but almost jet-black foam rubber that looked like flexible sections of sewer pipe." In short, she was in full kook mode. Asked if she could sing, she said, "Can I sing? If I couldn't sing, would I have the nerve to come out here in a thing like this coat?"[88]

Arthur Laurents, the play's director, attributed "calculated spontaneity" to her—in the clothing, in the way her music "accordioned across the stage after her" when she unfurled it and then "the trilling giggle of feigned surprise," in the tucking of the gum under her seat before she began to sing. (He said he later checked that seat: no gum.) He called her a "poster girl for Spinster Incarnate" with her "bird's nest of scraggly hair and her gawky disorganized body." He would describe how she "sprawled" in her chair, flinging out her legs, and "chattering as though we out front were the audience on her talk show."[89] But of course that was the intended effect, as was the by now familiar surprise she elicited when she began singing and undermined the first impression. "We were hearing music and words," Weidman later wrote, "but we were experiencing what one gets only from great art: a moment of revealed truth."[90] When they asked her back that afternoon, she said, in true Streisand fashion, that she had a hair appointment.[91] Not even on the cusp of success would she allow herself to be subjugated.

But the fact was, as good as she had been, landing the role wasn't a slam dunk. Producer David Merrick had the conventional response to her: She was too ugly, despite the character's own physical shortcomings and insecurities. And not even Laurents, who was wary of being snowed by her kook act, was convinced. He, Weidman, and composer Harold Rome went to her opening at the Blue Angel to see how she performed before an audience, and it took four more auditions to soften Merrick.[92] Part of the indecision was that Miss Marmelstein as written was fifty years old—which was the "almost" in the role being almost perfect for Streisand, who was only nineteen. But Laurents, having seen her repeatedly now, was wary no longer. He asked Weidman if the character had to be fifty. And that was that.

Fifty or nineteen, Streisand knew Marmelstein's longing intimately. And she knew something else. She knew how to translate that longing into a form of attention-grabbing—yet again, the girl who nobody noticed was going to get noticed by poking fun at her own inconspicuousness. Already during rehearsals, Weidman and Harold Rome had added a song for her, "Miss Marmelstein," a funny caterwaul of grievance, because, Weidman said, they knew the audience would be watching her anyway. And Streisand took that song with the unshakable determination to make it a showstopper. She would later say that she came up with the ingenious idea of singing the song in an office chair with casters, rolling herself across the stage, and that she had to fight Laurents to let her do it that way. More chutzpah from a teenage supporting player. Laurents would say that the chair was choreographer Herbert Ross's idea and that he never fought it.[93] Either way, it was different because Streisand made it different.

Wholesale was not a particularly good show by critics' estimates. It opened in Philadelphia to disastrous reviews, which sent Laurents into a tirade at his cast, directing fire at Barbra as well. Weidman watched with dismay, as she sat there, her head bowed, her hands twitching in her lap in seemingly nervous misery, and decided he would console her—only to find that her hands were not wringing but drawing a floor plan of her new apartment. Laurents hadn't made a dent. "Barbra Streisand is going into the books, near the top of whatever list gets compiled," Weidman later wrote, "because she possesses one other ingredient necessary to stardom, and I discovered it on that dismal morning in Philadelphia: she is made of copper tubing."[94]

It was true that Streisand seemed unflappable at a time when her entire future was riding on her performance. That may have been because she had a certain youthful fearlessness and, more, because even though Laurents was railing at her, she realized that she was the show's unmistakable secret weapon— the girl whose number got the nightly cheers. When *Wholesale* opened on Broadway on March 22, 1962, she received a three-minute ovation after her song, and just like that, overnight, she was a Broadway sensation.

Making it in small nightclubs, making it on TV talk shows was one thing. Making it on Broadway, albeit in a show that was hardly a hit, was another. It was life changing. During rehearsals, she had stayed at friends' apartments because she had lost her own lease. Now she was able to rent a tiny railroad apartment of her own above Oscar's of the Seas fish restaurant on Third Avenue—a symmetry with the family fish business over which her parents had lived for the first two years of their marriage. And when she celebrated her twentieth birthday two months after the show's opening, it was with a celebrity-filled gala at the Lichee Tree restaurant on Eighth Street. Among the noncelebrity guests were Barry Dennen and Bob Schulenberg, and Dennen would recall that when they managed to edge their way through the crowd to the gift table, "we were astonished to find it piled high with presents and accompanying cards that numb the mind. . . . The gift table was like a Who's Who of People Worth Knowing."[95]

The attraction was her talent—her gutsy, funny Marmelstein. But she couldn't have been the gutsy, funny Marmelstein if there hadn't been that other element: her difference. What had once made her virtually unemployable in show business was now one of her greatest assets. Broadway was paying its respects to a one-of-a-kind, and the kind was a girl who, they knew, should not have made it in a world circumscribed by convention. So they were not only celebrating her immense talent. They were celebrating her immense will. Streisand became a Broadway star playing an outsized Jewish *mieskeit*, and she was unlikely to have become a star any other way. She wasn't fitting herself into old prescriptions for stardom. She had written herself a new prescription. It is fair to say that no one had ever found stardom in a role that was so obviously a negation of stardom.

And she found something else in *Wholesale*. She found romance. She found it with the show's leading man, a young

Brooklynite like herself named Elliott Gould, who remembered seeing her during that outrageous audition and thinking that she looked like a "young Fagin." But Gould recognized in her an ally, another wounded soul using show business as a balm, and he was smitten. "She scared me, but I really dug her," he would say. "I think I was the first person who ever did." By the time the show closed, they were living together in that railroad apartment.[96]

Still, for all the accolades and for all her outward confidence, her insecurities ran so deep that they had not abated. She could have afforded a better apartment than the sixty-dollar-a-month walk-up, but she was never sure how long success would last. By one account, on weekends during the summer run of *Wholesale*, she played a resort in Connecticut with a group called the Four Young Men from Montana.[97] And when she went to shop at the chic Bergdorf Goodman department store on Fifth Avenue, the salespeople refused to wait on her because she didn't look like one of their clientele. "I'll be a success when I'm famous enough to get waited on at Bergdorf Goodman," she said.[98]

It wouldn't be long.

3

Tsezingen Zikh

THOUGH BARBRA Streisand was scarcely twenty, just about everyone in show business now knew her and loved her. Everyone believed she was a comer. She received a Tony nomination as Best Supporting Actress in a Musical for her performance as Miss Marmelstein, and there was astonishment when she lost to Phyllis Newman, the wife of Broadway royalty lyricist Adolph Green, for *Subways Are for Sleeping.* In the meantime, she returned to the Bon Soir, where she had gotten $175 a week, and now was a headliner there at $1,250 a week, and she was given a five-week engagement at the Blue Angel that summer.

Critics raved. "By the time her act was half finished," wrote Charles McHarry in the *Daily News* of her Bon Soir appearance, "it was obvious to guests in the packed cellar that Barbra will be picking her spots from now on."[1] *Time* described how she "squirmed onto a stool and let her coltish legs dangle, ankles flapping. She twisted her bony fingers through her hair and blessed her audience with a tired smile. Then she sang—and at the first note, her voice erased all the gawkiness of her presence onstage."[2] Syndicated columnist Robert Ruark, opening by labeling her nose more "moose than muse," went on to call her "the hottest thing to hit the entertainment field since Lena Horne erupted," and predicted, "She will be around 50 years from now if good songs are still written to be sung by good singers."[3] By the time *Wholesale* closed, Streisand was making five thousand dollars a week on the nightclub circuit and getting a raft of television invitations.[4]

Still, *Wholesale* would prove to be something of a mixed blessing. Although it won her acclaim, it didn't get her any closer to her real goal, which was movie stardom. *Wholesale* was a supporting role, a character role, a comic role, and Streisand didn't want to be a comedienne. Moreover, it was an ethnic role, and though she couldn't have hid her Jewishness if she wanted to, and she clearly didn't want to in that part, she also didn't want to be a professional Jew either, a Molly Picon or Gertrude Berg—someone who appealed almost exclusively to Jewish audiences and who could only hope to be a satellite in the larger Hollywood constellation. She never saw herself as a satellite, not even when she was a little girl dreaming of her future.

What *Wholesale* did get her were those singing engagements. But Streisand had always had that disdainful attitude toward singing, even as she recognized her talent. To her, singing was still just a road to acting—a "floozy job," she called it. She often arrived at her shows just before going on, and one accompanist thought she had "belligerence" toward singing, which she did.[5] "When I was singing, I always felt, This is not who I am," she told Chaim Potok. "I'm not a singer. I'm an actress."[6]

But there were no acting jobs coming in, only the nightclub offers. Marty Erlichman, her manager, kept trying to get her a recording contract now that she had gained notice. He

61

aimed high. He wanted Columbia Records, where Goddard Lieberson, a recording industry legend, was the virtual dictator. It is unclear who first brought her to Lieberson's attention. According to biographer Shaun Considine, Erlichman arranged a meeting, which Lieberson, on seeing her, thought was a "joke." He said, "I kept waiting for the punchline."[7] Arthur Laurents, the *Wholesale* director and a friend of Lieberson's, wrote that he was the one who had sent Streisand to see him, but Lieberson sent him a note: "Barbra Streisand is indeed very talented but I'm afraid she's too special for records," by which he presumably meant too kooky or too Jewish.[8] Undeterred, she auditioned a second time for Lieberson at Columbia's studio on Seventh Avenue. This time producer John Hammond, who had been instrumental in furthering careers from Billie Holiday to Bob Dylan, sat in and concluded, "It's a wonderful voice, but she's coming on too young and too soon."[9] She auditioned a third time, but Lieberson was no more inclined to sign her than he had been before.

Why was Lieberson, who was said to have exquisite taste, so resistant to her? Most charitably, one could say, as Laurents would, that Streisand was "an acquired taste" Lieberson hadn't acquired. Laurents took composer-lyricist Stephen Sondheim to hear her at the Bon Soir and said that Sondheim found her voice "too pinched and nasal."[10] But some thought there was another reason why Lieberson rejected her, and it had to do with his religion and his sense of status. Lieberson was a *haute* Jew, and like many *haute* Jews, he was not particularly enamored of aggressive, showy Jews like Streisand who seemed to confirm the negative stereotypes. Columbia publicist Peter Reilly told biographer Shaun Considine that Lieberson "moved with the Stravinskys, the Leonard Bernsteins, the Moss Harts. . . . She embarrassed Lieberson and his group. They didn't know it was an act with Barbra. To her it was all theater."[11] On this last point, Reilly was wrong. It was theater, but it wasn't *all* theater.

She didn't change who she was; she exaggerated it. And yet there was irony in that the Jewishness so critical to Streisand's persona and to her appeal was the primary hurdle to her recording contract—this woman who would wind up selling more records than any other female vocalist.

If this interpretation of Lieberson's coolness is true, it was in defiance of her obvious brilliance as a singer. According to biographer James Spada, after Lieberson's repeated rejections, Columbia's artist and repertoire director David Kapralik happened to catch her during one of her *PM East* appearances and was astonished by her voice. In another version, he caught her during an appearance on *The Garry Moore Show*, a variety program hosted by the one-time radio personality and quiz show moderator. Tellingly, Moore acknowledged the lingering kook persona by introducing her saying that she was as good singing "straight numbers" as she was being "zany." Moore had a segment on his show called "That Wonderful Year," which saluted a selected year through skits and songs, and it was writer Ken Welch who suggested that Streisand sing "Happy Days Are Here Again" for the show's celebration of 1932, but not as a tune of triumph. Rather, he said, she should sing it as a dirge. She did, and it became arguably the most important song in her repertoire.[12]

Seeing her performance, Kapralik later said that she affected him more than any performer since Edith Piaf. He managed to pressure Lieberson into seeing her on the closing night of her Blue Angel appearance, where she sang "Happy Days" and the room went wild.[13] This time Lieberson conceded. Streisand clearly had something. As columnist Radie Harris of the *Hollywood Reporter* said after also catching her at the Blue Angel, "Why would anyone who looks like that think she has a future in show business? . . . And then she got up to sing, and I knew why. Barbra Streisand was suddenly beautiful."[14]

Erlichman's negotiations with Lieberson were instructive.

63

He had asked for a hundred thousand dollars. Lieberson may have finally surrendered, but he wasn't going to give this untested kid that kind of money. By this time, Erlichman certainly could have gone elsewhere. Streisand now had a reputation. He didn't. He wanted the best. And neither he nor Streisand thought money was the main objective. She wanted greatness, acknowledgment, respect, and, of course, that road to Hollywood. So they settled for twenty thousand dollars, along with a clause that gave her complete creative control of her first album. In short, she traded money for the opportunity to determine her destiny.

In doing so, however, she got her first blowback, and it had something to do with her Jewishness, too. There were gripes within Columbia that Streisand was granted that control only because she was being abetted by Jews in the recording business who saw her as a form of revenge—exactly the way some of her fans saw her. (Evidently these gripers didn't know how the Jewish Lieberson had done everything he could *not* to help her.) One critic told biographer William Mann, "They wanted to have their say about what was beautiful, what was talented. For so long they had been self-conscious about being Jewish themselves, always having to promote these pretty blond gentile girls with perky little noses, and then along came Barbra and they suddenly had a chance to build up a real obvious Jewish girl."[15] It was yet another diss of Streisand, even though this one was a reversal: She couldn't possibly have made it because of her talent. She had to have been the beneficiary of a Jewish entertainment mafia.

It was true that Streisand, to the extent she put herself in anyone's hands, put herself in the hands of Jews. Dennen was a Jew. So were Schulenberg and Erlichman and her new publicist, Lee Solters, who was Sinatra's publicist, too. Her favorite composer, Harold Arlen, was a Jew. And now Lieberson. Her first album's producer, Mike Berniker, was a Brooklyn Jew, and the album's arranger, Peter Matz, was a Pittsburgh Jew. No doubt there was a comfort to being surrounded by Jews after being judged so harshly by gentile standards of beauty, even though, in truth, the Jews hadn't been much kinder.

But that Jewish phalanx would not provide protection at Columbia, where she was deeply resented as outside the mainstream, though the only thing that really could have placed her there was her Jewishness. Columbia execs griped that she and Bob Dylan, another Jew, were the "two the fags and radicals brought in."[16] Others asked, "Why doesn't someone give her a bath, wash her hair, buy her a dress?"[17] And Columbia provided no financial support either. The album, which she recorded over three days late in January 1963, shortly after *Wholesale* closed, was made for eighteen thousand dollars, a way for Columbia to hedge its relatively small bet, and it would not allow her a full band, only selected musicians.[18] "Look! We can't spend a lot of money on this," Berniker told Matz. "We don't know if this woman is going to sell records."[19]

She was shy. By one account, when she recorded, she had a screen around her so she could not be seen.[20] "She was so young, just twenty years old," Berniker told biographer Christopher Andersen, "that, of course, she had all the misgivings and insecurities that anyone that age would have. At the same time, she had this unbelievable, utter self-confidence"—that old combination of insecurity and self-belief that had proved so potent.[21] Citing Marlon Brando's sense of surprise in his performances, she herself would later say of control, "There is a difference between preconceiving everything and having it in control, and when it's slightly out of control."[22]

The Barbra Streisand Album, which is now a certified classic, was definitely slightly out of control. It consisted primarily of the songs she had been singing for two years in clubs, among them her standard "A Sleepin' Bee"; "Cry Me a River," which

Barry Dennen insisted she was singing for him when the two broke off their romantic relationship; torchy songs, "Soon It's Gonna Rain" and "A Taste of Honey"; an up-tempo bluesy song, "Keepin' Out of Mischief Now"; and three novelty numbers, Cole Porter's "Come to the Supermarket in Old Peking," "Who's Afraid of the Big Bad Wolf?" with which she had closed her act and sung with comic brio, and "Happy Days Are Here Again," now her signature song. All three confirmed Columbia's fear that she wasn't going to be mainstream. But having made her career so far on her difference, she doubled down on that difference. No one else was singing "Old Peking," "Who's Afraid of the Big Bad Wolf?" or the funereal "Happy Days," certainly not the pert blond gentiles. The album was a huge risk.

"There is no sense of proportion to the recording," one critic would later complain. He was talking about the repertoire: "For every haunting 'A Sleepin' Bee,' there is a self-conscious 'Come to the Supermarket.'"[23] But there wasn't much proportion to the singing either. She was pulling out all the stops, singing as if her life depended on it, which, in a very real sense, it did. The pert blondes might get another chance. Streisand knew she wouldn't. That is part of the album's appeal now: We hear a young artist going for broke. But even Streisand would come to realize that the album was *too* much. "I hear that first record of mine," she would later tell *Playboy*, "where I'm *ge-shreying* [Yiddish for "screaming" or "crying"] and getting so emotional, I think, Oh, my God, how did they ever like me? I'm embarrassed by it."[24]

The fact is that Columbia *didn't* like her. They released a single of "Happy Days," then failed to promote it. They put her on tour in March, after the album's February 21 launch, then failed to have enough albums in the stores, even though she appeared for a full week as a guest host on *The Mike Douglas Show* and Douglas flogged the album relentlessly. She made two

66

more appearances on *The Tonight Show* and one on *The Ed Sullivan Show* on March 24. Still the album sales didn't take off.

But Streisand had always been a word-of-mouth entertainer. Someone would see her and then tell someone else, who would tell someone else, and so on, until she had her fan base. It may have been a function of the intimacy she engendered. And she had begun as a coterie entertainer, winning favor with those who were a little off-center as she herself was, rather than an entertainer with immediate mass appeal. By the time she hit the Hungry i in San Francisco, the word of mouth had built, the coterie had grown, and she was beginning to attract larger audiences, just as she had done in New York. And by the time she hit the Basin Street East, back in New York that May, with its 450-seat room and on the same bill with Benny Goodman, her album had become a full-fledged success, against the odds and against the foot-dragging of Columbia. Radio DJs had even begun playing "Happy Days," and *The Barbra Streisand Album* slowly climbed the *Billboard* album list until it hit number eight, making her the best-selling female vocalist in the country. It would stay on the list for twenty-four weeks and win her a gold record.[25]

Her manager, Marty Erlichman, would call *The Barbra Streisand Album* the "turning point" in her career—the moment she went from being a New York phenomenon to a performer with a "national reputation."[26] The proof may have been that President John F. Kennedy had caught her appearance on *The Dinah Shore Show* early that May—a performance of which one critic said she was a "Flatbush gamine with the tonsils of a fish peddler"—and asked that she be invited to perform at the White House Correspondents Dinner, where she sang five songs, including "Happy Days."[27] "How long have you been singing?" the president asked her afterward. "About as long as you've been president," she shot back.[28]

Now she was a recording artist. But even though the superlatives overwhelmed the criticisms—one TV reviewer called her "so far superior to any of her contemporaries that there is really no one even in her league"—the "fish peddler" comment signified there was still some resistance to her, still the sense that she was too outré, too much the kook, perhaps too overtly Jewish to win over middle America.[29] It was a conundrum for Streisand, who wanted success but wanted it, as always, on her terms, without sacrificing who she was and what made her different. But did the difference limit her audience?

She encountered that challenge when she opened for Liberace at the Riviera in Las Vegas that August. Despite his flamboyancy and his homosexuality—a fact that seemed to escape just about all of his fans—there probably wasn't a more *goyische* entertainer than Liberace, just as there probably wasn't a more Jewy one than Streisand. "We found out very quickly that Liberace's audience was not a Streisand audience," her accompanist, Peter Daniels, told biographer Shaun Considine. "They didn't know what to make of her." The kooky New York Jewish charm was lost on them, and Daniels called her first two shows "disastrous." So Liberace, who legitimately admired Streisand, stepped into the breach. He said that he would do an opening number, then introduce her as his protégée, essentially vouching for her and disarming the audience.[30] With Liberace's blessing, Streisand turned the situation.

But that was Vegas and the tourist trade. When she opened at the Cocoanut Grove at the Ambassador Hotel in Los Angeles, among the cognoscenti, her reputation preceded her. The audience was a who's who of moviedom, but Streisand didn't trim her sails to appease them. Instead, she took the stage by walking up the aisle from the back of the room, wearing a pink gingham dress intended as a spoof on *The Sound of Music*, then looked out at the audience, said she was the only one she didn't recognize, and delivered a line that couldn't help but bring down the house: "If I'd known you were going to be on both sides of me, I'd have gotten my nose fixed."[31] This was Streisand in her element, which was people who really appreciated her.

She was on a roll, and she knew it. Taping *The Judy Garland Show* the next month, Judy, who was clearly intimidated, nervously asked Streisand if there was anything more she could possibly want in life. To which Streisand blurted, "Yes, there is. I'd like to take over your show."[32] She effectively did, scoring with a brilliant duet with Garland that remains Streisand lore: Garland sang "Get Happy," while Streisand counterpointed with "Happy Days." It ended with Ethel Merman pretending to wander onto the set: one former diva, one current diva, and one future diva all sharing the stage. The murmurs about the show at CBS were so strong that the network decided to rearrange its schedule and rush it onto the air the following week.

If the summer of 1963 was a turning point for Streisand's career, as the Garland show indicated, it was also a turning point for her self-regard. For years she had labored under the burden of her looks, and she had feigned a steely disregard and fed that famous myopic self-absorption. A friend told *Time*, "She is like a filter that filters out everything except what relates to herself. If I said, 'There's been an earthquake in Brazil,' she would answer, 'Well, there aren't any Brazilians in the audience tonight, so it doesn't matter.'"[33] Arthur Laurents probably had it right when he observed, "Her opinion of her looks has been the measure of her dissatisfaction far more than the accepted chilly mother." He thought the key to the way she felt about herself was how she dressed. "As her opinion of herself climbed," he wrote, "her outrageously outlandish clothes disappeared." But he added: "Still, each morning she must look in her unrelenting mirror over the bathroom sink: Have a good day."[34]

Now that Streisand was gaining national recognition, her estimate of herself, even of her looks, seemed to grow. "When I'm good, when I'm pleased with my performance," she would say, "I feel powerful. I forget about being an ugly duckling."[35]

Another time, she was blunter: "What does it matter what critics or people say? If you felt you did good, then fuck 'em."[36] But critics were seldom unkind now. That summer she was fêted in both *Newsweek*, which compared her to Bea Lillie and Billie Holiday, and the *Saturday Evening Post* by Pete Hamill, to whom she admitted, "They tell me I'll eventually win everything. The Emmy for TV, the Grammy for records, the Tony on Broadway and the Oscar for movies. . . . And I guess a lot of those things will happen to me. I kind of feel they will."[37] They, of course, did. But many years later, when she gave a speech at Harvard and a young English major asked her how she could fight injustice when she was such an insider, she replied, no doubt thinking back to those early days before success, to those days when critics insulted her and audiences didn't understand her, that she didn't think she was exactly mainstream, but she added, with a whiff of nostalgia, that she was nonetheless "disappointed" when her days as a "cult figure" ended and the adulation was no longer limited to New York, Los Angeles, and San Francisco.[38] She was disappointed that she had crossed the line.

Streisand didn't forget the slights. She would say that she never remembered the good reviews but could recite verbatim the negative ones. When she recorded her second album that June, just as the first album was cresting, she remembered, too, the foot-dragging at Columbia to sign her and the insults once they did and the unwillingness to help her album even after she had recorded it. "She never forgot that they kept her dangling," said one executive. "And she paid them back measure for measure."[39] When an engineer complained that this novice was telling him how to do his job, she now parried, "To have ego means to believe in your own strengths."[40] When she had recorded her first album, no one had wanted to work with her because they thought it a foregone conclusion she would bomb. Now that she was a hit, no one wanted to work with her because they thought she would be difficult, which she was. One producer said she was a "horror to work with" and called her a "bully."[41] Only twenty-one, Streisand shot back with the defense she would always use when accused of being overbearing: "If you maintain a standard of work in order not to get knocked down for not maintaining a standard of work, then you get knocked down for being a prima donna."[42] It was the defense of every ethnic outsider, not least of all Jews, who had been lacerated for being pushy or aggressive.

Her attitude was a manifestation of her vindication, and her vindication now intensified her appeal among the groups who had first rallied around her: Jews, women, and gays. She was her own person. "In sharp contrast to the one-note Jewish Princess image promulgated by Jewish male writers," feminist historian June Sochen would note, "Streisand is a one-woman rebuttal."[43] Another historian, Felicia Herman, said that by indulging her Jewishness, essentially succeeding on her own terms again, she was "refusing to submit to assimilationist pressures."[44]

That appeal to gay men had initially been predicated on the connection of their sense of difference to hers. "Queers can identify with her so much not simply because she had a huge voice and star quality—so does Julie Andrews," wrote Janet Jakobsen of Barnard College, examining the affinity between Jewish outsiderness and gay outsiderness, "but because she's different. She isn't simply white and Christian. Barbra doesn't quite fit."[45] Streisand would come to the same conclusion herself. Asked by a student at the Actors Studio why she had such a large gay following, she said, "Because I was different." But then she paused and added, "And I made it."[46]

And I made it. To be different was one thing. To be different and having succeeded was another, and to be different and having succeeded enough to be able to throw one's weight around was something else again. She was the Joe Louis of Jews and gays, their knockout puncher, not only the one performer with whom they could identify but the performer whose triumph became their triumph. And though she had crossed the line into success, she had done so without leaving her fans or, for that matter, herself behind. Not for nothing did she title her fifth album and first television special *My Name Is Barbra*. It was her way of asserting herself and her past. She had become a symbol of power, and she would remain that way for the rest of her career, even as charges that she was "difficult" kept being hurled at her. Of course, she was difficult. She could afford to be difficult. Her fans loved her even more *because* she was difficult. The girl who had once dreamed vicariously through movie stars was becoming a vicarious vessel herself, but it wasn't glamour or beauty or sex appeal that she provided. It was the power of the formerly abused now ascendant. Streisand was their revenge.

None of this would have been possible if she hadn't been great—really great, unprecedentedly great. So the pressing question is what made her great: What made Streisand, almost from the inception of her singing career, so far superior to her competitors? What makes her even now the standard for female vocalists the way Frank Sinatra remains the standard for male vocalists? Why is there Barbra Streisand and then everyone else?

Greatness isn't easy to dissect because it is a gestalt—the product of everything. With Streisand, you could begin at the beginning with her purely physical gifts. The voice was a given. The composer Marvin Hamlisch, who was once Streisand's accompanist, remembered his first impression of her, which was that she could be "very funny." "But then comes that voice in capital letters, and everything stops. You just go, 'Oh, my God.'"[47] Tennis star Andre Agassi, who met Streisand when a mutual friend invited him to a party at her home, remembered the guests prodding her to sing and Streisand finally capitulating. And then the voice again—the power of the voice. "The

72

sound filled the room from the rafters to the floorboards. Everyone stopped talking. Glasses shook. Flatware rattled. The bones in my ribs and wrist vibrated. I briefly thought someone had put one of Barbra's albums on a Bose sound system and turned the volume up full blast. I couldn't believe a human being was capable of producing that much sound, that a human voice could pervade every square inch of a room."[48]

And in addition to the power, there was the range. Streisand scaled notes no other popular singer scaled and did so without losing the beauty of her tone. "Nobody sounds like her when she's up that high, with that kind of clarity and purity," songwriter Burt Bacharach once said. "You can tell right away it's her."[49] And then there was the seeming effortlessness of it, like Fred Astaire dancing or Michael Jordan shooting. It always startled people that she had had no formal training and didn't even give a nod to the physiology of singing. Asked by the *New York Times* music critic Anthony Tommasini whether she thought incessantly like opera singers about breathing deeply from her diaphragm, she said, "Never." Nor did she do vocal exercises.[50] To another inquisitor she said, "It just seems the right sounds come out of me in the right way."[51] The early Streisand may have strained for emotion. She didn't strain to sing.

Beyond the voice was the ear. Streisand herself would talk about her sensitive ears, which she traced to the first night that stepfather Louis Kind came home. She told her mother that she had a buzzing in her ears (psychosomatic?), and Diana gave her a hot water bottle to sleep on, but Streisand said her mother never asked about the buzzing again. Still, it persisted—"a secret hidden inside me, inside my head." She said she wrapped scarves around her ears, even in sweltering summer, which is when, she claimed, she got the reputation of being "different." *Still*, the buzz persisted. It made her *forbiss*—depressed. But she also said that the tinnitus made her acutely aware of sound, including, apparently, the sound of her own voice. "It's probably some messed-up nasal thing which gives me the quality in my voice."[52] And when she recorded, she would hear everything—every single note, every single instrument—so that she would come to think of her tinnitus as a "gift."

The gift that most admirers cite is her gift of interpretation. Ever since Barry Dennen, and maybe even before, she had acted a song rather than just sing it. It was said so frequently of her—and she said it so frequently herself—that it became a cliché. "Barbra is the first girl I have ever heard who is a great actress in each song," composer Jule Styne, who would write the score for *Funny Girl*, said of her. "She makes each song sound like a well-written three-act play [back to Dennen], stunningly performed in three minutes."[53] One might say that this was because she knew how to invest a lyric with real emotion, but it wasn't just a function of interpretation or using her actor's training; it was a function of the way Streisand reinvented the use of the voice. She may not have understood physiology, but she took her acting and instinctively found a way to express it through the mechanics of singing.

"Ms. Streisand sings as if she is speaking to you," critic Anthony Tommasini observed.[54] This was, indeed, one of the things that made her seem so unusual. Other singers, particularly opera singers, typically operate in what is called their "head voice," which is what allows them to hit those stratospheric notes. But the head voice is not a voice that can also allow them to express the sort of intimacy, that sense of ordinary speech, as Streisand did. They are rafter shakers. To sing intimately, they have to use what is called their "chest voice," which is what so many popular singers do. But very few singers are able to negotiate between the two: to use their head voice and their chest voice, which allows them the range to convey both the grandiose and the intimate, the powerful and the tender. Streisand did. "Previous singers, like Mary Martin and Julie Andrews, did use their middle register, their speaking voice," says composer Roger Ames. "But when Streisand came along, with this incredible capacity to mix the registration from low to high in a way that was higher than anybody had ever tried before . . . these notes are thrilling." She was doing what the great Italian tenors did: "go high without losing her modulation." This takes, Ames says, not only extraordinary vocal control but extraordinary physical strength.[55] (And breathing. Listen to her whisk through "Come to the Supermarket in Old Peking" seemingly without taking a breath, and think of the physical exertion that takes—think about it because she draws no attention to it.) The payoff was also extraordinary: the ability to take her voice anywhere. As Arthur Laurents wrote, "When she sang, she was simple; when she sang, she was vulnerable; when she sang, she was moving, funny, mesmerizing, anything she wanted to be."[56]

Those were the mechanics that enabled her to act the song. The rest was the acting itself, her special way with a lyric. Calling herself "an actress who sings," she once said, "I approach a song as an actress approaches a part. I try to move people when I sing. I try to make little pictures for them which they can feel and visualize."[57] And like all great actresses, her performances couldn't be mistaken for anyone else's. Frank Sinatra had said of Billie Holiday, "What she did was take a song and make it hers. She lived inside the song. It didn't matter who wrote the words or the music. She made it hers. . . . She made them *her* story."[58] That was Streisand's talent, too.

Singers don't typically provide overarching themes to their songs. At best, most of them select songs within a certain genre, which allows us to impute a tone or mood to the artist. Some are bluesy, some are cool, some are heart wrenching. Only the very greatest, like Holiday and Sinatra, can take the whole of their oeuvre, regardless of genre, and turn it into an ongoing story. Only the greatest can impose their will on any song. For Sinatra, as Gay Talese wrote, speaking of "In the Wee Small

Hours of the Morning," though he could just as easily have been speaking of any Sinatra tune, "it was a song that evoked loneliness and sensuality, and when blended with the dim lights and the alcohol and nicotine and late-night needs, it became an airy aphrodisiac."[59] Sinatra was the bard of loneliness and seduction and, in later years, of ring-a-ding cool. But even that cool was about loneliness. As Pete Hamill put it, "His ballads are all strategies for dealing with loneliness; his up-tempo performances are expressions of release from that loneliness. The former are almost all fueled by abandonment, odes to the girl who got away. The up-tempo tunes embrace the girl who has just not arrived."[60]

In the same way as Sinatra, her closest male counterpart in terms of popularity and influence, Streisand brought a theme to her songs. No matter what song she was singing, they were all "Streisandized." If Sinatra is the bard of loneliness and seduction, Streisand is the bard of pain and pining, and *her* up-tempo songs are expressions of her resilience in the face of that pain. Song after song after song tells the story of a lost love or a love never found—of the desperate need for connection, which is why, if Sinatra's natural habitat is, as Hamill has said, the bar at the midnight hour, Streisand's is her empty room, late at night where she mourns her losses and her never-weres. And this connected to audiences as powerfully as the fact of Streisand herself. She was not only an outsider. She sang about being one. "'I want—I need—why can't I—you can't stop me—will I ever have,'" wrote Streisand biographer Tom Santopietro of a collection of her songs. "These are the primal emotions the career retrospective makes clear the Streisand voice always and ineffably was able to carry."[61]

This is where her image and her music joined. This is where she sang her life. Her manager Marty Erlichman had said of her, using the conventional view of her looks, "Barbra is the girl guys never look at twice." Then: "And when she sings about that—about being like an invisible woman—people break their necks trying to protect her."[62] That may have been true. But it wasn't just protectiveness that explained their responsiveness. It was the conviction with which she expressed her pain—and her defiance. The music critic Gene Lees wrote of Sinatra that people said he sang those love songs "as if he believed them." "That was the secret," Lees concluded, calling it "a striking advance in the art of singing" and writing that "Sinatra was to American song what Montgomery Clift was to American acting."[63] What he meant was that Sinatra was a Method Singer in the way Clift was a Method Actor. They were authentic. They conveyed truth. And, again, so did Streisand.

Audiences believed her as they had believed Sinatra. They felt that the songs were not just being performed; they were being torn out of her because she had lived them. "She's telling you the story of her life every time she gets up there," a friend told Pete Hamill in an early profile. "And the facts of her life have made her very sensitive."[64] That was *her* secret. It was, of course, mostly true. She did bear wounds, and she would recall her childhood pain as a reservoir on which she kept drawing. "What hooks into a child is the want, is the yearning for, is that seeking-approval aspect that probably does permeate into one's adult life," she would tell an interviewer years later. In this, she was no less a Method Singer than Sinatra. And if she could sing about pain and longing because she experienced them, the young Streisand also had, like all great actresses, an enormous capacity for empathy that enabled her to sing about those things she hadn't yet experienced. "That's probably why I could sing love songs at eighteen. I didn't know from it. It was a yearning. It was what I imagined it should be like—which is, maybe, more powerful than the real thing."[65] "She can be four years old. Or 54. Or 20 or 30," said veteran vocal coach Judy Davis, who once assisted Streisand early in her career when Streisand's throat tightened. "She knows things she's not right to know for her age and experience. I felt this and I knew immediately she was a great star. I told her that. I told her that and she cried."[66]

Some of this might have been atavistic. In *The Jazz Singer*, Jake Rabinowitz, the cantor's son who becomes the popular singer Jack Robin, is told that he sings with a "tear in his voice," which is attributed to the suffering of the Jewish people. It is part of his fiber, and it is the ingredient that makes him special. Whether one could attribute it to her Jewishness or not, this was an apt description for Streisand, too. She sang with a tear in her voice—a deep connection between her heart and her throat. "When I sing, the emotional connection is made involuntarily," she once said. "When I sing, something happens, and I can't even tell you what is in that process, a certain musicality to the voice that is not even verbal."[67]

She was exposed, vulnerable. Early on she would tell an interviewer, "They always write about me as the girl with the Fu Manchu fingernails and the nose as long as an anteater's. That hurts far more than if anyone wrote that I was a terrible singer—which they never did." But she understood how imperative that hurt was to her singing. "If my vulnerability goes in real life," she went on, "it goes as a performer and an artist on stage too. I must retain the vulnerability or lose sensitivity as an artist."[68]

The vulnerability was a truth, and it was truth that Streisand was selling to audiences—the truth of her and their lives, of her heartbreak and their heartbreak, of her will and their will. "A lot of my success is built on this truth thing," she would say. "I can't lie. By being honest—somehow that transmits itself to people."[69] Another time she would say, "The audience cannot be lied to. . . . The slightest tinge of falseness, they go back from you, they retreat. The truth brings them closer. They don't know why, they can't intellectualize it, but they know the

78

moment is right or wrong."[70] No singer had ever been as truthful as Streisand.

That was the underpinning of everything. Without it, there was nothing, certainly no superstardom. But on top of that truth was the glorious technique—the "Streisandisms" that made her so vocally distinctive. There was the phrasing—the way she let a lyric unfold, as Gene Lees would say of Billie Holiday, "not according to the melodic structure of a song but according to the natural fall of the words."[71] There was the way she sang every single word with a different coloration and inflection. Think of how she sings the word "special" in "People"; she punches the first syllable and elongates the second and gives it a beautiful onomatopoeic treatment that makes "special" sound like something special, or the way she takes the word "feeling," beginning with the soft "f" and extends the word into three syllables so that you *feel* it. Or listen to the entirety of "Cry Me a River," where she sings the first verses as lament and the last as angry retribution: the same words with entirely different inflections and effect. Glenn Gould called her "one of the great italicizers; no phrase is left solely to its own devices."[72]

And there is her pronunciation, which is unlike the pronunciation of any other singer—a Jewish pronunciation. Most singers preferred a more homogenized sound. The Italian American Sinatra was sensitive to his ethnicity and to the disdain he thought it elicited. He told Hamill that he would be at a posh party, black tie, best crystal, "and I'd see a guy staring at me from the corner of the room, and I knew what word was in his head. The word was *guinea*."[73] It rankled him, but he also admitted that if he was angry, he was embarrassed—embarrassed by the "street" in his pronunciation. Gene Lees cited something else, a certain Italian "husk" in Sinatra's voice, a rough edge, a quality he also found in Anne Bancroft's and Brenda Vaccaro's voices and that was part of Sinatra's vocal equipment.[74] Great as he was, Sinatra tried to lose his street pronunciation and his husk. Presumably as compensation for the way he naturally talked, he learned to sing with what Hamill said was "impeccable diction," which, Sinatra claimed, he had learned from "watching movies."[75] He felt he had to deracinate himself as a singer, if not as a person.

Streisand was every bit as ethnic as Sinatra, but she didn't bear the same negative sensitivity to her Jewishness, and she certainly didn't try to disguise it in her diction any more than she had tried to disguise it in her appearance. If anything, she always sounded Jewish, not only when she was speaking but when she was singing. (It was the head voice, chest voice thing again—the ability to sound as if she were just talking rather than crooning, which also allowed her to move seamlessly from talking one line to singing the next one, sometimes right in the middle of a song.) Streisand had a lilt, a distinctively Yiddish rhythm that made her sound at times like the comedian Jackie Mason, at others like the Bowery Boys. As with the tear in the voice, it was part and parcel of who she was as a person and as a singer—the two inextricably bound. So there was a lot of Jewish Brooklyn in her pronunciations—the way, for example, she would take the word "more" in "People" and render it "mohe" way up in her nose, making the "r" disappear. Or the way she sang "person" as "puhson." (African singers had learned this trick, reshaping the inside of the mouth to make the more felicitous "uh" sound rather than the less lovely "ah" sound.) Or the way she sang "river" in "Cry Me a River" as "rivah," no final "r" again. Or the way she gave the word "corners" a long "o" in "The Way We Were." It gave her words a beauty, the musicality of Yiddish, but it also gave them personality and feeling. There was "street" in her diction.

And there was something else she did in her pronunciation that made her sound so different. Traditionally, singers abided by the rules of legato that demanded the continuous flow of notes and that short-changed consonants, which were "stoppers," in favor of vowels, which were better sounding and more smoothly connected. Streisand blew that up. Because she was looking for meaning in words, not just flow between them, she didn't feel obliged to sing legato, and this might have been the most revolutionary contribution she made to popular music. The pure sound really was subordinated to the acting.

But there was a problem—the reason why singers before Streisand hadn't abandoned legato—namely, that so much of spoken language doesn't sound all that great. Who wants to sing ugliness? You have those consonants, which are hard and unappealing, if unavoidable, and you have certain vowel sounds that are anything but pretty—the "eh" sound in an unstressed syllable. Think of the first "a" in "amazing," or the first syllable of "supply," or the "o" in "gallop," or the "a" in "sofa." These are emitted from way up in the vocal chords where the voice is thin and where very little effort needs to be expended. One linguist even labeled it the "laziest sound there is." Some English speakers found the "eh" sound so unpalatable that they eliminated it altogether: "caramel" became "car-mel," "different" became "diff-rent," "camera" became "cam-ra." Linguists have a name for this less-than-appealing sound. They call it *schwa*, from the Hebrew for the diacritical mark, an upside-down "e," that indicates the "eh" sound in that language. Appropriately, linguists appropriated the symbol in other languages to indicate how people really pronounce words.[76]

No singer wants to sing schwa, so they perform their best vocal gymnastics to avoid it. Streisand, however, was the singer who sang as if she were speaking to you. She couldn't very well exorcise schwa. So she did something else. She changed the sound in her mouth when she sang this vowel. She would take the schwa and bring it from the vocal chords up into her soft palate to make it fuller and richer and softer, transforming it from the "eh" to an "uh" or even "ah." Listen, for example, to how she lengthens and softens the nearly silent "o" in "people," or how she holds the "o" in "world" until it extinguishes the schwa. It is magical. She takes the ugly and makes it beautiful. Taking the supposedly ugly and making it beautiful, of course, was the essence of her entire life, and it made for the perfect confluence of the woman and her work. Streisand was simply doing in her vocals what she had always done and what almost no one else could do. As composer Roger Ames put it, "She set the bar."[77]

It was a high bar. Over the next year, she would release three more albums, while her first, the pathbreaking *Barbra Streisand Album*, would win the Grammy for Album of the Year. She would also win the Grammy that year for Best Female Vocalist and win twice more in the two years thereafter. She no longer had to play a kook to get attention. She was now regarded as an artist. "The kookie quality is, it seems to me," a critic wrote, "merely a protective cover for the artist underneath. . . . She has put on a kookie façade to dispel the commercial inanities around her."[78] By this assessment, she didn't need that façade anymore.

A few years later, Jerome Robbins would rhapsodize over her in what had become a new consensus. "She always surprises. Her performances astound, arouse, fulfill. When she sings, she is as honest and frighteningly direct with her feelings as if one time she was, is or will be in bed with you." And he asked questions that a lot of people might have been mulling of a young singing sensation still only in her early twenties: "What will become of this woman? She is still unfinished. Where will she go and what will she do? With all her talent and radiance, glamour, uniqueness, passion and wit and spontaneity, she is still forming. There is more to come, things will change, something will happen. The next is not going to be like the last; she promises more and more surprises."[79]

Robbins would, of course, be proven right. But he was writing shortly after what might have been the biggest surprise of her career—the surprise that would lift her from the singing firmament into the brightest firmament of entertainment.

4

Bine Aktrise

FANNY BRICE got there first. Born on the Lower East Side to Jewish immigrants, she entered show business at nineteen through the only portal that would admit her: burlesque. Within a few years she graduated to the Ziegfeld Follies, where she was typecast as the comedienne, though she had other aspirations. She had a comedienne's expressive face with large eyes and a wide mouth and a long Semitic nose—a nose that she eventually fixed, claiming that she was "tired of being a sight gag," a pronouncement that prompted wit Dorothy Parker to opine that she "cut off her nose to spite her race."[1] "Flo" Ziegfeld did permit her to sing a torch song, "My Man," a song of slavish devotion that would become her signature and allow her, briefly, to escape her comic persona. But only briefly. In time, she would be best known for playing a character she originated in the Follies, a precocious child named Baby Snooks. She would perform in Snooks's romper even after she brought

84

the character to a popular radio program where the audience obviously couldn't see her, but in her personal life she was elegant, stylish, and refined, the opposite of her broad stage characters. That may have been the whole point. Though she didn't suffer quite the same abuse for her looks as Streisand had, she apparently did see herself as the homely girl without a beau, which sent her into the arms of a suave gambler and swindler named Nicky Arnstein, whom she married and whose defense she bankrolled when he was arrested and tried for securities fraud.

Brice died in 1951 of a cerebral hemorrhage at the age of fifty-nine. But she had left behind a memoir, and her daughter, Frances Arnstein, every bit as refined as her mother, was determined to bring that story to the musical stage. In this, she was abetted by her husband, the film producer Ray Stark. Stark had no stage experience, so he teamed with David Merrick, who did. They hired Isobel Lennart, a veteran screenwriter, to adapt the book, and the composer Jule Styne (*Gypsy*) and lyricist Bob Merrill (*Carnival!*) to write the score. Everyone involved fully realized that the show would rise or fall on the actress who played Brice. It was the role of a lifetime, navigating from comedy to tragedy and from the silly to the glamorous. It was the story of a woman's desire to be loved as a woman and, not incidentally, of a Jew's desire to be accepted as a star. And it was the story of intrepid will to survive the professional and the romantic difficulties. It was Brice's story, but it was Streisand's story, too. "This play is really about me," Streisand would say. "It simply happened to happen before to Fanny Brice."[2]

Though Streisand was only twenty-one and had only Miss Marmelstein on her Broadway résumé, as soon as word of the show leaked, her name was being floated as a possibility. Groucho Marx even mentioned it during Streisand's *Tonight Show* appearance. In addition to the similarities of their personal stories and, of course, their unmistakable Jewishness, Streisand

85

looked like Brice, had some of Brice's mannerisms, and shared her outsized kooky stage personality. Streisand just seemed to summon Brice. According to Streisand biographer William Mann, whose chronicle of this period in her career is the most authoritative, the assistant stage manager on *I Can Get It for You Wholesale* asked the veteran actress Lillian Roth, who was featured in the show, whom Streisand reminded her of. Roth immediately thought of Brice.[3] Streisand felt the same affinity. She would tell *Playboy*, "I read conversations [of Brice's] that have never been published, and it was very peculiar, we were very much alike in a very deep area, in spirit. . . . Her essence and my essence were very similar."[4]

The timing for the casting couldn't have been better since Streisand's star was rising. When she had played Marmelstein she was, like Marmelstein, a strange, lonely girl, lamenting her neglect. The role was a fit—character and life intertwined. Now she was opting, as Brice had, for a breakthrough as a leading lady, and again, there was a fit. She desperately wanted the role, but there were many candidates. Jerome Robbins, who had been signed to direct the show, was lobbying for Anne Bancroft. Other names included Mary Martin, Mimi Hines, Kaye Stevens, Carol Burnett, Suzanne Pleshette, Paula Prentiss, and Kaye Ballard. Certainly, others could have played Brice. But only Streisand had lived Brice.

Of all the contenders, Streisand had an internal cheerleader: Jule Styne. And Styne had a motive. After seeing her at the Bon Soir, where, by one account, he attended every one of her performances, he began thinking of the songs he could write for her—for that voice. "I was writing the score for someone with that range, that dynamism, that sense of fun," he would say.[5] So he dragged Ray Stark to see *Wholesale*, and according to Mann, when Stark said that his Brice had to be more than funny, Styne dragged him to the Bon Soir to see her in torchy mode. Meanwhile, the play's writer, Isobel Lennart, asked her friend Doris

Vidor, the wife of film director Charles Vidor and the daughter of Harry Warner of Warner Bros., to see Streisand at the Blue Angel and report back. Vidor wrote her: "There is a sadness and a deep emotional impact this girl projects to the audience that is very unique." She concluded that Streisand *was* a young Fanny Brice.[6]

But Streisand understood that the person she really had to convince was Brice's daughter and Stark's wife, Frances. When she flew to California for her appearance on *The Dinah Shore Show* in May 1963, Streisand made a point of meeting Fran Stark. Stark was not impressed. She asserted that Streisand would never play her mother.[7] Another Streisand biographer, Anne Edwards, adduced a reason for Fran Stark's hostility, and it was a deeply ironic one, though one that certainly resonated with her mother's aspirations: She thought that Streisand looked and acted too Jewish to be Brice.[8] Streisand certainly would have appreciated that irony in regard to Brice and even more in regard to herself. The girl who was always called too Jewish to play anyone but Jews was herself too Jewish to play a Jew who sought to temper her Jewishness.

Still, the congruencies between Brice and Streisand were so powerful and Streisand's show business march that year so triumphant that she landed the part. It didn't take her long to assert herself. During the preproduction, David Merrick, with whom she had signed her contract, left the show to concentrate on *Hello, Dolly!* and sold his *Funny Girl* rights to Stark. Since Stark didn't have her under contract, Streisand now had bargaining power, which she exercised. Her agent and attorney renegotiated her contract up from $3,500 a week to $7,500 and added perks like a personal hairdresser and driver. Once again, it was Streisand flexing her muscles and avenging the years of mistreatment. And it was her first real diva moment—the first of many to come.[9]

Stark paid because, like everyone attached to the production, he had come to the conclusion that *Funny Girl* needed Streisand, not just because she was the talented engine of the show, but because she was living the performance in a way no other actress possibly could. In a show that was narratively meta, there were a number of meta moments: Streisand singing "People," a wistful valentine to interdependence from a woman who seemed to need no one and may have regretted it; "Sadie, Sadie," in which she crows how lucky she was to have landed her handsome hubby; "His Love Makes Me Beautiful," a comic number with a less-than-comic subtext about beauty as a reflection of affection; and, perhaps above all, "I'm the Greatest Star," Brice's assertion of her unrecognized super-talent, which was also Streisand's assertion of her once-unrecognized super-talent.

The meta-ness of Streisand playing the lead in a story that could have been (and was) her own would be matched by the meta-ness of the difficulties of mounting a play about the difficulties of mounting a career. After staging the show, Robbins quit and then, when Stark berated him, demanded that nothing he devised could be used in the production, which meant they essentially had to go back to square one. Stark tried to engage choreographer-turned-director Bob Fosse to direct, but he declined. Finally, he wound up with Garson Kanin, the screenwriter and playwright who was married to actress Ruth Gordon. It was not the best choice for a young actress embarking on a potentially star-making role in a massive musical. Kanin, by his own admission, was passive. He said it was by design. He wanted to give Streisand the room to find herself. Streisand, for her part, took the passivity to be ineffectuality. Lost, looking for direction, she was thrown back on her own devices and forced to take control of her own performance. She was also forced to demand changes in the script. According to Mann, she called it "artistic responsibility."[10] Others weren't as charitable.

She was confused. She told Merrill and Styne that she didn't want to sing "People" or "Don't Rain on My Parade," the two songs that would become the show's classics. Merrill was enraged. Styne, who still loved her, asked her to reconsider.[11] And if she was confused, she was also determined. When, during the show's Boston tryout, Kanin found her belting "Don't Rain on My Parade" in between the matinee and evening performances and advised she rest her voice, Streisand snapped, "Goddammit! . . . I gotta get this fucking thing right." She later apologized but discovered that the conductor had not hit the right tempo, throwing her off.[12] She knew her performance wasn't perfect, that she wasn't quite getting it, and that she couldn't direct herself. So she asked Alan Miller, her old acting teacher, if he would watch her and coach her, keeping his presence a secret from Kanin. "Barbra was in real trouble," Miller would remember. "She was behaving like a rank amateur up there on stage. It was appalling."[13] And no matter what Streisand did, everyone realized that the second act, the act in which her career rise gave way to her marital entanglement with Arnstein, was a mess, lacking energy and drama.

When the play opened in Boston, critics were unkind, calling the show overlong and unshapely, and hammering at the second act. But another thing on which they all agreed was that they loved Streisand. Now the issue was whether the show could be improved as a vehicle for its star. In the event, this would require massive rewriting and a new director. Kanin left. Succumbing to Stark's pleas, Robbins returned for the next stop in Philadelphia. Now the real razing and renovation began, basically reconstructing everything around Streisand. Robbins seemed intoxicated by her, even as he recognized her bullheadedness. "She reads [new pages] and like an instantaneous translator, she calculates how all the myriad changes will affect the emotional and physical patterns," he later wrote. "When she finishes reading, her reactions are immediate and violent—loving or hating them—and she will not change her mind. Not that day. During the rehearsal, in her untidy, exploratory, meteoric fashion, she goes way out, never afraid to let herself go anywhere or try anything. . . . That night onstage, in place of the messy, grubby girl, a sorceress sails through every change without hesitation, leaving wallowing fellow players in her wake."[14]

It was obviously her show, now even more so, but leaving "fellow players in her wake" was a problem. Most of them resented it. In the original book, Nora, the beautiful showgirl, tells Fanny that she is braced for the day when she has lost her looks—to which Fanny says that she herself has no looks to lose, a typical Streisand line. Nora counters that Fanny likes being around the beautiful girls so that she can entice men away from them, proving that her own beauty is more than skin deep—another typical Streisand line. But Streisand was evidently so threatened that she apparently had Nora's role trimmed—more meta.[15]

That was the least of it, however. In yet another meta touch, Elliott Gould, Streisand's former *Wholesale* star, whom she had married during that high-flying summer of 1963, was playing in real life Arnstein to her Brice. The two Jews were perfectly compatible so long as Streisand, like Brice, wasn't a star. They were less compatible when the solar eclipse began. Gould fell into gambling, drugs, and psychoanalysis very much as Arnstein, feeling emasculated by his wife, fell into his financial shenanigans, at least as the play told it. But there was one more fillip. Streisand and her costar, Sydney Chaplin, son of Charlie, who played Arnstein, had begun an affair. Just as Brice won Arnstein on the force of her personality and her talent, Streisand won Chaplin. Chaplin said as much. On meeting her, he realized that "she didn't find herself attractive and was compensating with this enormous drive to succeed," which apparently he did find attractive.[16]

But it was far less attractive as Streisand's role expanded and Chaplin's was whittled—whittled until he had only a single song while Streisand was singing the entire score. (On opening night she would be onstage for 111 out of 132 minutes.) Now there was tension not only between Streisand and Gould but between Streisand and Chaplin. This was added to the tension of the show itself, which was still very much a work in progress. New scenes, new songs, lost scenes, lost songs—this became a daily occurrence once the show moved to its previews in New York. Streisand admitted to the *New York Times* that she was a "little tired" as the opening approached and she had to absorb the multitude of changes, though many marveled, as Robbins did, at how quickly she adapted.[17] (By one account, she and Chaplin rehearsed a new version of the last scene the day before opening, the forty-first version, and never played it onstage until that night.)[18] But for all the changes, one thing remained. Audiences loved Streisand. Columnist Dorothy Kilgallen said she so milked the curtain calls that they were "like rituals performed in a Buddhist temple."[19] But it wasn't Buddha audiences were worshipping.

On opening night, March 26, 1964, at the Winter Garden Theatre, after five postponements as Robbins wrestled the show into shape, Barbra Streisand stepped from entertainment into history, and from a stage into the American imagination. Streisand had been a popular singer—a *very* popular singer. In New York she had also been an icon for the marginalized and minorities. But that night, delivering what many believed was one of the greatest performances ever on Broadway, she became an institution. In a *Time* cover story the next week aptly titled "The Girl," as if there were no other, Ray Kennedy described her entrance: "In the moment's pause before she disappears as quickly as she came, she leaves an image in the eye—of a carelessly stacked girl with a long nose and bones awry, wearing a lumpy brown leopard-trimmed coat and looking like the star of nothing. But there is something in her clear, elliptical gaze that is beyond resistance. It invites too much sympathy to be as aggressive as it seems. People watching it can almost hear the last few ticks before Barbra Streisand explodes."[20]

And what a detonation. "She establishes more than a well-recollected Fanny Brice. She establishes Barbra Streisand," who "turns the air around her into a cloud of tired ions." Her voice "pushes the walls out, and it pulls them in." Kennedy cited what others had seen in Streisand beyond her talent, her "bravery" as well as her vulnerability, and he repeated what was now also becoming a commonplace: "People start to nudge one another and say, 'This girl is beautiful.'"[21] *Cue* magazine called her "Magnificent, sublime, radiant, extraordinary, electric—what puny adjectives to describe Barbra Streisand."[22] In the *Times*, drama critic Walter Kerr wrote, "Everybody knew that Barbra Streisand would be a star, and so she is."[23] *Life* exulted that the "entire gorgeous, rattletrap show-business Establishment blew sky high" for Streisand, and it called her "Cinderella at the ball, every hopeless kid's hopeless dream come true."[24] When, at show's end that opening night, she sang a reprise of "Don't Rain on My Parade," surely an anthem for all the things for which Streisand had stood, the audience erupted and she received twenty-three curtain calls.[25]

The reception testified to just how far Streisand had extended the Jewish metaphor—so far that the metaphor disappeared into the thing it signified. Though just about everyone involved with the show, from Stark to Robbins to Lennart to Styne to Streisand, was Jewish, and though it was about a Jewish entertainer, and though it starred the most overtly Jewish of singers outside of the Yiddish theater, the one word that no reviewer wrote in commending the show was "Jewish," even though without its Jewish underpinnings, the show was emotionally incomprehensible. Rather, *Funny Girl* became, as *Times* critic Howard Taubman stressed in his daily review, a show business story of a rising star wrapped around the story of a doomed romance, and not, as it so patently was, a Jewish story of an outsider trying to win acceptance in a world of beauty and glamour wrapped around the story of romance doomed by a driven Jewish woman's success. As he put it, "*Funny Girl* is most fun when it is reveling in Fanny's preoccupation with show business," which missed completely the show's real fun, Fanny (and Streisand) wooing the entertainment gods, and the real pathos, Fanny (and Streisand) striving to be loved.[26]

Loved she would be. Amid the accolades, only two people seemed unimpressed. One was Diana Streisand, who told a reporter on opening night that Barbra got her talent from her mother, but who prompted Streisand to complain during *Funny Girl*'s run, "Even today she calls me and says, 'So-and-so in the office says he read something nice about you in the papers.' But it never seems to mean anything to *her* personally."[27] The other person was Streisand herself, still negotiating between superiority and inferiority. Even the smallest criticism would elicit her to ask: "So am I great or am I lousy? I gotta know."[28] And she would still, even now, recall to a reporter the casting directors who had dismissed her in favor of prettier girls and say, "There are people who tell me I'm beautiful this way," meaning with her unfixed nose, adding, "Well, they're wrong. Beautiful I'm not and never will be."[29]

And yet she made her triumph seem inevitable. Speaking to the same *Times* reporter the day after the opening, Streisand talked about the sense of anticlimax after all the previews and her fear of getting bored with the show, but she also spoke of her destiny. "I always knew I hadda be famous and rich—the best," she said. "I knew I couldn't live just being medium." And then she spoke of the responsibility of being a success: "People will no longer come to see a new talent they've heard about. I now have to live up to their concept of a great success. I'm not the underdog, the homely kid from Brooklyn they can root for anymore. I'm fair game."[30]

"A Born Loser's Success and Precarious Love": that was the title of *Life* magazine's bouquet to her that May, and it was the Homeric story that would become *the* story about Streisand. "When five years ago, 16-year-old Barbra decided to leave Flatbush, invade Broadway and aim for the stars," wrote Shana Alexander, "she had every mark of a loser. She was homely, kooky, friendless, scared and broke. She had a big nose, skinny legs, no boyfriends, a conviction that she was about to die from a mysterious disease, no place to sleep but a folding cot and, worst of all, a supersensitive brain which could exquisitely comprehend precisely how much of a loser she actually was." Her only recourse, wrote Alexander, was success: "straight through to the top of the tent."[31] This tale, most of it true, was what made her success not just a show business victory but a cultural one and what made Streisand more than an entertainer. Again, the word "Jew" wasn't mentioned. But basically, Streisand was the marginalized girl who had, yet again, beaten the odds, tremendous odds—of course, playing a girl who had beaten tremendous odds.

It made her Broadway success special just as it had made her recording success special. Without that backstory, Streisand wouldn't have been Streisand. Now she was the toast of Broadway. She received a Tony nomination for Best Actress in a Musical. (She would lose to Carol Channing for *Hello, Dolly!*— a blond gentile playing a Jewish matchmaker.) Within a month, she had recorded the cast album, which would sell four hundred thousand units in its first four weeks. She appeared on *What's My Line?* She won her Grammy for *The Barbra Streisand Album*. And she signed a five-million-dollar, ten-year deal with CBS to provide musical specials to the network. "I'm fuzzy on the details," she told the press of the contract, "but it gives me creative control. That's the main thing."[32]

The girl who had been told she was dirty and unkempt and a style mess had even become a fashion icon. By one account, "Hairdressers are being besieged with requests for Streisand wigs (Beatle, but kempt). Women's magazines are hastily assembling features on the Streisand fashion (threadbare) and the Streisand eye make-up (proto-Cleopatra). And it may be only a matter of time before plastic surgeons begin getting requests for the Streisand nose (long, Semitic and—most of all—like Everest, there)."[33] It was a reversal: fashion insiders imitating the fashion outsider.

And there was more. The girl who had dragged a cot from one friend's apartment to another, and who had finally found a railroad apartment of her own above the fish restaurant, now moved to a lavish penthouse duplex on Central Park West with a view of the park. As a *Vogue* reporter described it, there were five chandeliers, including one in the upstairs bathroom, an Aubusson rug in the living room, red damask wallpaper and an eighteenth-century French desk in the foyer, a Steinway in the den, a huge Jacobean bed on a platform in a bedroom (Streisand said, "It should be like the place Desdemona got strangled in") with green brocade walls, and a red paisley sofa, which matched a dress of hers. On the nightstand was a photo of Streisand licking a lollipop and inscribed: "Too Eleot I wuv you Barbrra." The reporter admitted, "My defenses crumbled."[34]

The apartment was ostentatious, an arriviste's idea of luxury, but Streisand's defense was that there had been "no intermediate stages in my life" to prepare her for the life she was now living.[35] And no time to acclimate herself to what had happened to her. She had gone directly and immediately from nightclub stardom to recording stardom to Broadway stardom. But these were still relatively small fiefdoms. That April, scarcely a year after *Funny Girl*'s opening, she would achieve stardom in the larger duchy of television. Her first special, "My Name Is Barbra," was designed, by Streisand, as a tour de force. There were no guest stars, no skits, and little patter. There was just Barbra singing in various locales—from a spare set, through which she raced singing "I'm Late," from *Alice in Wonderland*, to the schoolroom where children taunted her as "Crazy Barbra" and where she sang ironically, "I Wish I Were a Kid Again," to the Bergdorf Goodman department store, the store whose salesgirls had once denied her even after her *Wholesale* success, where she sang a medley of poverty songs—"Give Me the Simple Life," "I Got Plenty of Nothin'," "Brother, Can You Spare a Dime?" and "Nobody Knows You When You're Down and Out"—that served as counterpoint to the setting and a statement about it. Even in her special, she would wreak vengeance.

In the program's last act, she performed concert style in a plain black dress singing "Lover, Come Back to Me," "My Man," and her trademark, "Happy Days Are Here Again," which always betrayed its apparent sentiment in a way that seemed true to Streisand's own doubts about the staying power of happiness. This was Streisand in great voice and great performance—the distinctive phrasing, the Brooklyn Jewish intonations, the elongated words, the notes no other popular singer could possibly hope to reach, and the astonishing range that in one segment took her from singing "I'm Five," with the exact delivery of a five-year-old, to "People" before a full orchestra.

And just as she had conquered recordings and Broadway, she now conquered television. One critic called it "a pinnacle moment of American show business, in any form, in any period. She is so great, it is shocking, something like being in love." And he delivered the highest superlative of superlatives: "She may well be the most supremely talented and complete popular entertainer this country has ever produced."[36] "My Name Is

Barbra" would receive six Emmy nominations. It would win five, including Outstanding Achievement in Entertainment and Outstanding Achievement by an Actor or Performer. It was easy to forget that Streisand was still only twenty-four years old.

But she would discover that getting to the top would be easier than enjoying the stay there. First, there was her costar Sydney Chaplin, whose resentment of her stardom had not only ended their affair but launched open warfare. Offstage he was angry and snarling. Onstage he was brusque and dismissive, often whispering "nose" in her ear during their love scenes to agitate her.[37] (She filed a complaint with Actors' Equity against him, but, marginalized himself like the character he played, he wound up leaving the production before his contract expired.) And just as she had suspected, playing the same role eight times a week for months began to bore her, so she would change lines to keep herself engaged, even though it had the effect of throwing off the other actors. One night Ray Stark happened to be in the audience, heard the changes, and went backstage to scream at Streisand.[38] Some nights, she would decide to shorten the show. Some nights, she just went through the motions. When Arthur Laurents took his parents to see *Funny Girl*, the pit pianist David Shire said the audience ought to thank them since "it was the first full-out performance she had given in a week."[39] But despite her boredom, she was so terrified of missing a show and becoming the Wally Pipp to another actress's Lou Gehrig that she dragged herself out of a sickbed to perform one night after her understudy, Lainie Kazan, had been announced and after Kazan had already alerted her friends and the press. (Later, when Streisand's accompanist, Peter Daniels, began a romance with Kazan, Streisand cut him off.)[40]

And Streisand would recall one particular night, after she had scratched her cornea and was thinking of sitting out the performance, when she found a candy dish in her dressing room from her stepfather, Louis Kind, who had come to see the show. Now she insisted on going on and gave what she called the performance of her life. He didn't come backstage afterward, though she waited for him. She kept the candy dish for twenty-three years, then finally threw it away. She never saw or heard from him again.[41] She had won the war.

But there were other hostilities now, not only Chaplin's, but those of many in the cast who resented the star's late arrivals, her borrowing their makeup without asking, just as she had done in *Wholesale*, and her on-the-fly script changes. "I was the most hated girl on Broadway," she admitted.[42] And yet, for all her self-absorption, there was a sadness in this solipsism, too. Lainie Kazan told Streisand biographer Anne Edwards that Streisand always felt she was an "outsider" in her own show, and recalled how, after singing "People," she told the musical director that she finally understood. "I got it now," she said. "It's a duet. . . . I'm not alone up there. I've got you. I've got the whole orchestra."[43]

Yet in many ways, she was alone. The price of her success was that she had to carry every project she was in and that, she felt, she had to be great in every project because no one was going to cut her a break, especially now that she had made it. "I win awards and everything but one of these days something is going to bomb. It's a scary thing. It can all suddenly fall apart," she told a reporter.[44] Her longtime fans, those who did see the Jew in Streisand and the girl who had had to fight for her career, became even more vehement in their support. Every night a group of them, mainly self-described misfits, would huddle around the stage door to catch a glimpse of her as she arrived at and then left the theater.[45] These were her people, but they terrified her, though not as much as the people who had heard so much about her and came to see her with such high expectations. "It makes me feel that they're the monster and I'm their victim," she said.[46]

This was the vulnerable Streisand, the one who always felt how provisional her success was, but she was nevertheless right to anticipate the backlash after the ballyhoo. A reporter observing her as she taped her second television special, "Color Me Barbra," found her nervous and testy and fearful. When the director asked her to redo two songs after another concert sequence like the one in "My Name Is Barbra," she mutinied, demanding that he send off the audience. "I hate them. I hate them," she told her manager, Marty Erlichman, though what she really seemed to hate was what she thought was their demand for her perfection or, more accurately, her projection of her own demand for perfection onto them. The audience waited for a half-hour while Erlichman explained to her that the sequence needed them. Streisand finally returned, sang the numbers, thanked the crowd, then retreated to the control room where, ever the perfectionist herself, she snapped, "OK, let's see what we've got."[47]

It was another reporter, Rex Reed writing in the *New York Times* Arts and Leisure section the Sunday before the special aired, who was the first to take on the image of the homely girl made good and transform her into a spoiled narcissist, though it seemed a lot of the bile was Reed's umbrage at not being accorded the better treatment he thought he deserved. He said that Streisand kept him waiting for three-and-a-half hours before plopping into a chair, biting into a green banana, and telling him he had twenty minutes, most of which she spent, according to Reed, telling him how great the show would be and how she was doing it all her way. Reed was not amused by her obvious contempt for him, completely missing that Streisand had contempt for nearly everyone—a contempt born of the contempt she had had to endure and that she gave back, no doubt, simply to prove that she could. Streisand was supposed to be grateful, humble, a poor girl anointed. She was none of those things.

But what she didn't realize is that since the enthusiasm for her was predicated in some measure on the adversity she had overcome, any seeming arrogance would undermine that enthusiasm, in the press, if not among her own fans. It was a form of discrimination that a girl like Streisand, a poor Jewish girl with a big nose, had to be grateful, whereas beautiful stars, gentile stars, were entitled to act immodestly, and she would reserve some of her deepest contempt for those, like Reed, who didn't think she had the right to act immodestly or arrogantly. In time, she would certainly come to realize the effect this attitude had on her press coverage, but she didn't seem to care. She didn't feel she had to humble herself. She felt she had to be great.

But "Color Me Barbra," which aired three months after she left *Funny Girl*, revealed a few chinks in her armor. Despite generally favorable reviews, and despite the fact that the soundtrack album reached number three on *Billboard*'s chart and would receive Grammy nominations for Best Album and Best Female Vocal Performance, there would be no Emmys, just five nominations, and some carping. *Time* opined that her voice was "nasal," her taste in songs "appalling," and an hour of her was "45 minutes too much." But its most salient charge was a warning about the relationship between Streisand's performance and her image: "The Streisand talent is considerable, but it is getting lost in a myth," presumably the myth that she was infallible, which the press itself had promoted.[48] "Ten million people love you when you're an underdog on the way up," she had told Rex Reed, "but nine and a half million of them hate you when you hit the top."[49] Her infallibility was now her burden.

If Streisand felt terrorized by expectations, it had been a long reign of terror—the twenty-one months that she performed as Fanny Brice. They had been eventful months: her first television special, her first Grammy, her first Emmy nomination (for Outstanding Performance in Variety or Musical Program or Series for her *Judy Garland Show* appearance), and her first hit single, "People," which she had recorded before the show opened, even though she was incensed at Columbia for passing on the *Funny Girl* cast album and then for stalling three months to push the single as the label waited to see if the show would be a hit.

Now there were so many avenues to pursue, once she could shake loose of the musical. She gave her last Broadway performance on December 26, 1965, singing Brice's own anthem, "My Man," as her encore. Elliott Gould, sitting in the front row, said something that seemed very true to Streisand's persona, though odd to say of someone who was now certifiably a first-rank Broadway star: "Everybody was with her. Everybody was pulling for her."[50] And so ended Streisand on Broadway.

But much as she might have liked to be finished with the stage—she said she had a giant calendar and crossed off the days until she was through—she wasn't. Stark wanted her for the London production, and his bait was the lead in the movie version, which was bait Streisand couldn't ignore. So the following April, she opened in London for a fourteen-week sold-out run. Asked by a reporter nearly forty years later if she could relive any night in her career, she cited that one. There was a "strange atmosphere" at the opening. Princess Margaret was there, and "I felt that people were watching her watching me and that upset me." Then she came offstage and her close friend Cis Corman whispered to her: Streisand was pregnant. That was the verdict of a urine test Streisand had given Corman before the show and then forgotten. "So there I was," Streisand said, "standing there shaking people's hands on opening night, with Rex Harrison congratulating me, and I felt like all praise and congratulations were because I was pregnant. The exuberance I felt that night with this wonderful secret. . . . I'll never forget that."[51]

Yet even after the London production closed, and even after a truncated concert tour, for which Erlichman got her more money than any other singer had ever gotten, and even after taking time off to await the baby's birth, she wasn't finished with Fanny Brice. The objective hadn't been Broadway stardom, which, to Streisand, wasn't any more stardom than being a recording star or a nightclub star. Those entertainers, herself included, had scaled hills, not mountains. Real stardom was what she had dreamed about since she was a girl. Real stardom meant the movies. *Funny Girl* had never been about having a Broadway hit. It had been about landing the starring role in the movie version. Having fulfilled her obligations to Stark, she now got Stark to fulfill his promise to her, though he extracted a four-picture deal from her to do so. As Arthur Laurents put it, she considered the theater "a small town on the way to the big city of Hollywood."[52] Everything she had done so far pointed the way to that trip to that city.

5

Holivaud

SHE WAS right. Nightclubs were provincial. Broadway was provincial. Television less so, but still provincial. And yet because they appealed to their coteries, an urban Jewish girl like Streisand had a chance. Hollywood was different. Hollywood purveyed its images to the world. And Hollywood was assimilationist in a way that nightclubs, Broadway, and television were not. The American film industry had been created by eastern European Jewish immigrants who left their ethnicity, and often their religion, behind to generate the grand myth of an idealized, largely homogeneous America that they loved and that they felt they could comfortably inhabit. There was, of course, a great irony in this—basically that the America of our movie dreams was invented by men who were anything but typically American, at least in the popular image, and who would not have been granted status if they hadn't assimilated.[1] This made it difficult for Jews in the industry, especially difficult for those in front of the camera. Once the silent era passed, and with it films like *The Younger Generation* and *The Jazz Singer*, which were about the process of assimilation, Jewish characters were scarcely seen on-screen, much less an actress like Streisand, who was so overtly Jewish that she couldn't really play anything but a Jew.

This alone would have made Streisand a breakthrough star, and on her arrival in Hollywood, on May 10, 1967, she was treated that way—the way no other first-time movie star had ever been treated. It intimidated her. Ray Stark threw her a party at his mansion and invited the industry's biggest stars to pay tribute. "It was like I couldn't believe it," Streisand said years later. "Here I am meeting Cary Grant! Or Marlon Brando, the only actor I ever really idolized. These people were at a party for me?" But Streisand absented herself in a back room, only to read in the papers that she was arrogant. "The truth is, I was absolutely frozen to my seat."[2]

She had come to film *Funny Girl*. To direct, Stark had hired one of the most respected filmmakers in Hollywood, three-time Oscar winner William Wyler, also a Jew, though Wyler had never directed a musical. To costar as Nicky Arnstein, he had signed the Egyptian actor Omar Sharif, not a Jew, who had made an impression in *Lawrence of Arabia* and *Dr. Zhivago*. This wouldn't have ordinarily raised any issues, but that very week, the Six-Day War between Israel and Egypt began, and suddenly there was concern over whether Sharif should be fired, especially since he was playing against a Jewish actress. Wyler calmed the controversy by saying that in America, you didn't terminate someone because of his nationality, and that was that.[3]

But another war was brewing much closer to the picture. This was the war of perfection that twenty-five-year-old Streisand was waging on the set. Her reputation had preceded her. "When I came out here, everybody thought, 'Oh, she's got to be a bitch and have temper tantrums, be demanding and nasty,'" Streisand said. She claimed she had no intention of confirming that image. And yet she was aghast at how careless some of the crew could be. "Like on the morning of a scene, my dress isn't here yet, my hair isn't fixed properly, and they want me to go out anyway and film it," she complained. "*For posterity!* Listen, once it's on film, that's it. It's got to be perfect when the cameras are turned on you."[4] Others said that it wasn't just perfectionism that bothered them. It was Streisand's haughty attitude. Anne Francis, playing a showgirl, accidentally brushed up against her, after which Streisand allegedly upbraided her: "I've been told that a star is never touched in a scene like this."[5]

Wyler would call her "obstreperous," and there were those who wondered how he maintained his composure when this neophyte seemed to be ordering him around. (Joyce Haber wrote a scathing article in *New York* magazine titled, "Barbra's Directing Her First Movie.") But Wyler actually defended her, saying that she was edgy because she was terrified, and also that, more than any other actress with whom he had worked, she was an absolute stickler for detail, right down to the color of her nail polish.[6] After Streisand began telling him where to set the lights, the veteran cinematographer Harry Stradling agreed with Wyler. "Sure, she's tough," he said. "But she has an unerring eye."[7] But there was more to Streisand's approach than nerves and perfection. There was her sense that she *needed* to take control, just as she did on her albums and her television specials, to keep the enterprise on track. "One flicker of doubt and everybody gets doubtful," she told *Newsweek* critic Joseph Morgenstern. "And most people are followers. They need you to be sure. They might resent you for being sure, but they need you to be sure. They would fall apart if you weren't sure."[8]

Hollywood was filled with prima donnas who ordered people about. Streisand may have been mistaken for one of those (sometimes she may have been one of those), but she knew exactly how much was at stake here, as it always seemed to be for her, and, as always, how little margin for error she had: none. This wasn't about arrogance. This was about survival. Watching her on set, Pete Hamill was amazed. He said she treated the script the "way a great performer treats an old standard. She was looking deeply into it, past the glib surface, and locating the emotion that was there at the start, before repetition and second-rate artists had corrupted it. She did almost a dozen takes of the scene, and each time it came out fresh. The hired audience of extras was dazzled. So was I."[9]

But Hamill would also observe something else on that set—call it the "starification" of Streisand. "When Streisand wanted to sit down, someone was there with the chair," he wrote. "When she sat down makeup people surrounded her, patting the dampness of her face, straightening a loose hair, checking the shoes, handing her a script." And he saw that "she had grown used to it. She was Barbra Streisand Superstar now, and she didn't need anybody."[10] In truth, she never had.

She had been filming less than a month when she flew to New York on an off-day that would certify just how big a star she was becoming. The occasion was a free concert in Central Park—she called it a "happening"—that was being taped for her next CBS television special. Despite a downpour earlier that day, an estimated 135,000 fans showed up at the Sheep Meadow, easily besting Leonard Bernstein's previous record of 75,000, and called the largest gathering ever for a single performer. But it wasn't just how many people showed up or the fact that they began chanting "Streisand Park! Streisand Park!" or the way they mooned over her or applauded her every move. It was Streisand herself—the confidence she seemed to have, the control she seemed to exercise, the glamour she exuded, and yet the intimacy she created with the crowd, the aura in which she was enveloped. It is hard to imagine anyone else, save perhaps Sinatra, pulling it off. It wasn't entertainment. It was an audience with royalty.[11]

With the release of *Funny Girl* in September 1968, she had ascended to royalty or better: She was a movie star—that long-held dream. And something else. In the assimilationist world of Hollywood, she was the unassimilated star. Her victory as the unassimilated was surely Streisand's, and part of that uncanny ability of hers to use her outsiderness. But it was a victory that had two other engines. One was the film industry's own struggles in the late 1960s—a time during which the audience was narrowed significantly, so that the studios, which traditionally had appealed to the broadest possible audience, were now looking to swaths of the audience for box office, especially young people, women, even blacks.[12] Among the top-grossing movies the year of *Funny Girl*'s release were *Funny Girl* itself (number two), and also *Midnight Cowboy;* Franco Zeffirelli's *Romeo and Juliet*, with a young, age-appropriate cast; *Goodbye, Columbus*, from Philip Roth's novella about a relationship between a poor Jewish boy and a rich Jewish girl; and *Easy Rider*. None of these but *Funny Girl* was a typical Hollywood blockbuster, and the blockbuster, *Funny Girl*, after all, was a Jewish movie.

But the Hollywood success of *Funny Girl* was a function of a larger cultural change in America as well. The civil rights era of the 1960s had promoted the idea of a black identity that didn't get rendered in the melting pot, which, in turn, gave rise to the pluralistic concept of the salad bowl, the rainbow, or the mosaic—whatever one wanted to call the celebration of a more polyglot and heterogeneous America. Just as those movie audiences were declining, the mosaic was expanding. Streisand certainly benefited from this idea, as a number of ethnic entertainers would, including Streisand's husband, Elliott Gould, and her former acting classmate Dustin Hoffman. For really the first time in Hollywood, it was acceptable to be identifiably ethnic without also being comic—to have actors who resembled the audience. In fact, it is highly doubtful that Streisand's movie stardom would have been possible without this cultural change—a change to which, of course, she contributed.

Funny Girl introduced Streisand to her largest audience yet, and if she had arrived in Hollywood with more fanfare than any novice, with the film's release she would receive more critical fanfare than any novice. Reviewers were rapturous. Joseph Morgenstern in a *Newsweek* cover story enthused, "The cameras in 'Funny Girl' unmasked an artist even more gifted than she was supposed to be. I remember worrying about superlatives in my review. Would I make a fool of myself by calling it the most accomplished, original and enjoyable musical comedy performance ever put on film? I searched my memory and finally decided that what the hell, it simply was the greatest; why not say so?"[13] Stanley Kauffmann in the *New Republic*, commenting on the interplay between her dramatic gifts and her comic ones, said of her, "in one person, Punch and Judy." He even paid her this backhanded compliment: "She is a bit irritating because she is evidently conceited—evidence that filters through from the screen, not from the press—and it's always irritating when a conceited person is as good as he (she) thinks."[14] In the *Times*, Renata Adler said the movie treated Streisand "rather fondly, improbably and even patronizingly, as though they were firing off a gilded broccoli," and though Adler wrote that the "movie almost does her in," she also said, "Miss Streisand's talent is very poignant and strong."[15]

The shrewdest analysis, not surprisingly, may have come from the *New Yorker*'s film critic Pauline Kael. Noting the hard times in movies and the dearth of real stars that had been one of the great pleasures of going to the movies, she cited Streisand as an answer, then quickly dispensed with what she called the "ugly duckling myth," and finally delivered her classic Streisand line: "The 'message' of Barbra Streisand in 'Funny

Girl' is that talent is beauty." She went on: "And this isn't some comforting message for plain people; it's what show business is all about. Barbra Streisand is much more beautiful than 'pretty' people." She saw in Streisand the same sassy, wise-cracking quality of 1930s and 1940s stars like Claudette Colbert, Carole Lombard, and Jean Arthur—which is to say an active intelligence that most actresses or actors just don't have. (Though Kael didn't say it, one loves Streisand's brain as much as her talent: intelligence is beauty, too.) And then she gushed over Streisand's openness, which makes the film's tragic second half so heartbreaking. "She conceals nothing; she's fiercely, almost frighteningly direct"—something her admirers had said of her singing as well.[16] In a later review, Kael would touch the very source of Streisand's appeal, writing, "She is like thousands of girls one sees in the subway, but more so; she is both archetype and an original, and that's what makes her a star." Or put another way: Streisand is uniquely *us*.[17]

Funny Girl, Streisand's breakthrough success, would provide the template for every film she made thereafter, which is also to say that every film Streisand would make, even a late one like *Guilt Trip*, was a way for Streisand to act out her personal story and to infuse herself into the picture just as she infused herself into every song she sang. That may be the "openness" that Kael detected in her; her emotions are always naked because she makes her characters so close to herself. In *Funny Girl* the entire story seems to be Streisand's. She is a less-than-beautiful Jewish girl who manages to win the heart of a handsome man by virtue of her talent, her intellect, her drive, her spunk, her moral force—in short, her superiority over the prettier girls. But the relationship is usually unstable, often because the Streisand character, like Streisand herself, is often "too much" for her lover to contend with. (How many Jewish women have heard that complaint? How many Yiddish words refer to a woman's "too muchness"?) She is left at the end of the film, hurt but also unbroken. Alas, the strength that damages the relationship is the same quality that allows her to plod on. "You're stronger than the whole world," Arnstein tells Fanny, which he intends as half-compliment, half-criticism. And since nearly all of her films are romances, underlying them is inevitably an examination of male and female roles—roles to which Streisand either cannot or will not conform. In effect, her films are about role reversals, about active women and passive men, which is why Fanny mutters, "You're gorgeous," when she first sees Arnstein, typically a man's line to a woman. Arnstein wants a compliant wife. He gets a tornado. "You never lose," he says to Fanny, testifying to the thing that undoes him, except, of course, that she has lost the relationship.

This would become basic Streisand: Streisand 101. But it is in the film's details, the repetitions of hurt, the casual abuse, the self-deprecation that serves as self-defense, the desperation, the pressure to be "less than" rather than "too much"—all of which are Streisand's every bit as much as they are Brice's—that make the performance memorable and that almost raise the movie itself, which is pedestrian in so many ways, into a work of tragic majesty. Despite its comic moments, most of which are Fanny overcoming the prejudices against her or outwitting the conventional minds who cannot see her talent, the film subsists on Brice's/Streisand's pain and her will and her consciousness of being who she is in a world that doesn't necessarily honor her virtues. In one of the first scenes, young Fanny stands in front of a mirror primping, while her mother and her mother's card-playing cronies behind her—a bit of trademark William Wyler deep focus—sing "If a Girl Isn't Pretty," which lists the indignities such a plain girl will suffer. But Fanny parries: "The whole world will look at me!" Later, addressing a stage manager who fires her, she says, "I'm a bagel on a plate full of onion rolls," and still later, she muses, "Do you think beautiful girls are going to be in fashion forever?"—not whether they are going to be *beautiful* forever, but whether they will be in fashion. (Here the film like the play is obviously flaunting its own prescience.) And: After singing the song that expresses her confidence, "I'm the Greatest Star," tears well in her eyes because it takes so much to believe what she is saying. And: Arnstein asks her to dinner and says he will wait while she changes. "I'd have to change so much, nobody could wait that long," says Fanny. And: When Ziegfeld asks her to sing, "His Love Makes Me Beautiful," Fanny demurs because she can't see herself that way. And: In "Sadie, Sadie," she sings, "To tell the truth, it hurt my pride. The groom was prettier than the bride." And then there are the frequent references to her nose. When Ziegfeld offers her stardom, Fanny ripostes, "I haven't suffered enough yet." The audience knows differently. She has suffered plenty.

But then there is that finale: Streisand/Brice singing "My Man" about the man who has wronged her, the man she has lost because he isn't enough of a man to cope with her. And here we see that final Streisand fillip, the one that had become familiar in her previous songs, the one that made her the voice of the put-upon but also of the defiant, the one that would prevent her from being a long-suffering Camille. As Morgenstern described the moment, "She started small, injured, all tremblytearful as if there were nothing else to do with an old chestnut about a lovelorn lady. Before the end of the first chorus, however, her funny girl made a decision to sing herself back to life. Her voice soared defiantly, a spirit lost and found in the space of a few bars." You could, he wrote, be "wiped out" by the shameless sentiment or "by the virtuosity of an actress looking lovely, feminine and vulnerable at the same time she was belting out a ballad with the force of a mighty Wurlitzer."[18]

That was Streisand. Like William Faulkner's Dilsey, she prevails. She always prevails.

Having finished the film version of one of the two greatest Broadway musicals with the two greatest female roles of 1964, Streisand went directly into the film version of the second, yet another Jew. The hue and cry over Streisand landing the role of Dolly Levi in *Hello, Dolly!* for which Carol Channing had beaten her for the Tony, was loud, and the seeming sense of injustice raw. The role, the media bellowed, belonged to Channing. The problem was that the studio was not going to gamble a hugely expensive movie on an actress who had never scored a film success and who, in any case, seemed not to be scaled to the intimacy of movies. These weren't problems for Streisand. Even before *Funny Girl* had been released, she was a star-in-waiting.

But Streisand had her own doubts about taking the part. At twenty-five she felt she was too young to play a widowed matchmaker angling for a romance of her own. Ernie Lehman, the screenwriter who adapted the play for the film, told biographer Anne Edwards that Streisand complained, "There is no way I can play Dolly Levi in a way that makes sense of the woman."[19] In this, as in most things in her career, Streisand was absolutely right. Dolly Levi was the one character she played who did not follow the Streisand path. She was not a scorned woman, an ugly duckling who becomes a swan, or a woman braving her way through pain; she was, as the title song shows, a legend. And whatever pain she felt had to be impasted on the film in reveries to her late husband rather than arise from it organically. It wasn't that Streisand was too young for Dolly; it was that Dolly was from the outset too hard and impregnable a character for Streisand. It is defiance without the pain, though it is always the pain that makes the defiance so moving. Or put another way, she was a gentile's stereotype of a Jewish woman—a woman without sensitivity.

It was not a particularly happy experience for Streisand. The dancer Gene Kelly directed, but like Garson Kanin on *Funny Girl*, he left the characterization to Streisand, an especially unfortunate choice since the character didn't have those Streisand characteristics the way Fanny Brice did. As she had told Lehman, she couldn't find the character in a way that made sense, by which she was really saying, she couldn't find this character in herself. That led to a pastiche that included everything from her Jackie Mason Yiddishisms to Mae West sexual purring. It is the first time that you see her effort.

But there was another issue: the clash of her new Hollywood with old Hollywood. Her costar, Walter Matthau, the antithesis of a Streisand leading man, detested her from the outset—detested the reverence she was accorded, detested the power she was able to exert, detested the perfection with which she approached her performance. "You don't have to be great all the time," he snapped at her in one of his kinder moments.[20] But she did have to be great all the time. She had nothing else to fall back on. In his less kind moments, he berated her for suggesting a line of dialogue: "You haven't got the talent of a butterfly's fart," he said, in what is surely one of the most inaccurate insults ever. Streisand was so distraught, Lehman had to console her.[21] Yet as much as Matthau might have liked to think that he was upholding Hollywood professionalism—this against a woman who was a consummate professional, perhaps too consummate—in fact he was revealing his own wounds over how long it had taken him to succeed and his own grievances over his lack of power. As one person on the set told Nora Ephron for a piece on Streisand, "It's a very simple story. She's twenty-six years old and she's the biggest star in town. Can you imagine how a big spoiled baby like Matthau reacts to playing second fiddle to that?"[22] But it was the head of 20th Century Fox, Richard Zanuck, who put it into perspective for Matthau when Matthau complained about Streisand: "The film isn't called *Hello, Walter.*"[23]

Still, as unhappy as the production was, *Hello, Dolly!* was a successful film commercially, if not critically. Streisand took some knocks, some no doubt because she had won the role in the first place and some because the movie itself is a lumbering atrocity—a "staggeringly unimaginative effort," as Pauline Kael put it in her *New Yorker* review. But Kael spared Streisand the worst. "At the center of all the asexuality, impersonality, and noisy mediocrity," she wrote, "there is Streisand, an actress who uses song as an intensification of emotion. . . . Almost unbelievably, she turns this star role back into a woman, so that the show seems to be about something." Yet at the same time, Kael fretted. She wondered whether big, traditional, blockbuster musicals were the appropriate vehicle for a talent as nuanced and sensitive as Streisand. And she wrote that if Hollywood didn't find smaller musicals for Streisand, she might become a straight actress. "She would be abandoning her true singularity—her ability to extend a character in song."[24]

That abandonment, of course, was precisely what Streisand had desired all along. She didn't want to be pigeonholed. She wanted to fly.

Now that she was a movie star, things changed. They changed in the way she was perceived. She had already begun the transformation, but *Funny Girl* completed it. The girl who had succeeded on the basis of her difference was suddenly called beautiful. "She looks lovely on screen and off," wrote Joseph Morgenstern in his *Newsweek* cover story, "so much so that you wonder what happened to her and when. Had she been taking ugly pills for her 'Funny Girl' role and then quit cold turkey?" His answer was that she had so played up her unattractiveness that the audience, and presumably the press, took their cues from her.[25] Similarly, Arthur Laurents, her director on *I Can Get It for You Wholesale*, recounted Streisand asking him rhetorically why she couldn't play the lead in that play and then answering, "It's because I'm not pretty, isn't it?" And Laurents admitted to himself that it was true. "That year the audience wouldn't have accepted her as the heroine. Two years later, she was in fashion, a contemporary Nefertiti."[26]

Even before her movie fame, Jerome Robbins, her *Funny Girl* director, was mesmerized. "The kook's looks are ravishing. Her beauty astounds, composed of impossibly unconventional features. Her movements are wildly bizarre and completely elegant. Her body is full of gawky angles and sensuous curves. It scrunches, elongates and turns on in spotlights. Her El Greco hands have studied Siamese dancing and observed the antennae of insects. She flings gestures about, sprinkling the air with outrageous patterns, but every movement is a totally accurate composition in space."[27] Harry Stradling, her *Funny Girl* cinematographer, told *Life*, "I like the nose. No, you can't make Barbra look like Marilyn Monroe. But she does have a beautiful face—because she's got something in back of it."[28]

It is a remarkable statement, but then the whole transformation of perception was remarkable. It wasn't just that Streisand had always been considered unattractive. She was a part of a tradition of unattractiveness. Jews had long been cited as being physically different from gentiles, physically less appealing than gentiles, their looks a signpost of degeneracy and disease. Unsurprisingly, for many Jews, their alleged physical inadequacies had been a source of self-loathing. And this was especially true of the Jewish nose. One nineteenth-century German anthropologist, Bernard Blechmann, determined that Jews even spoke differently from gentiles because of their noses: "The muscles which are used for speaking and laughing are inherently different from those of Christians."[29] It follows that the first modern rhinoplasty was performed by a German Jewish surgeon named Jacques Joseph in 1898. As cultural historian Sander Gilman put it, "The nose [became] one of the central loci of difference in seeing the Jew," and that difference was that the Jew was seen as ugly.[30]

No less an authority than *Vogue* picked up on this idea, and on Streisand's relationship to it. It called her "the romantic whose need to be a pretty woman made her a fascinating-looking woman," accurately identifying that the need "reaches out and takes the heart," and it attributed to her something truly amazing: "a whole new taste in beauty." "The starry hands, the splendid skin [this from a girl who suffered from terrible teenage acne], the shifting smile, the proud nose [proud!]— they're all a part of the irresistible force that powers her style." And *Vogue* cited the deeper changes in her that augmented her beauty. "There's detachment (now). There's a shining sureness (now). There's real concern for freshness and gleam and polish." The magazine admitted it didn't know what the new style would prompt—perhaps a "more searching, less automatic standard regarding the realms of elegance." It concluded appropriately, "Funny thing for a funny girl to set in motion."[31]

So Barbra Streisand had not only managed to make herself seem beautiful, which was a feat in itself given all those detractors. But she had somehow managed to change the entire definition of beauty. Morgenstern was only partly right when he had said that the change was largely a matter of a lifting of the veil from our eyes that had been placed by Streisand's own deprecation. It was also a matter of what historian David Kaufman would call the "sheer force of will aided by make-up, hairstyling, and high fashion."[32] But most of all it was a matter of Streisand, certainly in conjunction with feminism and changing ideals of femininity, convincing us that there were different kinds of beauty than the conventional ones, and that beauty constituted something more than just physical appearance or, rather, that physical appearance could become beautiful when informed with other qualities. Yes, Streisand had changed her look. Yes, she was the beneficiary of stylists. Yet this wasn't wholesale renovation. What made her truly beautiful was the growing conviction that there was so much beautiful within her. It was another of her revolutions. She made us see differently. As Gloria Steinem would say of her, "Barbra Streisand has changed the bland, pug-nosed American ideal, probably forever."[33] Forever.

That she did this while not forsaking her Jewish identity was also remarkable: "American integration without assimilation, the persistence of Jewish identity in the open society," as David Kaufman would describe it.[34] She still *looked* Jewish in the caricatured ideal of Jewishness, even though, as theater historian Henry Bial would assert, "There is little or no link between the biology of a Jewish body and the way in which that body is recognized as Jewish, whether on the movie screen or on the street corner."[35] She would tell an interviewer that she had found a photo of Fanny Brice just after her nose job with the caption "so she could play more leading parts."[36] Streisand got those parts without bobbing her nose. In fact, she said she once was approving an album cover and noticed that the photo had been retouched, her nose reduced. "Somebody at the lab probably thought, This will please her. I told the lab people that if I'd wanted my nose fixed, I would have gone to a doctor."[37] The old nose was restored.

The toast of Hollywood still hadn't made peace with Hollywood. Dressing for the Oscars on the night she was nominated for *Funny Girl*, she asked her hairdresser, Fred Glaser, to tease her hair into a tall dome. When Glaser told her it looked "overdone," she said, "The whole town is phony, and if I lose they'll know I don't give a damn."[38] Of course, she did give a damn, and she won, tying with Katharine Hepburn, who had been nominated for *The Lion in Winter*. It was a conjunction of the old Hollywood and the new, only one that was much more satisfying than the conjunction with Matthau. Streisand made it her moment, ascending the podium in a transparent black Scasi pantsuit with a bow that would have fashionistas talking, and then addressing the statuette with her opening *Funny Girl* line: "Hello, gorgeous." But she also said something that unearthed all the hurts, albeit humorously. "Somebody once said to me—asked me—if I was happy, and I said, 'Are you kidding? I'd be miserable if I was happy.' And I'd like to thank all the members of the Academy for making me really miserable. Thank you!"[39]

It was true that Streisand often had her issues with happiness. Part of this, Streisand herself said, could be traced back to her father's death and to a pervasive sense of deprivation and punishment that flowed from it. "Whenever I would have an abscess in my tooth, I would go, Why me? I took it all so personally. Who was punishing me? It started off very early, and I'm still trying to change it." She even admitted she saw herself as a "victim."[40] Part of it may have had to do with something deep in Jewish consciousness—not even so much the long history of suffering in which every Jew is steeped, but the questioning, the doubt, the disappointment, the uncertainty, the threat, the anxiety, the pessimism that are so much a part of the Jewish sensibility and the likely source of Jakie Rabinowitz's "tear in his voice" as well as Groucho Marx's comic nihilism. A "true pessimistic religion" is how Jewish scholar Sander Gilman described it. The German philosopher Georg Hegel had implied that the Jews were an unhappy people because they stood outside the gates of salvation that Christianity had opened. Perhaps, but that "unhappiness," living without redemption and even doubting the whole possibility of redemption, may have also been one of the wellsprings that made Jews who they were.[41]

And possibly helped make Streisand who she was. "Barbra seemed constitutionally incapable of allowing herself any experience of joy," Barry Dennen wrote of her. "She was always searching for the dark underpinnings, the trip wire, the pimple on God's ass."[42] When she met the Maharishi Yogi, and he told her that a free consciousness will always flow to happiness, she quipped, in what could have served as a preview of her Oscar acceptance, "Well, I normally go toward the point of greatest unhappiness, so that must mean that unhappiness is the source of my greatest happiness."[43] Success didn't change that attitude. If anything, it seemed to reinforce it. Money was part of it. She had a poor Brooklyn Jewish girl's fantasy of what money would bring. "It's having a $12,000 fur coat instead of a $15 hand-me-down from a thrift shop," she would write. "It's getting a $15,000 weekly night club salary instead of $108 a week. It's being accepted for what I am, kooky clothes and all, and it's having top American fashion designers like Norman Norrell and Bill Blass make a fuss over me."[44] To Nora Ephron, she described success as "having ten honeydew melons and eating only the top half of each one."[45] But she complained to Rex Reed that the reality didn't match the fantasy. "I've always dreamed of a penthouse, right?" she told him. "So now I'm a big star and I got one and it's not much fun. I used to dream about terraces. Now I gotta spend $500 just to convert mine from summer to winter. Let me tell you, it's just as dirty with soot up there on the 22nd floor as it is down there on the bottom."[46]

And it wasn't just that the money didn't release her from her unhappiness, as she might have thought it would. It was that she couldn't even conceptualize the money. Marty Erlichman told Nora Ephron a story about securing a $120,000 deal for Streisand from a dog food company just for her doing a picture book on her own dog and singing two songs about dogs. Two hours' work, he said. She turned it down to go to the movies. Erlichman was perplexed. He said she would buy presents and then boil over discovering she could have spent four dollars less on each. "You're talking about saving sixty-four dollars, and

I just told you where you can make $120,000," he yelled. To which Streisand said, "Marty, I *understand* sixty-four dollars."[47]

Nor did success assuage her insecurities. One interviewer observed that she has a "constant need for reassurance, an ego that can't be sated, a strange vanity, and a frantic pride."[48] She wouldn't have disagreed. And yet she professed to hate the attention now that she had finally gotten it. "I guess a lot of actors loved to be looked at and asked for autographs," she told one reporter. "I'm totally opposite. I know what's in the fans' heads. They don't want to be disappointed in anyone, and reality is always disappointing." And she commented on how people asking for her autograph would often ask a person she was with, "Are you anybody?" and said, "I don't relate easily."[49] But, of course, she did relate. She knew exactly what it was like to be a nobody.

And she said she didn't feel like a star—a real star. "I don't know that I'm like a famous person or star," she told Chaim Potok after she had been a star for nearly twenty years. "I feel just like a workaholic. Sometimes when I was around people like Sophia Loren or Elizabeth Taylor, they were like stars to me. They acted in a certain kind of way, you know? Like you see in the movies. They're very comfortable with the press, with photographers. You see pictures in the paper of Jackie Onassis or Elizabeth Taylor. They're always smiling like ladies. You see pictures of me, it's like, you know, leave me alone, get outta here, why are you taking my picture?"[50] To others, she said she felt as if she didn't really have a personality—from the woman with the outsized personality. "I think maybe I have nothing," she said, which is very close to a line her character says in *On a Clear Day You Can See Forever:* "I'm like nothing . . . No character."[51] To Kevin Sessums of *Vanity Fair,* she said that she had performed the role of Medea when she was fifteen in an acting class and that she had always remembered one of the lines: "I have this hole in the middle of myself."[52]

And beyond the insecurities about herself, there were the continuing insecurities about her career. "Everything is momentary," she told another interviewer after her *Funny Girl* film triumph. "You do a good picture, great; you do a lousy one, nobody wants you. That's why you have to have a husband, children and antique furniture."[53] The only way she could fill the hole and protect the future was work—hard work, unrelenting work, laboring-over-the-smallest-details work, work that was easy to mistake for narcissism and self-centeredness because it was a form of narcissism and self-centeredness. Recording "Autumn Leaves" for the *Je M'appelle Barbra* album with French composer Michel Legrand, she did twenty-eight takes over three-and-a-half hours, then spent four hours more listening to all of them.[54] A recording engineer who worked with her during her London *Funny Girl* run said that her self-involvement was a requirement for her success. "You can't do it any other way. I remember, from the moment she got up in the morning to the moment she went to bed at night, it was me-me-me-me."[55]

And yet, for all the overt displays of egotism, she was terrified. "You name it, I'm scared of it," she told another interviewer. "Skiing, hikes, coldness, water, heat, everything. I'm afraid of the world, probably." She added, "That's why I stay here in my little house most of the time. Simple fear."[56] The star who had conquered Hollywood, the star who was often described now as an egomaniac, was fragile. But that powerful combination of fragility and the bravado with which she compensated had propelled her success. Without both, she wouldn't have been Streisand.

In her first two films, she did much of her acting through her singing, which was not how Streisand preferred it to be. For her third film, she dispensed with singing. *The Owl and the Pussycat* was adapted by Buck Henry, cowriter of *The Graduate*, from a mildly successful Broadway comedy by Bill Manhoff.

George Segal plays Felix, a squirrely aspiring novelist who works in a bookstore. Streisand plays Doris, a brassy neighbor who is a prostitute, and, she says, sometime model-actress. The two, the would-be intellectual and the ditz, inevitably run afoul of one another, get evicted from their apartments when they complain about each other, find love, lose love, and then, in the final reckoning, refind love when they dispense with the illusions they have tried to maintain and speak honestly. He will not be a major novelist. She has never been a model or actress. They simply are who they are.

It is, once again, pure Streisand, filled with autobiographical moments and lines. The moments are largely spots of kookiness she exhibits, the superiority she exercises over the more conventional people in the film, primarily Felix's upper-crust girlfriend and her parents, and the disparagement she suffers, mainly at Felix's hands. The penultimate scene, in which he berates her and subjugates her, is painful to watch and extremely unpleasant, made more unpleasant for anyone who appreciated Streisand's own subjugation. The lines are references to her aspirations and her looks. "Do you think I'm pretty?" she asks Felix. To which she answers herself, "I'm not really. I just make you think that I am. . . . You've got to act pretty." By her third movie, this focus on appearance has already become a Streisand trademark.

As for the performance itself, it is pure Brooklyn Jewish, with the sort of quicksilver stream-of-consciousness non sequiturs that no female star but Streisand could possibly deliver. She is aggressive, strident, disparaging, loquacious, and she makes no concessions to the mainstream audience. Pauline Kael, already a Streisand enthusiast, found the performance exciting. "Her clipped diction is so full of controlled tension," Kael wrote, "that her lines never go slack; the words come out impetuously fast and hit such surprising notes that she creates her own suspense. She's a living, talking cliff-hanger; we're kept alert catching the inflections, hoping that the laughter in the theater won't make us lose anything."[57]

The Owl and the Pussycat was another commercial success, not because of its unwillingness to make those concessions, but most likely in spite of it. Years later, Streisand would say that it gave her the "creeps" watching performers who "desperately wanted the audience to like them." She admitted, "That's not what I'm about. Take actors: they're often at their most charismatic when they're doing very simple exercises. When they vomit out emotions, it's such a turn-off."[58]

That was a measure of her confidence as a performer. She acted to please herself. But there was a downside to that, and it was evident in many of her subsequent pictures. Comparing Streisand to Catherine the Great, "who ruled alone and was a shrewd political operator, intolerant of any invasion of her turf," Camille Paglia noted that successful artists, like rulers, "start out so individualistic, following their own instincts; but the point comes when they are so used to doing their own thing and not seeking advice from good people that they screw up."[59] Streisand may have made some of these films out of conviction, but many of them are messes, screw-ups, and nearly all of them between *The Owl and the Pussycat* and *The Way We Were* are piffle.

On a Clear Day You Can See Forever, from the Alan Jay Lerner and Burton Lane 1965 Broadway musical about a young woman who has a past life as an early nineteenth-century seductress and the psychiatrist who falls in love with that seductress, is a hapless film, butchered by the studio, which hacked off such big pieces that the narrative barely holds together. But there is some sublime music, and Streisand, as the young woman who has no idea she harbors a past life, is her usual eccentric self whose "Yiddish intonations," wrote Vincent Canby in the *New York Times*, "are so thick they sound like a speech defect." Canby also noted, "Barbra Streisand, a performer who sometimes seems too big for movies as well as for life, portrays a girl who is so full of life that she leads a succession of lives."[60] Her costar, Yves Montand, later complained, as Streisand's male costars often would, that in this case her bigness meant she overshadowed the movie. "They gave Streisand everything she wanted, and more. It was eventually decided to change it from a movie version of the play into a picture for her: a Barbra Streisand picture."[61] What Montand didn't seem to realize is that there was no other reason to make it.

As for *What's Up, Doc?* Streisand, against what she said was her own better judgment, decided to sign on largely because it was directed by Peter Bogdanovich, a wunderkind coming off the success of *The Last Picture Show*, and because she wanted to star with Ryan O'Neal. But she admitted that she didn't see what was funny in Bogdanovich's noisy, ramshackle remake of the Howard Hawks's screwball comedy *Bringing Up Baby*, which had starred Cary Grant and Katharine Hepburn as, respectively, a paleontologist with a rare dinosaur bone and the nutty woman who bedevils him, and Streisand's main contributions were to be adorably and uncontrollably winsome (or obnoxious, depending on where you stood on Streisand), and to sing Cole Porter's "You're the Top" under the credits, and "As Time Goes By." Other than that, the film, as Streisand detected, feels desperate—chaos mistaken for mirth. But not even abominable Streisand, which this film is, could hurt the box office. It was the third-highest-grossing picture of 1972.

Even before the release of *What's Up, Doc? Mad* magazine had renamed Streisand "Bubbly Strident" in a parody titled "On a Clear Day You Can See a Funny Girl Singing Hello Dolly Forever," with the implication that she kept playing the same character over and over and over again, running roughshod over the movie itself. *Mad* wasn't far off. Every movie Streisand made, the awful ones as well as the good ones, was unmistakably a Streisand movie—a movie in which her personality dominated, as is usually the case in star vehicles, but also in which her theme dominated, which is not always the case, even for major stars. Streisand worked for some highly regarded directors—William Wyler in *Funny Girl* and Vincente Minnelli in *On a Clear Day*, to name two. But she is always the auteur, the major creative force, and in her films, no less than in her music, she provides the governing idea, the overarching continuity, not only because her performances are usually the raison d'être for the movies, or because the narratives are all shaped around her in that *Funny Girl* configuration, but also and primarily because the meanings of the films are shaped around her or, rather, erupt from her.

These are not necessarily the same themes that inform her music: the themes of heartache and defiance. For a visual medium, every one of Barbra Streisand's early movies, at some level, is about, naturally, appearances—about how appearances can deceive, how they can trap, how they can and must be overcome. And every Streisand film is about honesty—about looking past appearances to some kind of emotional gravamen, which is the truest basis for love. And every Streisand film is about the societal version of appearance and dishonesty, which is convention—be they gender conventions or moral conventions or conventions of beauty. In a vestige of her old kookiness, even a disaster like *What's Up, Doc?* is basically about Streisand defying and then destroying conventions, which are inevitably constrictive, and finding personal liberation. And last, every Streisand film is a tribute to will, the ram that batters down those conventions as well as interpersonal barriers, for if there is no more unconventional leading lady than Streisand, there is no more driven or intractable one either. As Ryan O'Neal says at the end of *What's Up, Doc?* when he finally succumbs to the woman who has seemingly crushed his entire life underfoot, "You can't fight a tidal wave." Streisand is always a tidal wave, and in the end, even though her films are realistic enough to acknowledge that honesty and determination may not be enough, they hold a brief for those personal qualities she exemplifies. That is the primary message of Streisand's early films: finding and fighting for one's truth, even if one has to pay a price for doing so.

It is a message that is easily entangled with Streisand's Jewishness. The emphasis on the deceptiveness of appearances, the challenge to convention, the virtue of honesty, and the power of will are all characteristics that have been identified with Jewishness, not always approvingly. And, indeed, the criticisms of Streisand's stridency, which grew as her career grew, like those criticisms of her appearance, sometimes come uncomfortably close to anti-Semitism. The critic John Simon, undoubtedly the leader of the virulently anti-Streisand chorus, hated her looks, calling her "arrogantly, exultantly ugly" and claiming that he could not "accept a romantic heroine who is both knock-kneed and ankleless (maybe one of those things, but not both!), short-waisted and shapeless, scrag-toothed and with a horse face centering on a nose that looks like Brancusi's Rooster cast in liverwurst." But as much as he hated those looks, he also hated her persona—that Jewish persona. "Miss Streisand comes on as fundamentally Jewish as Woody Allen," he wrote in a critique of her film *Up the Sandbox*, in which she played a frustrated housewife with the gentile name Margaret Reynolds, "only she represents the other side of a stereotype that, like a coin, has two sides. Whereas Allen is the beleaguered, repressed, self-depreciating little man, masochistically wallowing in his littleness, weakness, homeliness, Miss Streisand is the shrewd, aggressive shrew, domineering to the point of sadism, blithely unaware of her ugliness or bullying everyone into accepting it as beauty." As if to spare himself the charge that so readily comes to mind, he called for filmmakers to stop "caricaturing" Jews, though it is interesting that the caricature that roused his ire was the Jew triumphant.[62]

To prove that Streisand just couldn't win, others castigated her for not being Jewish enough, and for providing, in the feminist scholar Felicia Herman's words, "sentimentalized, reductive views of both Jews and women that neutralize their purported criticism of the hegemony of WASP culture and the predominance of sexism. . . . Jewishness in Streisand's films seems confined at the most to a kind of secular liberalism or a 'superior' morality that leaves no room for the particularism of the Jewish experience, religious, cultural, or otherwise; at the least, Jewishness is equated only with stereotypical 'Jewish' features and behaviors: a nose, an accent, a mention of a bagel."[63]

Putting aside that no studio was going to finance Streisand making movies exclusively for a Jewish audience that comprised less than 2 percent of the American population any more than Streisand would have wanted to make them, Herman may have missed the point even more than Simon, who took many of Streisand's qualities that appealed to audiences and simply demonized them—a case of the conventional counterattacking. The point was that Streisand did exhibit those Jewish characteristics and that she valorized them. She really was, among all the other things, a bagel on a plate of onion rolls, which was yet another aspect of the Jewish metaphor she purveyed—not only different, not only louder and bolder and more honest and even freer, not only less timid, less guarded, and less conventional, but also, finally as a result, more powerful and, yes, better. Streisand made audiences feel that the odd bagel was more desirable than the ordinary onion roll. It was an extraordinary achievement.

6

Supervuman

PERHAPS BECAUSE the distance between the characters she played and the person she seemed to be was practically nonexistent, the charge of "moral superiority," which was issued against her characters, was one Barbra Streisand would become accustomed to hearing about herself. And when she began sounding off on politics, she took especially severe heat from those who disagreed with her. There was an idea, by no means limited to criticisms of Streisand, that entertainers had no business addressing any issues outside of show business. "Like a great many other people who have done very well in show business," Jonathan Yardley of the *Washington Post* wrote sneeringly in a perfect expression of this attitude, "Streisand has fallen into the trap of mistaking emotions for ideas, of assuming that because she feels something, she must think it as well. . . . She can feel any old thing she wants to feel, and she can even pretend her feelings are thoughts, but none of this entitles her to be taken seriously as anything except an entertainer."[1]

But it wasn't just that Streisand had the temerity to express her political opinions. The real anger was over the kinds of opinions she expressed, which were invariably and robustly liberal. This made Streisand into a liberal icon whose "ultimate song," wrote one admirer, "is that she has been using her voice in a manner that becomes a record of permission, hers and ours."[2] Of course, this also turned Streisand into a conservative target. One right-wing pundit, Laura Ingraham, even titled one of her books *Shut Up and Sing*, with the subtitle *How Elites from Hollywood, Politics and the UN Are Subverting America*. What undoubtedly made the conservative attacks so vehement is the same thing that made critical attacks like John Simon's so vehement: Streisand was the biggest star. That really seemed to rile her detractors. But Jewish studies scholar David Kaufman detected something more than right-wing animus in the attacks on Streisand's politics. Kaufman cited a syllogism that Jews are generally liberal, and that liberalism is thought by conservatives to be basically reflexive and irrational, and that, therefore, Jews are irrational, and he thought the syllogism helped explain the "unusual degree of negative comment and even outright hostility directed toward Streisand over the years—though couched as homophobia or sexism or anti-liberalism, the common denominator is anti-Semitism."[3]

The syllogism may have had some validity if one removed the alleged Jewish irrationality. Streisand's liberalism certainly owed a great deal to her Jewishness. She told political reporter Jack Newfield that when she attended yeshiva in Brooklyn as a little girl, "I was taught about the concept of *tikkun olam*—the responsibility for repairing the world. I was taught about charity, about putting money in a *pushke* for the needy. I was taught to invite a stranger to share your Sabbath dinner."[4] These weren't just obligatory prescriptions or religious lip service. They were the very principles that animated Jewish life, in large part because Jews fully understood that in a world that largely reviled them, they were dependent on one another. This was the tragic lesson of Jewish history. Their survival was predicated on a better world, a more charitable world, a more welcoming and forgiving world. And these principles animated Jewish politics as well, which were typically left-wing and often utopian as a result. In this, Streisand was, for once, not unusual. She was a quintessential liberal urban Jew. As Camille Paglia observed, "Streisand's radical politics go back to the passionate Jewish liberalism that pervaded 1950s avant-garde circles and descended in turn from labor-union agitation in the 1930s. . . . Even her crisp, emphatic diction is immediately recognizable as the old voice of Jewish political activism."[5]

Moreover, she was the quintessential Hollywood liberal Jew. Liberal politics had come to the film industry primarily via the New York Jewish writers who were beckoned to the West Coast by the advent of the talking picture in the late 1920s and early 1930s when Hollywood was suddenly in desperate need of men who could string words together. Most of these men were of a certain ilk. Many of them had grown up poor in New York. Many had been newsmen, novelists, and playwrights, and many had worked within the socialist Jewish milieu that was so hospitable to artists with a message. They transplanted that milieu to Los Angeles when they came, forming a left-wing cadre within the belly of the glamorous capitalist beast, and they both recognized the irony and were tormented by it. In fact, their left-wing politics may have been powered by the torment of their feeling that they were prostituting their talent but at the same time of their not wanting to give up the pay they got for it. Whatever else they did, and despite the strenuous efforts of people both outside the industry and within it to exorcise them via blacklists and other mechanisms, they made a bequest to Hollywood politics that would remain for decades, which was its liberal activism. Streisand was a recipient of that bequest.

Active she was. Asked by James Lipton of the Actors Studio

what was her chief "turn off," Streisand replied, "Apathy." No one would ever have accused her of that, either in performance or in politics. But Streisand was also no blind idealist when it came to politics or, for that matter, life. Like the characters she played, she pushed back, though not unmindful that there was a price to pay. "I'm a pretty pragmatic person, grounded in reality," she told Michael Shnayerson of *Vanity Fair*. "I'm an earth sign, Taurus. I don't like swimming underwater or flying in the air. It's about accepting things as they are, but always striving to better them. Suffering [how often that word is associated with Streisand] is the resistance to what is. If you want to suffer less, you have to come to grips with what is."[6]

Streisand seemed willing to suffer for the right cause. There was the black boy she dated in high school. There was the time in 1960 that she went to the Townhouse Club on Staten Island where the proprietor let her perform until he stopped her because the crowd was growing hostile to a black friend she had brought with her.[7] These were just ad hoc gestures. By one account, her formal indoctrination into politics began the next year when Lorraine Gordon, the wife of the owner of the Blue Angel, invited her to join a group protesting nuclear weapons.[8] That inclined her. In May 1963, she was singing for President Kennedy, and she sang "People" at Lyndon Johnson's inauguration in 1965.

But Streisand was hardly what you would call a political doyenne—yet. She said that started in 1969 when she campaigned for John Lindsay, a liberal Republican, in the New York City mayoral race. "I've been an activist ever since," she told a reporter.[9] The next year, her close friend and confidante, Cis Corman, introduced her to Bella Abzug, a liberal feminist firebrand who was running in the Democratic primary for Congress in the nineteenth district, and Streisand mounted a flatbed truck to campaign with her through the streets of the district. In 1972, Warren Beatty, with whom she had a brief fling, cajoled her into appearing at a fundraising concert for Democratic presidential nominee George McGovern at the Forum in Inglewood outside Los Angeles, even though Streisand by this time had stopped performing publicly. (The concert would become part of Streisand lore, not because she headlined a bill that included Carole King and James Taylor, but because she pretended to smoke marijuana while discoursing on how she had to summon her strength to perform.)[10] The next year, she agreed to perform at the estate of producer Jennings Lang to raise money for the defense fund for Daniel Ellsberg, who had leaked the Pentagon Papers to the press, and raised fifty thousand dollars.

She wouldn't perform publicly again for another thirteen years.

According to a Texas preacher's son named Andy Tiemann, any boy in Texas in the mid-1970s who wanted to make out with a girl needed three things: "an all-encompassing knowledge and adoration of the New Testament; membership in good standing with the Fellowship of Christian Athletes; and the ability to converse intelligently about Barbra Streisand." Tiemann admitted that he was confounded why nice Southern Baptist girls were absolutely batty about this New York Jew—that is, until Debbie Hartfelder told him why. Hartfelder's father was an alcoholic and her mother a "doormat," which, Tiemann said, was pretty much the situation for most of those North Dallas girls. "If only Barbra Streisand were her mother," Hartfelder told him, "everything would be just fine because nobody but nobody would bully Streisand. No man would dare. If they did, she'd eat them alive and not even burp. Streisand was a real woman because Streisand knew how to take care of herself."[11]

Of course, that wasn't true only in Texas. Streisand had that attraction for a lot of women, just as she seemed to terrify a lot of men. Power was one of the primary subtexts of her work. None of this, however, was especially political, at least not at the outset. It was just a function of who Streisand was and who her characters were—that stridency they both had. She could be insulted, but she couldn't be bested. Maybe this was a lesson she had learned from her mother's own doormat status under the feet of Louis Kind. Maybe it was another part of her Jewish heritage where women were often characterized as tough and domineering. Either way, as David Kaufman observed, Streisand was a feminist before there was such a thing as a feminist movement.[12] She was a born feminist.

The movement was something else. Not at all incidentally, Jewish women—among them Phyllis Chesler, Bella Abzug, and Letty Cottin Pogrebin—had been the spearheads for modern American feminism, which could be dated from 1963, when a freelance journalist and suburban New York housewife named Betty Freidan wrote *The Feminine Mystique*, which exposed the frustrations of intelligent, talented women who had been sentenced to the prison of homemaking. This especially resonated with Jewish women, many of whom were educated but had no better luck breaking into the professional world than Streisand had had breaking into show business. Some of them, including Freidan, cited their Jewishness as an inspiration for their feminism—"a passion against injustice," as Freidan put it, fueled by "feelings of the injustice of anti-Semitism," though a degree of antifemale injustice could be found within Judaism itself, which was patriarchal, a subject Streisand would address in *Yentl*.[13] One Orthodox prayer began, "I thank Thee, Lord, I was not created a woman." Some Jewish feminists specifically cited the disregard with which they were greeted as Jewish women as a spur. Writer Anne Roiphe said that Jewish women were in the feminist forefront because of the "pain and anguish" they felt over the "way they had been portrayed"—usually as man-killers, like Streisand, or as pampered Jewish American Princesses, and always as ugly.[14] The fight for women's liberation was, in some measure, a fight to be liberated from these stereotypes.

Streisand said that she never thought about the feminist movement. "I didn't even realize that I was fighting this battle all the time. I just took it very personally," she would say. "I didn't even separate it from the fact that I was a woman having a hard time in a male society. Then they started to burn the bras, and I thought it was ridiculous, although I now understand it in the whole picture of revolution. One has to go to these crazy extremes to come back to the middle."[15]

As incredible as that may seem for someone as self-aware as Streisand, it didn't take long for her to become identified with the movement and to become one of its foremost heroines. A film like *Up the Sandbox*, about a dissatisfied housewife who fantasizes far-flung adventures, or a song like "Much More" ("I want much more than keeping house") is explicitly feminist in sentiment. This was a matter of confluence: Streisand helping to create an image for the movement and the movement helping to create a context for the image. (It was also, not incidentally, something else for conservatives to hate about Streisand, since feminism gave her another convention to smash.) In the process, the Streisand persona got politicized. Her assertiveness, her unwillingness to be domesticated, her obdurate determination in the face of the abuse hurled at her, her demands, and her capacity to out-man any man were all manifestations of power, which, from a feminist perspective, also made them political actions. Oh, to be Barbra Streisand! That was what the Debbie Hartfelders of the world were dreaming.

But Streisand not only connected with Jewish feminism. She connected to another Jewish hero, which, in her feminized version, also appealed to those Debbie Hartfelders: Superman. Superman was created in 1938 by two Jewish teenagers from Cleveland, Jerry Siegel and Joe Shuster. In discussing the character's origins, Siegel, sounding very much like the teenaged Streisand, said, "I had crushes on several attractive girls who either didn't know I existed or didn't care I existed. It occurred to me: What if I was real terrific? What if I had something special going for me?"[16] Thus did Clark Kent, a "gendered stereotype of Jewish inferiority," in the words of philosophy professor Harry Brod, become Superman: "Superman exists to counter the notion that strength or manliness and Jewishness are incompatible."[17] In many ways, Streisand would become Superwoman, and lest one doubt that she was aware of the comparison, she would later title an album *Superman*, which featured her in nothing but a Superman T-shirt and knee socks. The *mieskeit* Streisand was her Clark Kent; the aggressive, beautiful, seemingly bigger-than-life Streisand was her Superwoman, and like the comic book identities, the second counteracted the stereotype of the ugly, unfeminine Jewess—the stereotype she had borne. Women seemed to perceive her that way. She was the living embodiment of the other becoming the overwhelming, and this spoke more to Streisand's feminism than any of her films or songs possibly could.

Streisand took to the role. She seemed to like the idea of being not only the biggest woman in Hollywood but the toughest. And she liked the idea of calling out both the media and the male Hollywood power brokers on their sexism. Addressing the American Academy of Achievement in 1992 on the occasion of receiving an award, she made her bluntest statement about the hypocrisy in the way women were treated differently from men, and a lot of what she said had direct application to the things that had been said about her.

> A man is commanding, a woman is demanding.
> A man is forceful, a woman is pushy.
> He's assertive, she's aggressive.
> He strategizes, she manipulates.
> He shows leadership, she's controlling.
> He's committed, she's obsessed.

He's persevering, she's relentless.
He sticks to his guns, she's stubborn.

And she added, "If a man wants to get it right, he's looked up to and respected. If a woman wants to get it right, she's difficult and impossible." She certainly knew whereof she spoke. (Nor could it have been lost on her that one could have made the same list substituting "gentile" for man and "Jew" for woman.)

She concluded by offering the kind of vision that had long since become feminist boilerplate but that, again, drew power from the woman who was saying it—a woman who had lived it. "I look forward to a society that is color- and gender-blind, that judges us by the value of our work, not the length of our legs. That accepts the fact that a woman can be many, many things: strong and vulnerable, intelligent and sexy, opinionated and flexible, angry and forgiving, deep thinking as well as deep feeling." That woman, after all, was Streisand herself.[18]

In a life of convergences, the personal Barbra, the professional Barbra, and the political Barbra all converged in what would prove to be one of her finest films, *The Way We Were*. The project began inauspiciously when Ray Stark, who still had Streisand under contract for two more pictures on her *Funny Girl* deal, asked Arthur Laurents ("charmed" is how Laurents described Stark's approach) to devise a plot for Streisand. Even as he pitched the idea to her—about a Brooklyn woman who teaches blind children to sing—he said he knew it was terrible. But he also said that as he made the pitch, he realized that Streisand reminded him of someone—someone he had known in his college days at Cornell, a political firebrand by the name of Fanny Price (really!). At that moment, he would write, "I knew that Fanny Price was going to be transformed into the hero of the picture I was going to write for her." He didn't have a story yet, but he was sure that the story would come.[19]

It did—the story of the campus radical, renamed Katie Morosky, and the campus jock she pursues, with the upper-crust, certifiably WASP-y name of Hubbell Gardner. Not surprisingly, Streisand loved his treatment. Laurents said he was the one who recommended that Sydney Pollack, who had received an Oscar nomination for the atmospheric Depression parable *They Shoot Horses, Don't They?* direct, though Pollack himself later said that Streisand wanted him because he had a long connection to the fabled acting teacher Sandy Meisner, and Streisand was eager to hone her acting abilities.[20] In any case, once onboard, Pollack, who was close to Robert Redford, then attempted to recruit Redford to play Gardner.[21] The casting of the most Jewish of Jewish actresses and the most gentile of gentile actors was irresistible. It was also pure Streisand—the furthest extension of the *Funny Girl* template as well as the ultimate role reversal. She was the muscular one, he the passive blond.

Which, according to some accounts, is exactly what irked Redford. Redford told Pollack that the Gardner role was thin, basically a straight man to Streisand. (He had good reason to feel that way; every one of Streisand's romantic leads had been a straight man to her.) Pollack argued that he was wrong. "This isn't a fuzzy piece for Barbra Streisand," he said he told Redford. "This is substantial—what do you know—it's political. I pressured and pressured him all summer as soon as we got back from Cannes," where the two had been promoting the film *Jeremiah Johnson*. But Redford admitted another problem. Streisand was untested as a serious actress. He told Pollack, "Her reputation is as a very controlling person. She will direct herself. It will never work."[22]

In effect, the movie became another of Streisand's metas— this time an effort to push back against her because she was too powerful, an effort to reassert male dominance over her. Pollack finally won Redford, but only by conceding to enlarge his role and shift the movie's focus from Streisand. Laurents, who was gay and Jewish and an admirer of Streisand's, warned Pollack: "The picture is Barbra's no matter what you do because the story is hers. Be careful you don't destroy it trying to give it to him."[23] Then Laurents was fired.

To fix the script to Redford's satisfaction, Pollack brought out a platoon of writers including the former Hollywood Ten member and blacklistee Dalton Trumbo, playwright and Oscar-winning screenwriter Paddy Chayefsky, and Francis Ford Coppola. Two-time future Oscar-winner Alvin Sargent, however, was the one who provided what Redford said he desperately needed: a scene that gave him a point of view to rival Streisand's character's moral vision.[24] It was set in Union Station in Los Angeles, where Katie is returning from a trip to Washington, DC, to support those called to testify about their political leanings before the House Un-American Activities Committee. Katie argues that one must defend one's principles. Hubbell argues back that it doesn't make any difference, that in the final analysis no one really cares, that the world goes on, and that basically she is engaged in political theater, not the morality she thinks. "I'm telling you, people, people, are more important than any goddam witchhunt—you and me."

Another meta occurred during the shooting. Like her character, Streisand was infatuated with Redford. One person on the set said, "It was obvious that Barbra was just too, too crazy about Bob. She had a hard time controlling her emotions, and when she played scenes with him, like the fireside courtship scene in Malibu, she was drooling."[25] Redford didn't reciprocate, but the two were, Pollack said, extremely respectful of each other, each telling him how much better his/her costar was in the picture than he or she was.[26]

By the time the film was being cut, Streisand had become manageable, Laurents felt too manageable. He had come back onto the picture during the editing and heard that Streisand had been "constantly debating and pleading with Sydney for the restoration of pieces of scenes, of lines he cut. Not her lines necessarily, lines she felt vital to the piece."[27] But Streisand, who was not known for backing down, was reluctant, he said, to challenge Pollack and Redford. Laurents wasn't. One of the lines for which she had fought was a line Katie says in the Union Station argument when Hubbell badgers her about her insistence on principles. "People *are* their principles," she rebuts. It was a key line—the line that differentiates the two lovers. Laurents knew he would have little sway, but he cajoled Streisand into insisting on it. And she won.

There were other battles to come—these fought after the previews, which were less than enthusiastically received. Pollack, Streisand, and Redford had been making a film that was essentially, in their eyes, political. Pollack had called it the first Hollywood film to tackle the blacklist. The film had a lot of political debate in it. But even though the wounds may have still seemed fresh in Hollywood, audiences were bored by rehashing old battles. So Pollack quickly recut the movie, removing large chunks of the political material. The political movie suddenly was, ostensibly at least, not so political anymore. It wasn't about the lefties fighting a system that demanded conformity. It was now a romance, which is what Streisand movies always were.

To some, this may have seemed a desecration. Laurents certainly seemed to feel that way. But it may actually have been a case of the material finding its proper genre. As a political film, *The Way We Were* would have been constricted and programmatic. As a romance, it addressed a conflict that was much larger than that between unreconstructed left-wingers, on one side, and unapologetic right-wingers and reformed lefties, on the other, and it did so in a way that was intelligent, evenhanded, emotional, and complex. Stripped of its political lineaments, *The Way We Were* became a film about the tension between morality and aesthetics.

This was a subject with a long and illustrious tradition in American literature. It is one of the primary tensions in the great novels of Henry James, who often pits essentially innocent and basically moral figures against aesthetic ones, and who identifies these with America and Europe respectively—the new, uncorrupted nation and the old, desiccated continent. It is also one of the tensions in the work of F. Scott Fitzgerald, whose great protagonist Jay Gatsby forswears the moral underpinnings of his life for the aesthetic ones that he thinks will bring him the love he desires. And beyond literature, it is one of the themes that run through the films of Streisand, though nowhere else as overtly or dramatically as in *The Way We Were*. This is clearly what upset Redford when he first read the script. Katie Morosky is a vocal moral force. Hubbell Gardner, who is physically perfect, is an aesthetic one. How could he possibly win?

To some extent, he is right. Katie is, after all, played by a woman who by this time was closely identified with the put-upon and who invariably portrayed women in the right. In all her previous films, she is the voice of sanity and truth. In this film, arguably better than in any of her other films, she deploys that righteousness and truthfulness to powerful effect. Katie is smart, she is willful, she is judgmental in the cause of helping her lover see what she believes is the best of himself. It is not for nothing that one of the film's most poignant lines is when Hubbell commiserates with his college friend and now producer on the breakup of the man's marriage (to a beautiful woman, of course), and the friend says, "It's not like, you know, losing *somebody*—Katie—that would be a loss." She is unquestionably the film's moral arbiter: the Jewish outsider who sees what the insiders cannot see and who says what the insiders will not say. Here morality is beauty.

Then there is the gentile. Hubbell is a golden boy, literally, but his looks belie his sensitivity. Though Katie strives to be a writer, her moral force seems to smother her talent. She is a plodder on the page as in life. Hubbell's writing, in contrast, is as effortless as he is. "In a way, he was like the country he lived in," goes the Fitzgeraldian first line of a story he writes for his English class near the beginning of the film. "Everything came too easily to him." (David Kaufman observes, aptly, that the romance between them is "emblematic of Jews' desire to be accepted and even loved by America," as that line suggests, though one could also say that the romance is emblematic of certain gentiles' desire to be accepted and even loved by Jews.)[28] Hubbell's ease is both his blessing and his curse. Because things come so easily, he doesn't know their value. Because nothing comes easily for Jewish Katie, she knows the value of everything. "I don't know how you do it," he says to her. To which Katie says, truthfully, "You're jealous." Hubbell begins the film with both talent and even some ambition. He wants to be a novelist. Katie obviously is smitten with Hubbell's looks and manner; seeing him tipsy in his crisp navy dress whites and inviting him to her apartment because he doesn't have a place to stay, she crawls in bed with him. It is, again, the sort of seduction scene that is usually reserved for a man. But in an odd case of Streisand, for once, having to look past a *man's* appearance for some deeper attraction, Katie falls in love, not with his beauty, but with his talent and his dreams. His writing and her ardent belief in it provide the interface between them.

As in most great romances, they love in the other what each of them does not have, a profound case of opposites attracting. But that is precisely what makes the relationship impossible. Hubbell goes to Hollywood to adapt his novel for the movies, losing his ambition and rapidly becoming another writer-for-hire. Though he comes to loathe himself for doing so, as many of the old New York Jewish writers did, he comes to loathe

Katie more for continuing to push him so hard when he has given up the fight, though what he really loathes is his guilt in having failed her. In truth, he never had Katie's moral force or determination, which is why he is so willing to compromise. For the man for whom everything came too easily, maintaining his integrity is too hard.

But, to the film's credit, this doesn't make Hubbell's position any less valid than Katie's. Yes, he is basically an aesthete, but Katie is so morally implacable that she makes no room for his fallibilities or those of anyone else. She can't help but judge —judge his friends, judge his industry, judge him. She can't help but be a scold. She is just, to use that term often thrown at Streisand, "too much"—too much for his good and too much for her own good. She wants to change. She wants to satisfy him. But she is finally too much herself to be able to do so.

In a film of dichotomies—Jew and gentile, poor and rich, brunette and blond, active and passive, loud and soft, complacent and provocative, and, above all, morally driven and aesthetically driven—the gulf between them is just too great to bridge. They love each other. They cannot really love anyone else. They see the virtue in each other. They complete each other, even *over*complete each other. He knows that she is special and that her moral force is vibrant and exciting; her judgment is the only one that really counts. She knows that he is gifted and that he sees the world with more equanimity and generosity than she does. And when Hubbell has an affair with his friend's ravishing wife, we realize, and he realizes, that it isn't love or sex or sympathy or anything other than escaping his wife's censure and finding someone who isn't always demanding the best of him. *It's not like losing somebody—Katie—that would be a loss.* And yet he does. And she him. Years after their breakup, in what amounts to an epilogue in front of the Plaza Hotel, he winds up with a pert young blonde of the sort Streisand had always vanquished, and she winds up with a Jewish doctor—partners whose sensibilities match their own rather than challenge their own.

It is a great scene, a heartbreaking scene, a memorable scene, a definitive Streisand scene. *New York Times* film critic Manohla Dargis would write forty years later that like a "lot of women, I suspect, I fell in love with her while watching *The Way We Were*," citing that scene as the deal maker: "Their misty reunion years later in front of the Plaza Hotel, during which she tenderly brushes his hair across his forehead, exquisitely captures the enduring heartache of loving the wrong man."[29]

This is tragedy, but it is also self-criticism. If no film of Streisand's captures her in full as *The Way We Were* does, neither do any of her films, with the possible exception of *Yentl*, express so fully the way in which her characters' strengths, so often conflated with her own, also become their weaknesses. That she has made a movie doing so is a sign of her self-confidence. Nicky Arnstein was never Fanny's equal, so his inability to accept her too-muchness was his deficiency: a shallow man who can't cope with a strong woman. Hubbell Gardner, on the other hand, is Katie's equal. He can't cope with a hectoring woman who, in Jewish fashion, is on an unrelenting mission to repair the world when all he wants to do is live as peaceably as possible within it. *The Way We Were* is Streisand's way of saying that she pays a price for her moralizing, for her perfectionism, for her gutsiness, for her ardency, for her stridency, for her lack of conformity—for all the things her fans had come to love about her and about her characters. She pays a price to be Barbra Streisand.

She paid a price from the critics, too. *The Way We Were* was not well received. Reviewers had no doubt heard about the film's editing problems and seemed to fasten on what they saw as a narrative lumpiness. Even Streisand admirer Pauline Kael of the *New Yorker* called the film a "fluke—a torpedoed ship full of gaping holes, which comes snugly into port," which she attributed to Streisand. Noting how much Katie's faults replicated Streisand's alleged faults, she wrote, "The tricky thing about the role of Katie Morosky is that Streisand must emphasize just that element in her own persona which repelled some people initially; her fast sass is defensive and aggressive in the same breath. But it's part of her gradual conquest of the movie public that this won't put people off now."[30] Vincent Canby in the *New York Times* felt just the opposite. "The only thing that limits Barbra Streisand as a movie superstar is that she's not really an actress, not even much of a comedienne," he wrote. "She's an impersonator. When the impersonation fits the contours of the public personality—tough, driving, ambitious, shrewd, self-mocking—the performance can be effective as it was in 'Funny Girl.'" But in *The Way We Were* she was asked to act, and Canby didn't feel she was up to it.[31]

Nevertheless, the Academy of Motion Picture Arts and Sciences gave Streisand her second Best Actress nomination. By this time, however, there was already a breach opening between how her fans felt about her and how the industry was feeling about her, though the feelings seemed to emanate from the same place: Streisand's much-bruited toughness. On Oscar night, she lost to Glenda Jackson for a middling comedy, *A Touch of Class*. Streisand later didn't mince words. "I felt I deserved the award," she said with typical candor. "I was the best of those five for the year."[32] She was right.

There was, of course, a lot of Katie Morosky in Barbra Streisand. Like Katie, Streisand would never give up the fight, but she was fighting undercover, supporting favored candidates like Abzug and giving donations, until 1986 after the explosion of the nuclear energy plant in Chernobyl in the Soviet Union. "I was very upset," Streisand told Jack Newfield, "so I called Marilyn Bergman [her friend and lyricist for *The Way We Were*] and we started talking about the world and nuclear disarmament." This is precisely the sort of thing that drove conservatives crazy. How dare she! But Streisand wound up joining a liberal fundraising and advocacy group called the Hollywood Women's Political Committee, which had been organized by women in entertainment in 1984 shortly after Geraldine Ferraro's nomination for the vice presidency on the Democratic ticket, and she began educating herself on political issues the way she had educated herself on artistic matters when she was a teenager in Manhattan. Marilyn Bergman got Streisand to thinking how she could have maximum effect on the things that mattered to her, and that led to her decision to stage a concert at her Malibu home to raise money for six prochoice, antinuclear Democratic Senate candidates, both by charging five thousand dollars per couple for the privilege of hearing her sing and by selling the broadcast rights to the HBO cable network.[33]

This wasn't as easy for Streisand as it may have sounded. She had come to hate appearing in public, ever since her famous Central Park concert in 1967, when there was a reported Palestinian Liberation Organization threat against her. The only force that could impel her was politics, which is why she performed at the McGovern fundraiser. Now she was called on again. As she told guests in a tape-recorded invitation to the concert, "I could never imagine myself wanting to sing in public again, but then, I could never imagine with all our advanced technology the starvation of bodies and minds and the possibility of nuclear winters in our lives—I could no longer remain silent." The concert became known as "One Voice," after Streisand's comment that we cannot forget the "importance of one voice, of each of our voices, and the enormous difference it can make in all our lives—in history."[34]

The "One Voice" concert, staged on September 6, 1986, raised over eight million dollars. More, it energized Streisand. "When she did that concert and saw the tremendous power she could have—the power to effect change," Bella Abzug said later, "that's when Barbra decided she was ready to kick some Republican butt."[35] Streisand formed a foundation to raise money for the causes in which she believed: civil liberties and human rights, women's issues, AIDS, gay and lesbian rights, the American Civil Liberties Union, the environment, youth, and many others. As with her political consciousness, she again cited the traditions of Jewish charity, which is, she said, "linked to justice and an obligation to mend the world," and to the history of oppression with which, as a Jew, she identified. Within a decade, the Streisand Foundation had raised over thirteen million dollars for her causes, which would prompt Jack Newfield to write, "When measured against all other celebrity icons, history will judge that Barbra Streisand used her gigantic fame, wealth and power to fight for justice. She not only sings proud, she thinks and acts proud."[36]

And talked proud—a veritable entertainment Katie Morosky. When Colorado passed an amendment to its constitution in 1992 allowing discrimination against gays, Streisand loudly called for a boycott of the state, which hit the entertainment industry where it hurt, since many of its members had homes in Aspen. They weren't happy. John Denver called her a "hypocrite." Jack Nicholson, who had two houses in Aspen, called the boycott "rubbish." But Streisand would not be dissuaded in her politics just as she would not be dissuaded in her art.[37]

It could be argued that not since John Wayne, another actor whose life was conflated with his roles, had an entertainer been so closely identified with a political position as Streisand was. But she didn't reach that point until Bill Clinton's presidency. Clinton and Streisand had deep commonalities. Like Streisand, Clinton never knew his father, who had died before Bill was born, and he was subject to many of the same psychological deficits as Streisand was; and like Streisand, he also had an abusive stepfather, which made him subject to many of the same compensations as Streisand was, especially the overdrive. They were both wounded overstrivers. Clinton had not been Streisand's first choice for the Democratic nomination. Iowa senator Tom Harkin, an old-fashioned liberal, was. But Streisand had met Clinton at the home of Interscope Records owner and film producer Ted Field and was impressed. When Harkin dropped out, she switched to Clinton, even headlining a benefit for him—her first public performance since the "One Voice" concert. It raised $1.5 million for the campaign.[38]

The right had excoriated Streisand in 1986. Tom Santopietro, one of her biographers, even called the "One Voice" concert a "turning point in the coverage of Streisand." Henceforth, he wrote, perceptions of her would be "filtered through the lens of 'diva as the ultimate Hollywood liberal,'" thus attempting to tarnish liberalism by associating it with Streisand's reputation.[39] Then there were the renewed charges that she was out of her depth, to which Streisand responded angrily. "When I directed a movie," she said, "it was as if I was being told how dare I attempt to infiltrate a man's domain. Now it's, 'How dare I be interested in politics.'"[40] The political criticism even extended to the outfit she wore to Bill Clinton's inaugural where, once again, she performed. That outfit, wrote Anne Taylor Fleming in the *New York Times*, "sent a disturbing signal to—and about—American women." It was a "three-piece pinstriped male power suit, with a feminine touch"—that touch being a slit up the side and a "definite hint of cleavage" in her vest. As she sang, Taylor noted a "mixed metaphor," which was a "woman letting us know that underneath her peekaboo power suit, underneath all her bravado and accomplishments, she is still an accessible femme fatale." So Streisand was being "devious" and exhibiting "ambivalence" about having to "conform to someone's notion of what it means to be female today."[41]

What it really demonstrated is not Streisand's ambivalence

but the ambivalence about her—about being a woman who is stronger than most men. That is why Camille Paglia called Streisand singing her hit "Evergreen" at the inaugural "one of the supreme moments in popular entertainment." Watching her, Paglia wrote, Streisand fans were thinking, "'Look at what we've missed for the past twenty-five years!' She looked spectacular wearing a business suit with big padded shoulders and a long slit up the thigh. I was delirious. She was all man and all woman." And Paglia saw it as something else. It was a reassertion of the younger Streisand—the bolder, less romantic Streisand who had emerged in the movies. "She's gone full circle."[42]

Streisand was not someone who was ashamed of her lack of formal education, though like many Jews, she had what Arthur Laurents said was an "exaggerated respect for a degree." Laurents said that when she first moved to Hollywood, she asked him for a reading list, and he recommended Aleksandr Solzhenitsyn's *One Day in the Life of Ivan Denisovich* and *Cancer Ward*. When Solzhenitsyn won the Nobel Prize, Laurents said that Streisand called him excitedly and gushed, "Hey, your guy won!" but admitted that she hadn't read his books.[43] But Streisand was nevertheless a willing student. Ever since her personal tutorials that began with "One Voice," she had studied politics. Bill Schneider, a CNN political analyst, told *Vanity Fair* that he met her at a dinner party after Clinton's election and she peppered him with questions—intelligent questions. He said that he saw her again backstage after a concert, and the "first words out of her mouth were: 'What the hell is Alan Greenspan [the Fed Chairman] doing raising interest rates?'" Schneider was impressed. He felt she had a "genuine interest in finding out more."[44]

But when Harvard's John F. Kennedy School of Government invited her to speak early in 1995, the media didn't know exactly what to make of it. Naturally, the invitation drew some howls of laughter from her critics on the right, and even in a liberal environment like Harvard's Cambridge, Streisand expected the worst. But she could never be bullied, and she determined to make her appearance a stout defense of liberalism at a time—after the midterm elections that had resulted in disastrous losses for the Democrats—when liberalism was hardly popular. She was also determined not to make the appearance a stunt, even though Harvard had to hold a lottery for tickets because demand exceeded supply. She prepared carefully. She had Peter Jennings, the ABC news anchor with whom she had once had a romance, read the speech and give advice.

Her talk, which was titled "The Artist as Citizen," was a presentation not only of Streisand's politics but also a candid confession of her feelings about public life. And it was vintage Streisand: outspoken, defiant, unapologetic, iconoclastic. She began by admitting that she was more frightened speaking before these Harvard intellectuals than singing in front of thousands of people, but calling it an honor to be invited to speak about "my convictions and not just my career." She referenced the 1994 election, which had elevated Republican Newt Gingrich into the Speaker's chair in the House of Representatives, and the threat it posed to the "progress of the recent past," singling out the conservatives' attack on the arts. In a career that had been largely predicated on disruption, she celebrated the arts, which, she said, existed "to challenge one to think, to provoke, even to disturb, in a constant search for the truth," and the great smasher of conventions called the conservatives' efforts to "force artists to conform to some rigid notion of 'mainstream American values'" a way to "weaken the very foundation of our democracy."

Artists were targets, she said. And citing a *New Republic* article that called Hollywood politics "uniformly idiotic," she thought the hostility to Hollywood activists was "all about jealousy." More, she defended her fellow actors' rights to speak out: "Why should the actor give up his role as citizen just because he is in show business?" She said that no one would dare deny other groups their say. And, in typical Streisand fashion, she called out the politicians and the media for their hypocrisy in courting celebrities, on the one hand, and then insulting them, on the other. "You can just hear them thinking—you make money, you're famous—you have to have political opinions too?"

And getting to the questions of why artists, including those in Hollywood, typically espoused liberal ideas, she cited the mission of the artist, which is to "explore the human condition." That required them to "inhabit other people's skins," and she said that did tend to "make us more sympathetic to politics that are more tolerant." "I'm not suggesting that actors run the country," she said, putting in a dig at Ronald Reagan. "We've already tried that." But she did hold a brief for having the country listen to Elizabeth Taylor, who raised money to fight AIDS, rather than listen to Senator Jesse Helms, "who has consistently fought legislation that would fund AIDS research."

She called out religious fundamentalists, too, for their narrow-mindedness: "What is dangerous about the far right is not that it takes religion seriously—most of us do—but rather that it condemns all other spiritual choices—the Buddhist, the Jew, the Muslim, and many others who consider themselves to be good Christians." It took chutzpah for a Jew to do that.

She noted how she had made her politics her art in movies like *Yentl*, in which she addressed the unequal treatment of women, and in a television movie she produced about Colonel Grethe Cammermeyer, who was discharged from the army for being gay. She talked about how she, and other entertainers, despite the charges otherwise, were "normal Americans": "We were not born in movie studios. . . . We've worked hard to get where we are, and we don't forget where we came from, whether it's Iowa, Cincinnati or Brooklyn."

And then, sounding exactly like Katie Morosky when Katie upbraided Hubbell's friends for making callous comments after the announcement of FDR's death, she declared that she was proud to be a "liberal." "Why is that so terrible these days? The liberals were the liberators—they fought slavery, fought for women to have the right to vote, fought against Hitler, Stalin, fought to end segregation, fought to end apartheid. Thanks to liberals we have Social Security, public education, consumer and environmental protection, Medicare and Medicaid, the minimum wage law, unemployment compensation. Liberals put an end to child labor, and they even gave us the five-day work week. What's to be ashamed of? Such a record should be worn as a badge of honor."

She was frank, too, about her image: "What can I say—I have opinions. No one has to agree. I just like being involved. After many years of self-scrutiny, I've realized that the most satisfying feelings come from things outside myself." And she concluded with a line from President Kennedy that the artist "must often sail against the currents of his time," which is "not a popular role." But Streisand assured the students that she would continue to speak out until the wrongs are righted.[45]

And she received a standing ovation.

It was a good day for her, one in which Streisand once again erased the line between her person and her persona and reestablished herself as a disrupter. *New York Times* columnist Frank Rich said that only when he read the speech away from Harvard did he appreciate "that Ms. Streisand may be the last unreconstructed liberal on the hustings right now."[46] Streisand would have been happy to hear that. Unreconstructed is what she always sought to be.

7

Shaygetz

IT WAS about wish fulfillment—not only Barbra Streisand's, but her fans'. That had always been the transaction between stars on the screen and the audience in their seats. It had been Streisand's own transaction when she was a girl and watched Vivien Leigh as Scarlett O'Hara. But the transaction between Streisand and her fans was different from that between most stars and their fans. Most other stars were likely to have dazzled in life as well as on-screen. Typically, they were attractive, confident, charismatic, doted on—which are among the reasons they could even think of themselves as becoming stars in the first place. Their fans might have projected dreams upon them, but those fans could not possibly or realistically have hoped to be them. Moreover, fans assumed that their favorite stars' lives were as gilded and glamorous when those stars were offscreen as their personas were. They had everything one could possibly want—looks, fame, respect, power, money, ease, and, not least of all, love.

None of this was necessarily true for Streisand. Because she seemed as if she were one of their own, an ordinary-looking girl with extraordinary talent, fans couldn't assume that her life was charmed. This applied to romance as well. Other stars dated and married beautiful or handsome fellow stars. That was in the Darwinian order of things, and it constituted a large part of the fans' vicarious and voyeuristic pleasure, so much so that movie magazines like *Photoplay* largely existed to purvey that order. But Streisand? Her journey to stardom had been an anomaly, and the hurdles to becoming a star in life seemed equally daunting. That was all the more reason her fans had a stake in whether she could find romantic success as well as stardom—because her success would be their success, her proof, their proof. Streisand herself, of course, had a stake in making her life replicate the stage and screen. This was wish fulfillment of a much different order than usual. This was wish fulfillment that sought to overturn the old Darwinian state of affairs.

Streisand had always harbored doubts as large as her dreams, not least of which were doubts about her romantic future. "Will I ever get a guy? Do you think anyone could love this face?" she would ask her roommate Elaine Sobel when Streisand came to Manhattan.[1] Another friend told Streisand biographer Anne Edwards, "Barbra's greatest tragedy and her greatest blessing is that she was not born beautiful. That is something with which she may never come to terms."[2] When it came to sex, Streisand admitted she was conflicted because in her family, by which she meant her mother, "sex was taboo." You didn't even hold hands with a boy, which, she said, forced her to "develop a fantasy life." And it forced her to think of sex and love as unitary.[3] It took her a while to shed that idea. By one account, she had her sexual initiation with a fellow student at the Theatre Studio, a short, good-looking young man named Roy Scott who had a reputation as a womanizer. Scott told Streisand biographer James Spada, "She was growing up, dawning, learning to be a woman." But, he added, "She thought she was ugly, with her nose and all. I would tell her no, that she was a very pretty and attractive girl."[4]

It wasn't easy for her to believe that, and her relationships didn't make it any easier. Her first serious romance was with Barry Dennen, who would claim that he was her mentor not only in music but in love. Dennen said that the young Streisand had never learned "feminine wiles" or how to flirt or how to get a man to do what she wanted.[5] But even though she moved in with him, the affair was troubled—troubled because Dennen felt Streisand was self-involved (she missed his last performance in *Twelfth Night* in Shakespeare in the Park, even though he had gotten her a seat) and ungrateful for his help, and because Streisand felt that he neglected her. But the break occurred when Dennen went back to California to visit his parents over the Christmas holiday in 1960 and decided to stay an extra week without telling her. As she would recall it, she arrived back at their apartment on New Year's Eve to find a man in their bathroom and came to the inevitable conclusion that her lover preferred men to her. Dennen would say that she told him she knew he was gay, but "for some reason, I thought that maybe I could change you."[6]

Streisand never talked much about it, understandably, but one can imagine the effect it would have had on a girl whose romantic confidence was low to begin with. Singer Eartha Kitt once asked Streisand during one of her appearances on *PM East* what happens when a "sleeping bee lies in the palm of your hand," referencing the song Streisand so often sang in those early days. Streisand answered evenly, "He stings you dead."[7] That was her idea of romance, which probably wasn't any different from the idea held by many of the young women who identified with her.

And then it changed. It changed the day that she auditioned for *I Can Get It for You Wholesale*. Elliott Gould was the play's lead, and he was sitting in the theater, deep in his seat, watching her do her shtick with the crazy outfit and purple lipstick and the music rolling across the stage and the gum stuck under the chair, and he said to himself, "A freak—a fantastic freak!" And when she was done, as Streisand later told it, "I sort of ran around the stage yelling my phone number and saying 'Wow! Will somebody call me, please! Even if I don't get the part, just call!' I'd gotten my first phone that day, and I was wild to get calls on it." That night, Gould called. He told her, "You said you wanted to get calls, so I called. You were brilliant." And that was that.[8]

Until the first day of rehearsal. "I thought he was funny looking," she would tell *Life* magazine. And childlike. He handed her a cigar. For Gould's part, he was infatuated. He was too frightened to ask her out on a proper date, but he did walk her to the subway after rehearsals. One night he took her to a horror movie, after which they ate at a Chinese restaurant, after which they walked around the skating rink at Rockefeller Center. It was very late. It began to snow. They had a snowball fight, and Gould rubbed her face with snow and kissed her— gently. She said it was "like out of a movie." Gould thought she was the "most innocent thing I'd ever seen," but "she was so strange that I was afraid."[9]

They were, in many ways, kindred spirits. Gould had grown up in Brooklyn, too. They were both Jews who understood the vicissitudes of being Jewish as well as the antagonisms toward it. They both had difficult upbringings, with Streisand's mother too aloof and Gould's too overbearing. Both felt abnormal; Gould slept in his parents' bedroom until he was twelve. Both suffered not only from feelings of otherness but also of inadequacy, and both had show business aspirations to compensate. And though neither knew it, *Wholesale* producer David Merrick had wanted to fire them both because he thought they were too ugly for Broadway. It was, in short, exactly the kind of romance that her fans might have imagined, if not exactly hoped, for their star—an ordinary romance for their ordinary girl.

Streisand didn't see it that way. To her, Gould, who was tall with dark, curly hair, was a catch. "Here I was, a girl from Brooklyn who never had guys chasing me, never went steady, and a loner," she would write. "And then the handsome leading man falls in love with me."[10] They moved in together, then married during her Liberace engagement in Las Vegas. But if the courtship had been like the movies, the marriage wasn't. *Wholesale*, the show in which he starred, turned out to be her break, not his, and the tensions and jealousies came early, even before they had wed. Barry Dennen said he saw the handwriting on the wall when he spotted a photo of them cavorting in the pool of the Beverly Hills Hotel shortly after the marriage, with Streisand riding on Gould's shoulders and her hands clamped over his eyes. It was an image worth a thousand words.

For those fans hoping for Streisand's romantic bliss—not the ordinary bliss of a homely Jewish girl but the bliss of a brilliant star—it would come. It would come after her *Funny Girl* triumph when Streisand was suddenly perceived no longer as unattractive but as beautiful. It was an astonishing occurrence—one that even Streisand herself never fully seemed to understand. "On the one hand, I'll be compared to Egyptian sculpture, and on the other hand, people think I'm awful looking," she said years later. "My opinion of myself is probably a little of both."[11] John Simon would continue to harp on her appearance, saying she looked like a "cross between an aardvark and an albino rat surmounted by a platinum-coated horse bun," and critic Stanley Kauffmann in the *New Republic* could counter the idea that "her talents make her beautiful" as "word juggling."[12] Speaking of *Funny Girl*, he wrote, "What is the theme of the show other than a homely girl's problems and triumphs? Why else was Miss Streisand, a relative unknown at the time, cast in the

Broadway show originally? And she is *Jewish* homely."[13] But even if Kauffmann's critique was justifiable (the show, after all, was called *Funny Girl*, not *Glamour Girl*), these were not only minority opinions now; they were the opposite of what most were saying about her.

There was the aesthetic context to this change in perception that had emerged after *Funny Girl*—the many references to the way she had transformed herself. "She simply decided to be beautiful, and now she is," photographer Richard Avedon, who photographed her for *Vogue*, said.[14] And there was a cultural impact to the change—that idea of becoming the standard bearer for a new conception of beauty. For Jewish women, this was particularly empowering. And not only beautiful, but, perhaps even more important, sexy—so sexy that she would grace the cover of *Playboy* magazine with the caption: "What's a Nice Jewish Girl Like Me Doing on the Cover of *Playboy?*" It was, wrote cultural historian and theater scholar Henry Bial, yet another Streisand milestone, but also a milestone for Jews, one he called the "apotheosis of an evolution of the way the Jewish body is perceived by an American audience." She had gone from "homely frump" in 1962 to cover girl in 1977. "Hence the presence of the label 'Jewish' on the magazine's cover carries a dual significance: on the one hand, it suggests that Streisand had become a sex symbol *in spite* of her Jewishness; on the other hand, it suggests that Streisand's Jewishness somehow contributes to her sex appeal."[15] In either case, the result was, as *New York Times* film critic Manohla Dargis wrote, a signal achievement: What Streisand did "indelibly, historically, was turn a Jewish woman into a sex symbol."[16] *Funny Girl* writer Isobel Lennart was more prosaic: "She's made life a lot better for a lot of homely girls," especially, presumably, Jewish ones.[17]

But there was a third context besides the aesthetic and cultural ones, and this had the most resonance for her fans. That was the romantic context. Streisand attracted men, or, rather, the post–*Funny Girl* Streisand attracted men. Omar Sharif, who played opposite her in the *Funny Girl* film, probably spoke for many of her romantic interests when he told one reporter frankly, "My first impression is that she's not very pretty. But after three days, I am honest, I found her physically beautiful, and I start lusting after this woman!"[18] As with her stage costar, Sydney Chaplin, Streisand had an affair with Sharif during the filming.

Simon's comment that Streisand "bullied" people into believing she was beautiful notwithstanding, she had the same effect on almost every one of her leading men and on men generally. Dennis Quaid, with whom she costarred in *All Night Long*, said, "She actually does have this glow about her."[19] What it all demonstrated is that Streisand had crossed over. She didn't have to *seem* beautiful or have her inner qualities bestow some kind of metaphysical beauty. She had become an object of desire. When her marriage to Elliott Gould collapsed in 1969, Streisand was now able to enter the same romantic world inhabited by conventionally beautiful stars, and she would remain there throughout her career. Hers was an impressive list of conquests: Ryan O'Neal, Warren Beatty, and Don Johnson, to name three of Hollywood's most famous Lotharios, and Canadian prime minister Pierre Trudeau, with whom she flirted from the gallery of Parliament. (She even thought, fancifully, if not entirely implausibly, of marrying him and becoming Canada's First Lady.) There were many others. "I'd be at her house, and the phone calls that would come in!" Ryan O'Neal's publicist told biographer James Spada. "Extraordinary men would be on the line."[20]

And *gentile* men. A large part of the wish fulfillment, both her audience's and hers, was not only that Streisand was beautiful and sexy but also that she could have any man she wanted. Romantically speaking, she had transcended her Jewishness. In Hollywood, this had almost been a rite of passage for Jews eager to be perceived as having assimilated. The old Jewish moguls had married Jewish women in their youths, before the men had attained power. Then, after their ascension to studio thrones, most of them jettisoned those Jewish wives for gentile ones. On-screen, Streisand had long since established her ability to captivate gentiles. After all, she won the heart of Robert Redford, the gentile's gentile, in *The Way We Were*, not to mention the hearts of a string of gentile leading men. Being gentile was almost obligatory to starring opposite Streisand because it was integral to the dream she purveyed on-screen: the girl who could have everything, including the perfect man, and that man, in typical American (and Jewish) idealization, was a WASP. But to have that dream realized in real life was the most dramatic demonstration of Streisand's power, not just the power of her talent but the power of her attractiveness. The irresistible force was truly irresistible.

Since her films had always been predicated on her physical undesirability being offset by her spiritual desirability, Streisand's new beauty clearly had an effect on her pictures. In *The Way We Were*, when Hubbell decides that Katie is just too strident for him and decides to break off the relationship, Katie calls him one night, tearfully, begging him to tell her what she did wrong, and she utters three lines that are brilliant both in the context of the movie and in the context of Streisand's emergence from her alleged homeliness. She says, "I know that I'm attractive, sort of. But I'm not attractive in the right way, am I? I mean, I don't have the right style for you." To which Hubbell says, "No, you don't have the right style." *Attractive, sort of.* The line, which no other female star could possibly have delivered with any conviction, is a heartbreaking confession, and yet a victory over the girl who hadn't been pretty enough. In a later film, the negligible boxing comedy *The Main Event*, she is no less bossy and brassy than in her earlier films, but she is no longer a wallflower. She is a bombshell in tight satin shorts that hug her derriere—more than attractive, sort of. And in *All Night Long*, she plays a busty, somewhat slatternly would-be country and western singer who speaks in a breathy Marilyn Monroe voice and has sex slathered all over her. These films display a different kind of Streisand, a lesser one who betrays the Streisand theme and her earlier movies' poignancy, and no doubt realizing it, she would revert to form in subsequent films like *Yentl, Prince of Tides,* and *The Mirror Has Two Faces* that give us back the old Streisand of self-doubt and self-effacement. But these other middling films, if nothing else, testify to Streisand's coming out, at least temporarily, into a more conventional form of feminine appeal. She isn't a beauty in these movies because we think of her as a star. She is a star in these movies because, among other things, we think of her as a beauty.

If fans seemed to relish Streisand's new romantic escapades as an elision from this screen life to real life, there was nevertheless criticism from some quarters of the romantic Streisand as a traitor to the female cause. Feminist scholar Felicia Herman complained that Streisand's "characters suppress their own needs for those of their men and willingly trade in their independence and individuality to 'get the guy,'" though Herman adds that the "strategy fails" because those characters have a very hard time subordinating themselves, even if they want to. In the end, they are usually punished for their "strong-willed behavior."[21] Of course, there was another way of interpreting this failure: that her characters just couldn't surrender because, unconsciously or not, Streisand knew what that would mean. It would mean the loss of her selfhood. Critic Molly Haskell cited a scene in *Funny Girl* where Streisand breaks a moment to precisely that effect. "When succumbing to the most voluptuous feelings of desire in the arms of the impossibly dreamy Omar Sharif in 'Funny Girl,' she suddenly crossed her eyes with Borscht-circuit bliss and her voice began to take on that heavy Yiddish intonation," which was her way of saying, Haskell believed, that

Streisand/Brice would always hold on to the deepest part of herself. Even as a sex object, she wouldn't be one of *them*.[22]

This was the on-screen Streisand. But the fact was that off-screen as well, loving her was a very complicated proposition, and usually a losing one. One of her early dates told her that she didn't like herself and "couldn't accept it when someone else liked her," which is why, he said, she had always preferred men who ignored her. Streisand admitted that he might have been right.[23] Another ex-lover told biographer Anne Edwards that the source of her sex appeal was the need she projected to be protected, but it was very hard to protect the famous, successful Barbra Streisand, not only from the world but from herself. He said it led to resentment and "a destructive, contradictory 'I'll show you!' attitude on her part."[24] Camille Paglia had another explanation for Streisand's romantic difficulties: they emanated from a basic dichotomy within her. "There has always been a conflict in Barbra Streisand, as in Oscar Wilde," she wrote, "between her populist politics and her aristocratic and tyrannical persona." In her early films, Streisand, she said, decked out like a "Russian duchess," was a "kind of drag queen herself," which Paglia attributed to a feeling that many women growing up share who "didn't feel particularly feminine," and by the "time you figure out what femininity is, you've become a female impersonator." This is also, Paglia said, what appealed to gay men: Streisand was both woman and man. But, appealing as this might have been to gay men, it is also why her relationships with heterosexual men invariably failed—because Streisand, like many great female stars, was "autocratic and autonomous. As artists, they need no one else."[25] Eventually, the men realized that they were superfluous.

Her divorce from Gould drew on these theories and on others. It was, as that early *Life* story announced in its title, a "precarious love" from the outset. "One side of Barbra needed men. The other was disdainful of men—and competitive toward them," Gould would say.[26] Another time he complained about a fear of showing weakness in front of her, and yet another that he was bored by her complaints about her unhappiness.[27] And yet another time he said he felt the marriage was destroyed by his loving her so unreservedly that he seemed desperate.[28] And if he loved her too much, he also blamed Streisand for not knowing how to love. He said that he once told her that her mother thought affection was a way to get something. Streisand said, "That's why I am the way I am."[29]

But there were those dichotomies, too, to consider. She was, by her own admission, a riven individual. Speaking of decorating, but just as applicable to romance, she once said that she had always had the impulse to "combine opposites": "I've always been interested in that dichotomy . . . masculine and feminine . . . simple and elaborate . . . rough and smooth."[30] "I have all these possibilities," she told Joseph Morgenstern of *Newsweek* in the same vein. "I'm slightly dumb. I'm very smart. I'm many things. You know?" And there was another dichotomy—between Jew and homogenized American. As Jewish scholar David Kaufman analyzed it, with particular reference to her performance in *On a Clear Day*, where she switches between the Jewish-y college student Daisy Gamble and her past life as the British Melinda Winifred Waine-Tentrees, "Jewishness, in this unique-to-Streisand performance, is an *essential* part of self, intrinsic and permanent, and at the same time is a *constructed* identity that can be deconstructed, a mask that can be taken off, an identity that one may escape. Streisand alone among American Jewish entertainers had it both ways." It is hard to think of a time when Streisand ever escaped her Jewishness, even when she was playing Marjorie Reynolds in *Up the Sandbox*; she was, after all, the most Jewish of entertainers. But Kaufman is correct in saying that Streisand's Jewishness existed on a continuum, and especially once she underwent her "beauty" transformation, she could deemphasize it when it suited her.

What other overtly Jewish entertainer could have recorded a hit Christmas album or would close a concert with "Silent Night," as she did for her Central Park Happening?

Romantically speaking, however, Streisand's dualities may surface most conspicuously not in Jew and American but in the concept of Streisand as Superman. If Streisand was both the bespectacled schlemiel Clark Kent and the *ubermensch* Superman, a dichotomy that had become a major part of her appeal, especially among women, it fell to her lovers to determine which of these they were romancing. Most often, they fell in love with Kent, as Gould had—with the Streisand who seemed awkward and innocent. But inevitably Kent would become Superman, and the relationship would change: the balance of gender power would change. (Hidden in this was the fact that, unaccountably, they couldn't see the Superman under the Kent disguise, bare as it was.) Her Superman intimidated men, which is no doubt one reason Walter Matthau tried to torment her with insults and sexual innuendoes. He was looking for the kryptonite—for the insecurities he could probe.

In her romantic relationships, too, intimidation was a constant hazard. Her affair with Sydney Chaplin, which had begun in *Funny Girl* rehearsals before she was a star, foundered once he and she realized that she would be a star. Chaplin couldn't take it. Similarly, Omar Sharif, playing the same role as Chaplin on-screen, said that he fell in love with her and then felt emasculated by her. He told an interviewer, "I think her biggest problem is that she wants to be a woman and she wants to be beautiful, and she is neither," another Matthau-like attempt to level the playing field.[31] But Sharif's biggest problem with Streisand may have been that she was a woman with the strength of a man, enjoying a success that clearly superseded his. "Too much" on-screen, she turned out to be "too much" in life as well. Tennis champion Andre Agassi, who found he and she had a lot in common, especially the hatred for the thing they did so well (his tennis and her singing), compared dating her to "wearing Hot Lava."[32] As Daisy/Melinda/Streisand is told in *On a Clear Day*, "It's not easy to be a strong woman, Melinda. A man will be strong for you to respect him, but weak for you to love him." But what happens when it is the woman who must be strong to be respected and weak to be loved?

Streisand's so-called manliness would become a meme about her, both in the media and in life. Her longtime lover Jon Peters would say explicitly that "she's almost like a man." It was one of the things, he said, that attracted him to her; he liked her strength.[33] Other female stars had been similarly characterized as manly; Bette Davis and Joan Crawford come to mind. But the media's emphasis on Streisand's toughness may have been intensified because it operated within the sexual and political context of feminism, which many men resented, and because it played into another popular stereotype, not only among the gentile press but among some Jewish men as well, that one could call the "Jewish woman syndrome." In this view, Jewish women were not only unattractive; they were also unfeminine. They were hard. They were bossy. They took control. This was Letty Cottin Pogrebin's "Jewish Big Mouth" who "lets everyone, especially the men in her life, know who she is and what she thinks" and whom Pogrebin explicitly connected to Streisand.[34] So Streisand's mannish behavior wasn't just personal; it was cultural. In many ways, the syndrome would define Streisand's public image for the rest of her career, and it would affect her romantic relationships too. It took a lot to withstand "hot lava." In effect, she was the Jewish Woman raised to the nth degree: too demanding and too domineering for most men. And if that weren't bad enough, she was also portrayed as someone whose demands were unreasonable and yet whose every whim needed to be satisfied or else. One word the press kept applying to her was "diva," which seemed especially damning when the so-called prima donna was a poor Jewish Brooklyn girl who seemingly didn't have the right to be haughty. Another, more secretive word was "bitch."

There were certainly women who lobbed this charge against her, notably Joyce Haber in her vicious piece on how Streisand supposedly commandeered *Funny Girl.* But most of the truly hateful coverage of Streisand, like most of her professional rivalry, came from men, Streisand would say insecure men, and she was probably right. Many men resented her—resented her power, resented her success, resented her popularity, even resented her talent, and they may have resented most of all, as Matthau evidently did, their not being able to figure out why she had all these things when, to them, she so clearly didn't deserve them. Nor was it just her success; it was her symbolism. She was so large a figure that she may have even been a lightning rod for male resentment against all the incursions that feminism had made into the male domain. And these men would continue to resent her throughout her career. Streisand was certainly no man-hater. Anything but. She was a true romantic. But there would be a lot of men who would be Streisand-haters—men who saw in her the kind of monster she was portrayed as being on *South Park*, men who knew that no one could possibly slay that monster.

None of this would likely have made her particularly attractive to men. And yet she obviously was, which leads one to believe that Robert Redford's more nuanced analysis of her effect on the opposite sex might have been closer to the mark than the broad-brush Streisand-as-man approach. "Her femininity brings out the masculinity in a man," he said, "and her masculinity brings out a man's femininity, vulnerability, romanticism, whatever you want to call it. . . . That's what it boils down to."[35] The first certainly explained part of her romantic appeal, while the second helped explain her romantic difficulties.

It was much easier not to operate as dichotomously as she did. And, romantically speaking, it was a lot easier to be a shrinking violet than a Venus flytrap.

Still, if the romances provided that wish fulfillment her fans seemed to want, the breakups provided their own, very different wish fulfillment. That was the fulfillment, not of being desired by handsome men, but of having the self-sufficiency to triumph over them, which was not dissimilar to the difference between Jews being accepted via assimilation and being accepted through self-assertion. "Actually, I believe that women are superior to men," Streisand told *Playboy*. "I don't even think we're equal," and she cited, among other things, that "emotionally and constitutionally . . . women are stronger than men." Men suffer more ulcers, heart attacks, breakdowns, and suicides. "Their façade"—their need to seem manly—"is killing them," is how she diagnosed it. It was an odd thing for a woman in show business, a woman who had had to erect her own facades, to say. But Streisand believed that women were "further along with their own liberation." They didn't have to play feminine roles anymore. "We accept the fact," she told *Playboy*, "that women can be weak yet strong, soft yet tough, shy yet aggressive." You didn't have to read between the lines to realize that what she was saying, too, was that she had come to terms with herself. Whether this was life imitating art or art imitating life was impossible to say. But all those dichotomous halves had finally begun to fit. Streisand at thirty was coming whole.

8

Rediskovering Iugnt

In many ways she was an old thirty. For years she had been racking up album success after album success—clearly the most popular female vocalist in America. Between April 1963 and April 1966, she released eight albums, all of which hit the top ten of *Billboard* magazine's chart and all of which earned her gold records representing a million dollars in sales.[1] But Streisand had arrived at roughly the same time as the Beatles, and they provided a challenge that made her defensive. "I'm not a fad," she said when the Beatles displaced her hit "People" on the charts. "I'm not singing rock 'n' roll, playing a strange instrument, or wearing my hair over my eye. My success is based on something real—talent."[2] It was an odd thing for the one-time kook to say, not to mention entirely wrongheaded.

But Streisand clearly felt threatened in an arena she had dominated. Sinatra had experienced the same threat when rock 'n' roll appeared—the threat of being irrelevant. "Rock-and-roll did not embrace his naturalism, the effect of a contained and inward drama," wrote critic Gene Lees in his own curmudgeon mode. "As amplification cranked up the volume of guitars and drums to a level dangerous to hearing, the singing became shrill, a distorted and grimaced music lacking in literacy or subtlety, a hysterical celebration of the mundane that all the press agentry in the world could not disguise."[3] Streisand's repertoire had from the outset been odd, with tunes like "Who's Afraid of the Big Bad Wolf?" and "Happy Days," but she had not been a rocker. Quite the contrary. "Look. I'm considered this kind of . . . institution thing," she would tell *Rolling Stone* in 1971. "I'm labeled, pigeon-holed. I play for middle-class audiences in Vegas. I made those definitely Establishment pictures— *Dolly, On a Clear Day, Funny Girl*. All of which tags me as a 'veteran performer.' But I ask you, 28, is that old? Is 28 all that old?"[4] (She was actually twenty-nine at the time.)

Normally not. But Streisand wasn't a normal twenty-eight- or twenty-nine-year-old, and certainly not a normal young woman in the 1960s and 1970s after the countercultural revolution swept American youth. For all her romances, she was something of a prude—a nice Jewish girl, as that *Playboy* cover had said. When there were rumors that she had once appeared in a pornographic movie, she laughed it off, calling it "preposterous," and telling *Playboy*, "Me—right?—who was an usher in a legitimate theater and hid my head so nobody would remember, after I had become famous, that I showed them to their seats!"[5] For another thing, she was wary of drugs, despite her bit at the McGovern fundraiser pretending to smoke a joint. According to biographer Shaun Considine, when a musician showed up during one of her recording sessions and started doing riffs, clearly under the influence of marijuana, Streisand asked, "Shouldn't he be arrested or something?"[6]

But Streisand didn't want to be stuck in the same musical rut either. She did her all-French album with composer Michel

Legrand in 1966, *Je M'appelle Barbra*, and a decade later she would record a classical album, simply titled *Classical Barbra*. (Glenn Gould praised her "courage" in doing so, yet also felt that she appeared "awed by the realization that she is now face to face with The Masters.")[7] These, however, weren't gambits that were likely to keep her relevant in the age of rock. In the interests of relevancy, her music publisher, Nat Shapiro, pushed her to record "Frank Mills" from *Hair*, preemptively, before the play had reached Broadway. Streisand did, then postponed the release until the show was a hit and the preemption was lost.[8] To the same end, Clive Davis, the president at the time of Columbia Records, Streisand's label, realizing how important a property she was and how modernizing her sound might be rewarding for both her and Columbia, pressed her to record a more contemporary album, suggestively titled *What about Today?* It even included songs from the composers she had previously dismissed, Paul McCartney and John Lennon ("Honey Pie," "With a Little Help from My Friends," and "Goodnight"), as well as a song from Paul Simon. But these were interlarded with songs by her friends the Bergmans, and even a song by the old master Harold Arlen. The result wasn't modernized Streisand so much as mishmash Streisand. Her eleventh album, it was the first not to be certified either gold or platinum, and it rose only as high as thirty-one on *Billboard*'s chart, just the second of her albums not to crash the top ten. In short, it was a disaster.

But Streisand was never one to be deterred, and neither was Clive Davis. He hooked her up with producer Richard Perry. Perry had produced everyone from Ella Fitzgerald to Fats Domino to Tiny Tim, whom he had discovered, and he had a similar effect on Streisand's musical education that Barry Dennen had had at the outset of her career: he introduced her to new sounds. Perry's and Streisand's first album, *Stoney End*, titled after the Laura Nyro song, which was Streisand's first number one single since "People," was both a return to success and a departure from it. This time there was no recidivism. The cuts were from Nyro and Joni Mitchell, Randy Newman, Carole King, Gordon Lightfoot, and Harry Nilsson—contemporary composers with a contemporary pop sound.

It took an adjustment—a big adjustment. For her older music, Streisand sang off the beat, as Sinatra did, dictating the interpretation and flow. This was what allowed her to invest so much emotion in her songs. The technical word for this sort of freedom or flexibility is "rubato," from the Italian "tempo rubato": literally "stolen time." Streisand was the master of rubato. She would slow down and speed up as the spirit moved her, rather than have the beat dictate to her. As composer Roger Ames put it, "Her greatness was her flirtation with the beat."9

Technically speaking, rock and pop were different from the music Streisand had generally sung, more different still with the advent of disco music at the very time Streisand was transitioning. In rock, you sang on the beat, not against it. You reinforced the rhythm. It was less about interpretation than punch. Disco intensified the punch. With the beat as the master, it was very rhythmically precise, and its precision rapidly infiltrated popular music generally. It didn't allow a singer to "flirt" with the beat, the way Streisand had in her earlier music, and when you hear these songs from *Stoney End* and other albums from the period, even though the voice is recognizable, the little Streisandisms—the rubato, even the legato—are largely missing. It was a moment of musical conformity in a career built on nonconformity. But *Stoney End* rose to number ten on *Billboard*'s chart. Streisand was musically relevant once again.

But she still wasn't young in the sense that other people in her generation were young. That may have been because Streisand had really missed her adolescence. "I became famous so young," she would tell an interviewer, "that I missed the social experiences most women have. And when I was in high school, I was very shy. Hardly went on a date. I met Elliott when I was nineteen, and we were together for eight years."[10] Whether it was the change in the music scene or a sense of personal lack of fulfillment, Streisand seemed to regret what she had never had.

And that is when she met Jon Peters.

John Peters was not the kind of man that a nice Jewish girl would take home to meet her parents, which may have been the point. He was the antithesis of a nice Jewish boy. His childhood was out of a 1950s movie about juvenile delinquency. Born in Sherman Oaks, California, half-Cherokee, half-Italian, he suffered the death of his father when he was eight. He was sentenced to a juvenile home simply because his mother couldn't control him, left school after the seventh grade, moved to New York, began working in a beauty salon, largely to be among beautiful women, and then returned to California to ply his trade. (As Streisand had dropped an "a" from her name, Peters would drop an "h" from his.) Meanwhile, he was married at sixteen and divorced at twenty-one. Eventually, he opened a salon of his own in Encino, which he was able to parlay into a string of salons. He called himself the "American Vidal Sassoon," after the British hair stylist. But his success had as much to do with his personality as his skill. He was rough and incorrigible, even vulgar, but charismatic. He was also something of a scamp and a rogue, which may have been a cover for his own insecurities (he said that when he was young in the salon business, he would "throw up before work every morning because I was so frightened") but which made him the perfect match for a successful woman trying to recover her lost youth. In effect, Peters was the wild teenage boyfriend that Streisand had never had.[11]

He first saw her when his wife at the time, the actress Lesley Ann Warren, who also happened to be Jewish, took him to a Streisand concert at the Hollywood Bowl. He was so smitten that he got word to her that he would do her hair for free. She never responded. But, as the story goes, she saw a cut she liked on a woman at a party and heard that Peters had styled it, so she called him and invited him to her house. It wasn't an auspicious meeting. She kept him waiting, and Peters let her know he wasn't happy about it. Yet Streisand seemed to like the idea of a man who wasn't intimidated by her, and hairstyling led to wardrobe styling, which led to romance.[12]

It was a hot romance, with Streisand now living out her delayed adolescence in public. One writer said, "She was really like a nineteen-year-old girl with a high school guy. He was her crush, and he treated her like a hot girlfriend. He was very sexy and physical with her. He would grab her like a woman. He never gave her that movie-star treatment, saying, 'Oh, Barbra, you're the greatest.'"[13] But it was more than romance. It was rejuvenation and reclamation. "I started off as one of the original beatniks," she told a writer. "Unfortunately, I sort of drifted into the establishment for a while. Now with Jon, who is very much a contemporary man, I'm picking up where I left off at the age of eighteen—back to my beaded bags and thrift shops."[14] She told another interviewer, "He was instrumental in a new, younger me. This hipper, more sexual character. But it was very entrepreneurial. Jon just had that in him."[15]

She was right that Peters was tweaking her image. He was the one who moved her from a beauty to something of a sexpot; she did her *Playboy* cover during their romance, as well as *The Main Event*, the film in which she is at her most overtly sexual. If her beauty transformation had countered the stereotype of the unattractive and unfeminine Jewish woman, this new transformation countered the stereotype of the unsexual Jewish woman. Streisand was now fully a sex object. (Of course, how many gentile female stars had had to assert their sexiness the way Streisand had?) And he moved her further from her Jewish persona, both on-screen and off, in another way. The man-killing Streisand of the Jewish Woman syndrome had, at least for the moment, become positively kittenish with Peters. "He's so strong, unbelievably strong," she gushed like a teenager. "But he can be scary. I never know what he's gonna do, y'know?"[16] This certainly didn't sound like the old Streisand.

And it went beyond image. Peters did what no one else could possibly have done before, what Streisand would never have allowed anyone to do before: he distracted her from her work. Director Herbert Ross, who had choreographed Streisand in the film version of *Funny Girl*, then directed her in *The Owl and the Pussycat*, and was now directing her in the *Funny Girl* sequel, *Funny Lady*, noted that she was a different person. "Her commitment was not one-thousand percent to the film," he said. "*Funny Lady* was virtually a movie that was made without her." He said that her commitment now was to Peters.[17] She made another film, *For Pete's Sake*, because she said she wanted to get out of Los Angeles and "figured I'd go to New York to escape."[18] *That* didn't sound like Streisand either.

Eventually, the romance and the career merged. His inexperience notwithstanding, Peters and Streisand decided that he would produce her next album, to be called *ButterFly*. But, by one account, Columbia deemed the record unreleasable, so the label had the songs remixed.[19] Then came the unthinkable: Peters took over her career from Marty Erlichman, her longtime manager. Peters was now setting Streisand's agenda. "You better check your act, and see if it's the money or the success which is the most important thing," he described his message to Streisand to a reporter. "Are your goals the things that you really want to achieve? You gotta evaluate all the time. Because the danger in dreams is that you just might get them."[20]

What Peters was referring to specifically was a film that he had pressed Streisand to make—a film that they would be producing together. In 1969, Streisand had joined megastars Paul Newman and Sidney Poitier, later to be joined by Steve

McQueen and Dustin Hoffman, in a company called First Artists, which would produce films on the same basis that United Artists had done with Charlie Chaplin, Douglas Fairbanks, Mary Pickford, and D. W. Griffith in the 1920s. The idea was to allow them to make films that they wanted to make and take a percentage of the gross, rather than work at the sufferance of the studio. What the partners of First Artists risked in salary, they gained in artistic freedom. Streisand had made films under the First Artists banner, but, despite all the depictions of her as diva, she complained that she had not exercised the control she had desired. And that was where Peters came in. Peters said she *should* exercise that control and *would* exercise that control on her next film—*his* film. He was encouraging her to become the woman everyone thought she was anyway.

The film he suggested was conceived when the husband-and-wife writers Joan Didion and John Gregory Dunne were driving in downtown LA and Dunne suddenly mused about remaking the Hollywood chestnut about a rising young female movie star who marries an older fading male movie star, *A Star Is Born*, as a rock and roll film with James Taylor and Carly Simon, who were married at the time. Once set in motion, the idea had a kind of unstoppable momentum, running through many cast considerations until it wound up, via Peters, with Streisand, who had already rejected it once. Peters said it was the story of their life—not a movie about careers moving in different directions, like the first *Star Is Born* from 1937 with Janet Gaynor and Fredric March, or the 1954 remake with Judy Garland and James Mason, but a movie about a woman who learns to trust a man and a man who learns how to trust his own femininity.[21] Streisand had her own take on the material. The pussycat with Peters wanted to be a tiger in the film and make it into another of her role reversal films—an aggressive woman and a passive man. "I wanted to portray her as taking what she wants," she told *Playboy*, "something that's a big thing for women today, especially sexually." She described how in the film's first love scene, "I wanted to be sort of Clint Eastwood—you know the guy always takes his belt off. That's why I have her on top. Why should a man always be the one shown opening his pants first?"[22]

It was yet another meta moment for Streisand—taking control of a film that she saw as being about taking control. Peters would later call it the "beginning of Barbra's examining her own power. It was the discovery period for her. And she started to realize that she could do it, she could take control of her own life. I was the tool in a way."[23] One of the first things she had to take control of was fighting for Peters as her coproducer, just as she had fought for him to produce her album. The ridicule was savage. "So what if Jon was a hairdresser," Streisand told *People* magazine defensively. "A lot of producers in Hollywood started off selling dresses in New York City. They said the same thing about me. 'How could she act when she's just a singer?' No one is just anything. The whole purpose of life is to grow, right?"[24]

The movie was a tussle. They had a hard time finding a male lead, until they settled on Kris Kristofferson, who had been an old romantic fling of Streisand's. "He's beautiful to look at," she said of his casting. "He can sing and play the guitar. And he's gentile, which seems to work with me—the Jew and the gentile."[25] (At one point, they put out feelers to Elvis Presley.) Then there was the script, which Streisand kept tinkering with, in part, one assumes, because she never could strike the right balance on-screen as in life between how forceful she wanted her character to be and how submissive. Too much of the first, and one didn't have a romance; too much of the second, and one didn't have a Streisand picture. Then there was the issue of the music. This was to be a rock musical, but Streisand, *Stoney End* aside, was not really a rock singer, and trying to find some happy medium between the kind of music Streisand traditionally made and the kind of music that would sustain a modern, youth-oriented movie was not easy and was never finally solved.

And then there was the issue of control. Peters and Streisand had settled on Jerry Schatzberg to direct, but he departed after conflicts, and they hired screenwriter Frank Pierson, coming off of the script for *Dog Day Afternoon*, probably hoping that because he was inexperienced behind the camera, having helmed only one movie previously, he would be more malleable. Depending on whose version one believed, he was either too malleable, thus not providing enough direction to the actors, or not malleable enough, usurping Peters's and Streisand's prerogatives and ignoring their suggestions. Either way, it was reported to be an extremely unhappy shoot.

And "reported" is the right word. A cover story in *New Times* magazine by Marie Brenner featured a bald Streisand—a "star is shorn"—and called the picture "Hollywood's biggest joke" nearly two full years before its release.[26] Worse, much worse, was a story in *New York* magazine and *New West* magazine, written by Pierson, no less, and titled "My Battles with Barbra and Jon," a month before the film's opening. If Pierson had seethed during production, the article was his revenge. "For us, the picture cost $6 million and a year of our lives," he wrote. "For the audience, it's $3.50 and an evening out. If it's a bum evening, it doesn't make me any better or worse as a person. But if you think the film is you, if it is your effort to transform your lover into a producer worthy of a superstar, if you think it is a home movie about your love and your hope and your deepest feelings, if it's your life that you laid out for the folks and they don't smile back, that's death." And Pierson was determined to be the gravedigger. Never had a director so publicly wanted to sabotage his own film—but then Pierson didn't think it was his film anymore, and, like Matthau, he wasn't happy about it. He called it a "nightmare that has no end."[27]

Every criticism that had ever been leveled at Streisand the Monster was reiterated here. She was a control freak. She wouldn't listen to constructive advice. She was vengeful, threatening Pierson that he would pay "for every lousy thing Ray Stark ever did to me." She was an egomaniac who actually re-edited the film, he said, to remove Kristofferson's close-ups and even his best scenes to make herself look better. It was scathing, and it was, Streisand felt, a breach of faith between director and actor, and a deep betrayal, not necessarily of her (she knew Pierson didn't care for her any more than she cared for him), but of the movie that she had labored over for three years, the movie that had come to represent her entire life, the movie that was the furthest expression of her creative control. "No other article has ever touched off this deep sense of injustice in me," she would tell *Playboy*. She said she felt like Edvard Munch's *The Scream*—"a scream with no sound."[28]

The expectations for the film by the diva-bitch Jewish Big Mouth and her hairdressing boyfriend couldn't have been lower. Critic Frank Rich wrote before the film's release that it was "riding into town on the largest wave of negative advance publicity since *Cleopatra*," the Elizabeth Taylor–Richard Burton debacle that had bankrupted 20th Century Fox.[29] Predisposed to hate it for everything it represented, which basically was hubris with a big mouth, the critics did. One review was titled "A Bore Is Starred." John Simon, writing in the conservative *National Review*, no lover of liberal Streisand anyway, used the occasion to expatiate yet again on Streisand's nose: "Oh, for the gift of Rostand's Cyrano to evoke the vastness of that nose alone as it cleaves the giant screen from east to west, bisects it from north to south. It zigzags across our horizon like a bolt of fleshy lightning; it towers like a ziggurat made of meat." He would go on to criticize her frizzy hair ("something like the wig of the fop in a Restoration comedy"), her voice ("continues to sound like Rice Krispies if they could talk"), and her acting ("Streisand's notion of acting is to bulldoze her way from one end of a line to the other"). Finally, admitting that she is "in fact beloved above all other female stars," he bemoaned a society with a "collective will to live in ugliness and self-debasement."[30] Streisand biographer James Spada said it might have been "the single worst review any performer had ever received."[31] Even so, Frank Rich in the *New York Post* wasn't much kinder. He called *A Star Is Born* "the work of a madwoman" and advised that if "you ever cared about Streisand, there's little fun in seeing her make a monumental ass of herself."[32]

But most critics hadn't really cared about Streisand since *Funny Girl.* Once she was no longer a poor, ugly duckling fighting for recognition against the odds, someone they could champion, they saw her as that egomaniac. One critic who did care was Pauline Kael. Kael, a disaffected Jewish woman herself, defended Streisand against Pierson's self-serving attack: "If the picture we got to see was anything less than great, it would be because Streisand and Peters had wrecked it in the final cut, while if it was *great*, we had him to congratulate." But she was no lover of the film, which she accused of "bland romanticism," seeing the "purity of their relationship" as a "vacuum." And she came finally to the conclusion that Streisand could no longer play Streisand—that she had simply outgrown her old persona. "Streisand has more talent than she knows what to do with, and the heart of a lion," wrote Kael. "But she's made a movie about the unassuming, unaffected person she wants us to think she is, and the image is so truthless, she can't play it."[33]

Kael may have been right. What most critics didn't see is that *A Star Is Born*, though a remake, wasn't really a remake of the old 1937 William Wellman movie or the George Cukor 1954 update. It was a remake of *Funny Girl*, with the same Streisand conflations, only modernized to accommodate the new world of rock and roll, along with the new attitudes of feminism and the new attitudes toward romance of Streisand herself. Streisand's Esther Hoffman is, like Fanny Brice, a nice Jewish girl striving to make a splash in show business, even though, of course, she is not the most conventionally beautiful performer. She is more assimilated than Fanny. She doesn't have quite the same Yiddish inflections to her speech or the frumpy Jewish manner. But what she has is talent and moxie and perfectionism and a certain kind of innocence, as Fanny had, which are the aphrodisiacs for the over-the-hill, boozy, coked-up singer, John Norman Howard, played by Kristofferson. She is, we imagine, what he once was; she has the purity he supposedly once had before he got wrecked by celebrity, another post-Brice feature of show business. In her, he sees his better self.

All of this is more or less consistent with Fanny and Nicky, though Nicky's self-destruction is less public than Howard's. And, as in *Funny Girl*, as Esther's star rises, it eclipses Howard's, and as Esther takes the alpha role in the relationship, Howard feels diminished. When he cheats on Esther, it is like Hubbell's infidelity to Katie; he cheats, not because he doesn't love her, but because, in a way, he loves her too much and can't live up to her expectations. (Streisand seems to have that effect on men.) But, like Fanny, Esther never loses faith in her lover. She remains a true believer. This is the vapidity, the vacuum, that Kael found at the middle of the film—and not at all incidentally, that some found in Streisand herself, now that she seemed to be under the sway of Jon Peters. In *The Way We Were* there is real friction, which is the friction of two different sensibilities. In *A Star Is Born*, there is no friction. The only thing that seems to separate them is his lack of success, which, the film suggests, is less his fault than the music industry's. Before she could possibly emasculate him, show business has.

Of course, here the role reversal is much more explicit than in *Funny Girl*. In a bathtub scene, Esther paints eyebrows on her man and rouges his cheeks. She wears suits and even a bowtie. She is the sexual aggressor, as she told *Playboy* she would be, and she proposes to him. And several songs are celebrations of feminine strength. But Peters was right when he said that the film was really about a woman trusting a man and a man trusting his own femininity, speaking of Streisand and himself. Still, the film isn't just about acceptance of one's other gender. Peters would have even been more on point if he had said the film was about how Streisand/Hoffman had to balance her power against her own femininity so as not to overwhelm her lover, and how Kristofferson/Howard had to balance his sensitivity against his masculinity so as not to be subordinate. In short, the film is about finding gender equivalence both within oneself but also between two people. Both *Funny Girl* and *A Star Is Born* end similarly, with the triumphant woman singing her devotion to the man who left her—"My Man" versus "With One More Look at You." In doing so, Fanny/Esther is attempting to temper and thus reconcile her male self with her female self.

Obviously, this issue had a special resonance for Streisand. No man could possibly be her equivalent in terms of show business success, so she was always having to reconcile, always having to find a balance. Her relationship to the pugnacious, macho Peters, who kept a pet lion, only magnified the issue, which made the movie an expensive form of couples' therapy. But while *A Star Is Born* is a movie about Streisand's romantic dilemma, it is also a movie about the Jewish woman's dilemma, since so much of Streisand's alleged stridency was attributed to her Jewishness. Just compare Streisand's unreserved performance to that of Janet Gaynor or Judy Garland, in which their characters are so recessive and obsequious to their men that their success almost seems accidental. It bears repeating that gentile women, even big, powerful stars, were seldom accused of devouring their men black widow–style the way Streisand supposedly did, both in life and on-screen. It was *Jewish* women who had the hardest time striking the balance between their masculine and feminine sides, *Jewish* women who couldn't find their softness no matter how hard they tried. That turns *A Star*

Is Born not just into a movie about a strong woman, not just into a movie about a strong woman named "Streisand," but into a movie about strong Jewish women everywhere who have to navigate the same treacherous waters as Esther Hoffman. When she loses her man, as always when Streisand loses her invariably gentile man, her Jewishness is what does her in.

So *A Star Is Born* was, went the critical consensus, an abomination, and not only an abomination, but the abomination of a star tripping on her own reckless power and, for someone who had usually been accused of being too controlling, being out of control. And yet for all the abuse heaped upon it, something bizarre happened. *A Star Is Born* turned out to be the biggest film success of Streisand's career to that point. It grossed $140 million, its soundtrack album was the biggest selling up to that time, and the hit ballad "Evergreen," which Streisand cowrote and for which she would win her second Oscar, wound up being the number one song.[34] Audiences, as John Simon had feared, loved the movie.

Why? If ever there was a film that testified to Streisand's popularity and to her ability to hit that audience nerve, *A Star Is Born*, which seemed to have had everything going against it, was it. Streisand herself would disavow the connection between the person she was and the characters she played. She would say, "People think that I'm really like my movies, that my roles are somehow an extension of myself. Totally false."[35] But anyone who knew anything about Streisand—and how could they not?—knew that she was totally wrong. As the critic Molly Haskell put it in a *New York Times* piece eighteen months before *A Star Is Born*'s release that asked the question "What Makes Streisand Queen of the Box Office?" "Streisand had a way—perhaps a genius—for exploiting the public's knowledge of her real-life background to help rationalize her screen persona." In her earlier films, she could get away with "extravagant sets and Prince Charming" because "we knew she had done duty as a poor ethnic and ugly duckling."[36]

The public had read those awful accounts of the making of *A Star Is Born* or, at the very least, heard about them. They had heard about Streisand's relationship with Jon Peters, heard the jibes directed against them, heard about how she was letting her boyfriend *produce* her albums and her movie, heard her rushing to his defense ("Do they think I would let Jon produce a record if I wasn't absolutely sure he could do it?"), and they saw that postponed adolescence she was enjoying with Peters.[37] They heard and saw all this, and they not only rallied to her; they cheered her for withstanding the abuse she took. As one of her biographers, Tom Santopietro, put it, "The critics saw a terrible film, but in Barbra audiences saw a woman mocked and misunderstood, a woman standing up for her own rights and daring to crash through the barriers in her way."[38] And so audiences loved *A Star Is Born* in part because they understood that neither Esther Hoffman nor Barbra Streisand would allow herself to be knocked down. This was a different dynamic from the old one that Haskell had identified and that had dominated Streisand's films—the downtrodden girl making good. This was the powerful girl, not as naive as Kael portrays her, whom people wanted to destroy. But it proved every bit as effective.

This public adulation didn't temper the press. If anything, it emboldened them. The reporters who had castigated Streisand for her independence and bossiness were now castigating her for being too dependent on her man, turning the Jewish Woman Syndrome inside out. The once implacable woman was now a fool for love. And Peters, for his part, was a gold-digging Svengali—Streisand's thuggish enabler in his quest to get a toehold in Hollywood. They were considered rough and abusive and cheap and peremptory. One story had it that Streisand arrived on the set of *Funny Lady* and announced that everyone to her left was fired.[39] Streisand protested, "I can't stand to fire people. I get this reputation for firing people, and I can never do it."[40]

But neither would Streisand make nice with the press. "I don't try to be liked," she once said.[41] She seldom gave interviews, complaining that she prized her private time, that she was usually misquoted, and that when a writer did submit a positive piece, "they don't print it because it's too sweet."[42] (*Playboy* interviewer Lawrence Grobel said that his interviews would "absorb the next six months of my life" because Streisand was so assiduous about everything, and he said the sessions were "at times battles.")[43] Molly Haskell concluded that her refusal to play by those rules was another part of her appeal. "She acts—and she has always acted—like a star," Haskell wrote, in what was truer of later Streisand than earlier Streisand. "At a time when most members of the movie colony were doing 'real people' routines, baring their souls on talk shows, and shuffling to the anti-establishment boogie, Streisand never followed the beat. She hadn't come all the way from Brooklyn for that!"[44]

In fact, Streisand had once agreed to make her first *Tonight Show* appearance in twelve years and then suddenly canceled the night of the show—she would later say due to nerves. Johnny Carson, the host, was furious and promised she would never be invited back. She wasn't, but Streisand didn't seem to care much. "You know what it's about?" she would ask Oprah Winfrey rhetorically, speaking of why the press had turned on her. "It's about the Aristotelian rule of drama. It's about the fall of kings and queens. The Greek tragedies are not written about the common man. They're written about the fall of people in high places. Part of me understands it: People want to see kings and queens fall because it's the great equalizer; it makes them less envious."[45] But, whether she now saw herself as a queen or not, ordinary people had never been envious of Streisand. The press had become the envious ones. They were the ones who were always trying now to make Streisand into a monster of control. In a notebook she kept, she scribbled, "The world envies success."[46]

And so she decided that if she was going to be excoriated for being overbearing, she might as well, finally, exercise the control the press always said she had exercised.

9

Macher

Anti-Semitism—that had always been Streisand's veiled explanation behind all the euphemisms like bossy, bitchy, controlling, tyrannical, egomaniacal, loud, cheap, and monstrous, and it didn't make any difference that Jews were also leveling these charges at her.[1] Jewish studies scholar Sander Gilman had noted that many Jews, upscale Jews, establishment Jews, had deplored what one of them, columnist Walter Lippmann, had called the "rich and vulgar and pretentious Jews of our big American cities" who are the "fountain of anti-Semitism"— "the latent hatred against crude wealth in the hands of shallow people."[2] Wealth, Streisand certainly had, but when she tried to sell her Central Park West penthouse and applied to buy a coop apartment, she was twice refused by boards—because, she was convinced, she was Jewish.[3] The antagonism could have been retribution for her never having downplayed her Jewishness or never having tried to pass. She was always the Jew extraordinaire. In the 2001 film *The Believer*, a group of neo-Nazis determine that Streisand is the first Jew they should murder.

But whether it was anti-Semitism or antifeminism or some other anti-, Streisand seemed to give her detractors a lot about which they felt they could be hostile. Camille Paglia, a Streisand defender, said that comedienne Roseanne Arnold, another loud and strong Jewish woman and, as Paglia put it, "no little chickadee," met Streisand and said she acted like the "queen of the United States," which Paglia thought was fitting. She said admiringly that Streisand "practically invented the modern concept of 'bitch.'"[4] Streisand wouldn't have quibbled with that. "Some people look at me and say, 'Success has gone to her head,'" she told an interviewer. "But that's not true. I've always been this way. I'm no good at dealing with people or being tactful. I say whatever is on my mind. I go by instinct. . . . I was like that when I was twelve."[5]

She was correct that she had always seemed to rub some people the wrong way. Jerome Weidman, author of *I Can Get It for You Wholesale*, said, "I have dealt with revolting people all my life," but added, "As far as I'm concerned, she has not earned the right to act that way."[6] But *Funny Girl* composer Jule Styne said Streisand's reputation for being difficult "comes from untalented people misunderstanding truly talented ones." Streisand's problem, he said, was that she was a show-off. "She was always shoving shovelsful of talent in your face." And he quoted Jerome Robbins: "He said she does everything wrong, but it comes out right."[7] Chaim Potok came to a similar conclusion, but through different reasoning. He saw her as someone who found greater creativity in "stratagems of self-abnegation that often border on self-torture," and sensed a narcissism in her: "alluring, playing at being charming, centered on one's own self, laboring relentlessly and expecting the same of others, too soon bored with achievement, too quickly disdainful of permanence, grasping at opposites, at times impatient to near ruthlessness with those of smaller mind or lesser vision."[8] To make matters worse, she was a self-confessed grump. "I complain a lot," she told *Playboy*. "And I have a negative approach to things. I see the black side rather than the white."[9]

Moreover, the talent that had helped make her an entertainment goddess also seemed to terrify some people. As early as *What's Up, Doc?* Pauline Kael detected a backlash against Streisand. (It actually came much later.) "There is a possible unpleasantness, of threat, in that red-hot talent—as there is in Liza Minnelli at full star strength—which produces unresolved feelings in us," Kael wrote, and she thought that the new film could make her likable to people who hadn't previously liked her because "here her charm has no drive." She was going soft, or at least softer.[10] Writing in *Vanity Fair* twenty years later, Michael Shnayerson described an ornate wooden frame that Streisand had hung on the wall of her Third Avenue walk-up during her first success and suggested that if one thought of Streisand's entire life as a "quest" to fill that frame, one could "start to come to terms with who Barbra is now and why she stirs more extreme reactions—of love, awe, envy, irritation— than any other star in the world." The reason is that she kept working on the portrait she wanted in that frame, never feeling it was finished, always trying new things, and, as a result, turning her life into a "meditation on self" that could seem "portentous and narcissistic."[11]

That quest Shnayerson described would lead detractors to claim that Streisand just didn't know her place, as antiquated an idea as that may sound now. As Streisand herself put it, "Somehow, I always had the feeling that, according to everyone else, whatever I was, was enough. People wanted me to stay put. They say, 'You sing, so what do you have to act for?' . . . 'You're an actress, now what do you want to produce for?' I got a lot of flak when I was executive producer on *A Star Is Born*, yet I was financially responsible for every penny of those six million dollars."[12] When, after *A Star Is Born*, Streisand finally decided to direct, she was demonstrating to detractors that once again she didn't know her place and inviting more derision. It certainly came.

Of course, most people assumed that Streisand had been directing herself all along, and to a great extent, she had. "I never thought about it back then," she told film critic Stephen Holden of the *New York Times*, "but I was always directing. I always saw how things should be."[13] Sydney Pollack, who directed her in *The Way We Were*, claimed that she drove him crazy. "Barbra knew about camera positions and editors' options and all that. So I directed, but they [meaning Streisand and Redford] would challenge it."[14] And yet she had her doubts. She called herself "emotionally fragile"—not a term most would have applied to her—and, apparently alluding to *A Star Is Born*, where she did a lot of the direction, she said that she takes things so seriously that "it becomes painful to me. . . . I get palpitations, I get ill. I get sick to my stomach. I get terrible headaches. I just become a mess. So then I say, What do I need this aggravation for? It's much easier just to act."[15]

But it wasn't easier because, even before *A Star Is Born*, Streisand seemed to be losing interest in acting—or in *just* acting. Herbert Ross had seen it in *Funny Lady* when she said her takes were good enough.[16] (Takes were never good enough for Streisand.) And Pauline Kael said she could detect it in her performance in *Funny Lady*—a failure of Streisand's once near-faultless "instinct . . . which has been playing her false lately." Kael thought she wore her costumes "like a man and turns herself into a transvestite." But in the end, the real problem, Kael admitted, was that "I fell out of like with Barbra Streisand." Streisand, she wrote, had lost her sensitivity and her "volatility." "Something rigid and overbearing and heavy seems to be settling into her manner. She may have gone past the time when she could play a character; maybe that's why she turns Fanny

Brice into a sacred monster. Has Streisand lost sight of the actress she could be?"[17] The answer might have been worse than Kael thought. She hadn't lost sight. She just didn't seem to care. She confessed to Potok, "As I get older, I find it more difficult to get dressed in the morning, put on make-up, act."[18]

Perhaps directing was inevitable for someone who wanted the control Streisand desired and someone who was as much of a perfectionist as Streisand was and someone who sought the challenges Streisand sought and someone who carried the responsibility Streisand carried on her projects anyway and someone who was as bored as Streisand seemed to be. All of that had led to *A Star Is Born*, where she shared the reins uncomfortably with Frank Pierson, and it would lead to her directing by herself. But if there was an inevitability to her becoming a director, there was also a kind of inevitability to the material she chose to direct for her first feature. She said she had read Isaac Bashevis Singer's story "Yentl the Yeshiva Boy," about a girl who poses as a young man to study the Talmud in early nineteenth-century Poland, in 1968 when a producer had sent it to her, and she was immediately captivated, even though her agent, Freddie Fields, told her it could never get made. Still, Streisand approached Ivan Passer, the Czech director who had relocated in the United States to work, about the possibility of directing the film. Passer told her that at twenty-seven, she was too old to play the role.[19] "Those were wonderful words to hear," she would say. "It was like I was a kid again, listening to experts say I wasn't suitable, that I would never make it in show business. I knew right there I was going to play Yentl. I would not be stopped."[20] It couldn't have been lost on Streisand that the story itself was about a girl who was told she could never study Talmud because, according to Orthodox tradition, women were barred from doing so. It was another meta—two women crashing a man's domain.

But the woman who said she wouldn't be stopped was. No

studio wanted to make the film. Sherry Lansing, the production head of 20th Century Fox and a Jew, told her, "The story's too ethnic, too esoteric. We just don't see Middle America paying to see this movie."[21] "Everybody told her she couldn't do it," said Jon Peters, who was one of the naysayers, and who saw the relationship end in part as a result of his lack of enthusiasm. "But Barbra was saying I'm going to drop everything and I'm going to work seven days a week, and I'm going to fight on the phone to raise money, and then I'm going away for two years, and I'm going to film in a Communist country with machine guns and tanks, and her mother's calling her crying and begging her not to go, but she's saying I'm going to do it anyway."[22]

That is pretty much the way it was. Streisand did finally get financing, from Orion Pictures, but only by agreeing to turn what she had envisioned as an intimate drama into a big musical with the stipulation that the budget not exceed thirteen million dollars. But when *Heaven's Gate* turned into a cinematic *Titanic*, a debacle that rattled Hollywood, Orion withdrew. Streisand pleaded with her former agents, Fields and David Begelman, who had taken over United Artists after *Heaven's Gate* nearly bankrupted the studio, and they agreed to provide the now fourteen-million-dollar budget but added a raft of conditions, including that Streisand contribute half a million dollars of her own money. "In order to make this movie," she told Potok, "I had to give up all of my so-called power." When Potok asked what power she yielded, Streisand enumerated that the studio had script approval, casting approval, even the final cut. "I had to eat shit, put it that way," she said. "You know what I mean? You want to do it, this is the way you get to do it."[23]

Now began the spadework—years of it, years to make sure that she wouldn't fall on her face, as her critics expected and hoped. Sydney Pollack told Streisand biographer Christopher Andersen, "For five years before production, she was talking to everybody she could about it. I'd go to a party, and she'd come over and say, 'Now, look, if I want to begin on the rooster on the weathervane on top of the church, how would I . . . ' She was consumed."[24] Eventually, before she went on location, she actually videotaped a run-through of each scene with all the camera movements.

But there was something else besides the technical skill she felt she needed to acquire. There was the religious component. Streisand was undeniably steeped in Jewishness, but she wasn't steeped in Judaism. Though she had attended yeshiva as a young girl, she was a secular Jew—a Jew by culture and feeling and instinct, not by religion. "*Ma nishatna halaylo hazeh mikol haleylos?* That's the only Hebrew I remember—it's from the Passover ceremony," she told *Playboy*. "I studied Hebrew. I went to Hebrew classes and I could read fluent Hebrew, but I didn't understand what I was saying, and I thought to myself, What is this all about?"[25] Now, playing an Orthodox Jew with a passion for Talmud, she had to learn.

So she sought out rabbis and Jewish scholars. (This is how she met Potok.) She read extensively on Jewish religious issues. She attended Hasidic weddings. She studied alongside Jason, her thirteen-year-old son, as he prepared for his Bar Mitzvah at a beachfront synagogue in Venice, California. "Our study sessions would often run for two hours or more as Scriptural texts and transmitted wisdom from ancient times engaged us ever more deeply," recalled Rabbi Daniel Lapin.[26] And through it all, she kept notes in children's composition books of what she was learning and of questions she felt she had to address. "Gentile thinks, so you're the chosen people huh?" went one note. "We are chosen not for privilege but for responsibility."[27]

And then, after all the years and all the preparation and all the consultation, she was ready. It had been a fact of Streisand's movie career that although not all her films were particularly good, all the good ones had been directed by Jews, which may not have been saying a lot since nearly all her films were directed by Jews. Since, after *Funny Girl*, Streisand could choose whomever she wanted to direct her in her films—with the possible exception of *Hello, Dolly!* which she made before *Funny Girl*'s release—this was clearly a choice. Though she never talked about it, presumably it was a matter of comfort and communication—perhaps of knowing that she wouldn't be judged as harshly by Jewish directors as by gentiles. (One of the things she did discuss was the lack of connection she felt to Peter Bogdanovich, who saw her only as a kook; Gene Kelly, who didn't seem to know what to make of her; and Frank Pierson, who was actually antagonistic to her.) The Jewish directors never bad-mouthed her, even when prompted, as William Wyler was.

But there was something else about them—about Wyler and Herb Ross and Irvin Kershner and Pollack and later Howard Zieff and Martin Ritt, who directed her in *Nuts*. They seemed to get her, to understand what she was about as a Jewish woman. When you think of Streisand, you generally think of how well she understood her persona and her effect on audiences, as Molly Haskell observed. She fully appreciated the metaphor of herself, a very large part of which was her Jewishness. But it is fair to say that her best directors, her Jewish directors, also understood that persona and its effect, and appreciated the metaphor. It was cultural bonding. She was usually well served by them. They became coreligionists in art.

No one, however, could serve her as well as she served herself, quite possibly because it would take a Jewish woman really to fathom the depths of a Jewish woman—the doubts and complexities and self-criticisms. The charges of narcissism notwithstanding, Streisand as director wasn't in love with Streisand as actress. She didn't dote on herself or try to make herself more beautiful, which would have been a betrayal of what she represented. If she understood her persona as an actress, she understood it even more analytically as a director. "I have two very different sides of my face," she would tell Anne Fadiman of *Life* magazine in an example of just how self-observant she was. "My left side is more feminine. My right side is more masculine. In the movie [*Yentl*] I had myself photographed from the right side to show a side of me that had hardly ever been seen. You know the scene after my father's funeral, where I look in the mirror and cut off my hair? I had a crack made in that mirror that would divide my face in half. Male and female."[28]

The division between male and female, both in terms of her relationships and in terms of her own halves, and how difficult it was to reconcile those, had long been one of Streisand's themes. Not only did she bring that theme, as one might have expected, to *Yentl*, but it became part of the process of making the film. The general expectation of director Streisand was that she would be a ball-breaker, a screamer. The truth was quite different. "I found myself being very soft-spoken, feeling even more feminine, than I have ever felt," she said. "More motherly, more nurturing, more loving. I had patience I never dreamed I would have."[29]

Pauline Kael made a point in her review of the film of saying that Streisand directed like a woman, which Kael intended as a compliment. Describing a scene in which Yentl, who has assumed the identity of the boy scholar Anshel, shares a bedroom with Avigdor (Mandy Patinkin), a fellow student with whom Yentl has fallen in love, Kael called the scene "simply different from scenes conceived and directed by men; it has a different flavor," and added, "The whole movie has a modulated emotionality that seems distinctively feminine."[30] Beyond talking about how motherly she felt making the film—a film in which a girl's halves are at war with each other—she also spoke about how natural directing felt to her, how instinctive, how uncerebral, which sounded very different from the quasi-military approach one heard from so many male directors. "You can't think too much about it—if you do, it's gone."[31]

And then there was the performance itself, which seemed

to benefit from Streisand's direction. Arthur Laurents had observed long ago, in *I Can Get It for You Wholesale*, that when "she sang or spoke, she was alive; when she had to listen, Miss Marmelstein went home and in her place stood Barbra Streisand, uncomfortable in a costume." His verdict was that Streisand didn't have the concentration to listen, which is why she had to be centralized in her productions.[32] Pauline Kael made a similar observation about how Streisand could overpower her characters if she didn't remain within them. "When Streisand is playing a character, it releases something in her—a self-doubt, a tentativeness, a delicacy," Kael wrote. And that is why her performance in *Yentl* was one of her best, Kael felt. "The basic concept of the movie lets her release herself, and as the yeshiva boy she's giddy and winsome." And Kael thought that the music, which was used largely as inner monologue, aided the performance: "Her singing has an ardent, beseeching quality— an intimacy. And her vocal fervor lifts the movie to the level of fantasy."[33]

But there could never be a Streisand movie now without a comeuppance. Some said that Streisand really didn't direct the film the way an auteur did—by stamping her vision on it. She was more of an editor. (A ridiculous claim when one thinks of how meticulously she laid out every shot in the film.) Another colleague said, "She always knew a good idea when she saw one, though she rarely originated one"—an idiotic idea, even if true, which it wasn't, since an artist will take inspiration wherever he or she can find it.[34] What really irritated Streisand was an interview she gave to the *Los Angeles Times* in which she said she had shown Steven Spielberg a rough cut and asked what he thought of the film—the *Times* omitted his answer (he thought the film was perfect)—thus making it seem as if Streisand had enlisted Spielberg's help to rescue the picture.[35] In any case, the idea behind all these comments and omissions was that

Streisand—a woman—couldn't possibly have directed the film without the assistance of men.

The worst criticism, the most stinging criticism, came from Isaac Bashevis Singer, who had written a screen treatment for *Yentl* that Streisand rejected and for which, in any case, he felt underpaid. Interviewing himself in the *New York Times*, Singer, accused of being something of a misogynist himself, unloaded on Streisand.[36] She received too much rabbinical advice, but "rabbis cannot replace a director." The singing disturbed him: "The passion for learning and the passion for singing are not much related in my mind." Streisand hogged the film: "The result is that Miss Streisand is always present, while poor Yentl is absent." (This is precisely the opposite of what Kael felt.) And the ending, in which Yentl leaves Poland for the United States, was a travesty: "What would Yentl have done in America? Worked in a sweatshop 12 hours a day where there is no time for learning?"[37]

If Singer had intended to hurt the movie—and what other intention could there have been?—he succeeded. *Yentl* received five Golden Globe nominations from the Hollywood Foreign Press Association, an Oscar precursor, and won for both Best Musical Picture and Best Director, making Streisand the first woman to win the award. "I am very Jewish and very pessimistic," she said afterward about her Oscar chances. "If I say I want to win it, I won't. So I'm saying nothing."[38] But by this time Singer had helped poison the well, giving license to anyone who wanted to punish Streisand for her hubris, and in Hollywood that amounted to a lot of people. *Yentl* received four Oscar nominations, but not Best Picture, Best Actress, or, worst of all for Streisand, Best Director. "Do you think they didn't see it?" she allegedly asked a friend. "Or they did see it and hate it? Or is it me?"[39] Basically, it was her. "You kept hearing at every lunch how she was spending too much, how she was an egomaniac, how it was all falling apart," actress and director Lee Grant told *People*. "And then, of course, when she came back, all the stories were the exact opposite. . . . She's a bigger-than-life person. I think there's a resistance to giving her her due."[40]

Streisand would have loved the recognition of a Best Directing Oscar, but she didn't make *Yentl* for that. She made it as a form of self-exploration and self-discovery, as she did most of her films. That is why she fought to get it made, spent half a million dollars of her own money, suffered the high-handedness of the studio and ceded final cut, took the rabbinical instruction, spent year after year after year in preparation (from 1968, when she first read the story, to 1984, when the film was released), and shot on location in Czechoslovakia, where the conditions could not have been more un-Hollywoodlike. In some measure, the film was a way to reclaim her father since Yentl has a wise, loving, and tolerant rabbi father, a guiding presence, clearly modeled after her fantasy of her own. Though he dies early in the film, he is the spiritual and intellectual foundation for Yentl, as she vocalizes in one of the film's most famous songs in the score by Alan and Marilyn Bergman and Michel Legrand, "Papa, Can You Hear Me?" It is part gratitude to her father, part expression of love, part acknowledgment of her fear now that she has to face the world alone, and part apology to him for her venturing forth in the guise of a man to do what women are forbidden to do. Yentl's father becomes an idealization of fatherhood for Streisand. "See, all these years I was just looking for a daddy in a way," she later said, "and then I realized I was never going to get him. It was only through *Yentl* that I had a chance to make a father." The film is dedicated to "my father—and all fathers"—ostensibly to the ones who give their children, especially their daughters, confidence and hope and protection.[41]

With the subtext within that dedication, and with Streisand's own feminist reputation, it is easy to misread *Yentl* as a feminist call to arms for women's equality. Superman Streisand, her Clark Kent/Anshel disguising her Superman/Yentl, is saying women are the equals if not the superiors of men, as Yentl is superior to her male Talmudic classmates, in part because she can ask the questions about justice that the men cannot ask since men have not suffered the injustice women suffer, and in part because she has sensitivities that the men cannot or will not let emerge. No one would deny that Streisand intends that to be one of the film's messages.

But it is not the film's primary message, and it is certainly not its most interesting one. *Yentl* is above all a film about the varieties of love and their complications—complicated precisely because we have these male and female components, psychologically and biologically speaking, and because we are forced into single male and female roles, socially and culturally speaking. If *Yentl* is about liberation, then, it is not just about liberating women from social and religious constrictions; it is about liberating everyone from the way they have been taught to view the world. *That* is a Streisand theme.

One feels this most movingly in the song "No Wonder He Loves Her," in which Yentl watches the beautiful Hadass (played by Amy Irving) serve her fiancé, Avigdor, at a dinner at Hadass's home. The song, Yentl's reverie, begins as a kind of feminist complaint: No *wonder* he loves her. She is obsequious and overly deferential to him, even averting her eyes. But as the song proceeds, Streisand's tone changes ever so slightly, the way it did in "Cry Me a River." The complaint turns to envy. Avigdor loves Hadass, not just because she is a doormat whose only desire is to please him, but because of her grace, her femininity, and her quiet charm. In a later dinner scene, this time between Anshel/Yentl and Hadass, there is yet another turn. Yentl feels an attraction to Hadass herself. Since Yentl had earlier, in a scene at a swimming hole where the boys go skinny-dipping, sung of Avigdor and about "The Way He Makes Me Feel," she is one confused young woman.

Which is exactly Streisand's point. Love is powerful and confusing because it can't be held in check by social conformity, even though social conformity can ultimately doom it. Yentl falls in love with the intelligence and strength of Avigdor but also with his sensitivity when he tells her that his brother had committed suicide, a death the revelation of which ends his betrothal to Hadass at her parents' insistence and which leads Avigdor to convince Anshel to marry Hadass instead, as a kind of place keeper for him until her parents relent. Hadass clearly loves Avigdor for some of the same reasons Yentl does, but she comes to love Anshel even more for his tenderness and understanding. And Yentl loves both Avigdor and Hadass. When she finally reveals herself to Hadass as a girl, she tells Hadass so—"I loved you"—to which Hadass replies, in one of the more daring moments in any musical, "I loved you, too." And make no mistake: there is an erotic component to the relationship.

It almost sounds as if *Yentl* is a farce with so many loves bouncing around—one wag called it "Tootsie on the Roof"—and it does have its farcical comic elements. But in the end, it is much closer to tragedy. And that is because when Yentl finally reveals herself to Avigdor and declares her love for him, and he declares his in return, clearly attracted to her intelligence, the love cannot be consummated. And it cannot be consummated because Avigdor immediately begins sketching a future for the couple—a future in which, obviously, Yentl sacrifices her education to be his helpmate. This is something Yentl is not willing or even able to do; it would be a betrayal of herself. In the end, then, love is not sufficient. In the end, Avigdor remains imprisoned by social norms and by his own psychological needs, as Streisand men often are: Nicky in *Funny Girl*, Hubbell in *The Way We Were*, John Norman Howard in *A Star Is Born*. The balance cannot be struck—the fundamental Streisand dilemma. There are not a lot of happy endings in Streisand movies, and there is not one here. What there are are hopeful endings. So Yentl leaves Avigdor and Hadass and heads to America. Though her love is lost, like Fanny and Katie and Esther, she soldiers on because she knows herself.

Knowing oneself was always a central motivation to Streisand's films. "Every film she directs involves a working out of a part of her own life," her close friend lyricist Marilyn Bergman said. "*Prince of Tides* is about family and forgiveness, about Barbra forgiving her father and her mother."[42] Mostly, however, it was her mother who needed forgiveness. "You can say, 'Well, my mother didn't understand me,'" she told Kevin Sessums of *Vanity Fair*. "But by her not understanding me, she's responsible for my success. I had to prove to my mother that you don't have to be so beautiful to be a movie star . . . or conventionally beautiful. That my arms . . . it doesn't matter if they're skinny. Now I look at her with enormous gratitude, and I can feel love. I have no more anger."[43]

Prince of Tides was adapted from Pat Conroy's best-selling 1986 novel about a South Carolina English teacher cum high school football coach named Tom Wingo who goes to New York when his sister, Savannah, a poet, attempts suicide. The trip brings him into contact with his sister's psychiatrist, Dr. Susan Lowenstein, who tries to determine what has driven Savannah to this despair. He is her "memory," Lowenstein says. These sessions lead to romance, though both Tom and Lowenstein are married—he to a dissatisfied doctor having an affair, she to a world-famous concert violinist. Of course, the affair is ill-fated, but like all Streisand film romances, it leads to understanding, if not completion. As Streisand described the film, it was about "coming to terms with people in our lives . . . our parents . . .our children . . . our mates . . . and even more important than that, as I am learning myself, it's about coming to terms with ourselves by accepting, loving and being in harmony with the child who still lives inside of us."[44] (Here Streisand was parroting the pop psychologist John Bradshaw, who had written *Championing Your Inner Child* and whose philosophy she had adopted.)[45] In the end, both Tom and Susan are liberated from their pasts and free to be themselves—not happy, yet again, but hopeful. "Before I met you," Tom says, "I was in a deep sleep and I didn't even know it." At film's end, he is awake.

It was all very Streisandesque. There was Tom's severe and demanding mother, right out of Streisand's life, who imposed a vow of silence on her son about a family trauma—a vow that wound up psychologically crippling him just as the trauma itself had crippled his sister. There were the role reversals—the football coach who must find his feminine side, and the psychiatrist who helps her son, played by Streisand's real-life son, Jason, find his masculine side by having Tom coach him. There were the deceptions of appearance—Tom's seeming machismo and Lowenstein's seemingly perfect life. There was the search for gender balance, and the exploration for some deeper personal truth. And there was the gentile-Jewish division yet again, another clash of sensibilities, though this time the question isn't whether Lowenstein can fit into a gentile world, as it was for Katie in *The Way We Were*, but whether Tom can fit into Lowenstein's elite Upper West Side world.[46] "If we are staying together, do I have to become Jewish?" he jokes, though there is substance beneath the quip. He *would* have to become Jewish, or at least find a Jewish sensibility in himself, as Savannah assumes a Jewish identity of a Holocaust survivor for a book of her poems, presumably to connect with Jewish feeling because she sympathizes with victimization. In any case, it is another Streisand example of Jewish understanding attempting to save a gentile from his own torpor: Jewishness as revivification. And when Tom tells Lowenstein—which is what he always calls her—that he is returning to his wife, not because he loves her more but because he has loved her longer, Lowenstein says, "I've got to find me a nice Jewish boy. You guys are killing me."

Coming seven years after *Yentl*, years in which the animus against Streisand seemed to have mitigated slightly, *Prince of Tides* received a mixed critical reception. Owen Glieberman, writing in *Entertainment Weekly*, spoke for the detractors in calling it a "big, messy, go-for-the-throat soap opera, the sort of movie in which every third scene feels like one of those soul-spilling climaxes they use for clips on Oscar night . . . a four-hankie therapy session."[47] Others also picked up on the therapy and Tom's breakthrough as he dredges up the awful childhood incident that blighted his family, and they found it inflated and implausible. It was Freudian movie magic.

Streisand, who had undergone therapy herself, was clearly a believer. "Obviously, I wasn't too self-aware in the past," she told *Playboy* ten years earlier, discussing the effects of her therapy. "This is a whole new kind of world opening up to me, which is acknowledging other people's realities." She admitted that she was "in the process of great change," part of which was losing her fear.[48] And comparing a scene in the film, where Lowenstein physically comforts Tom after he divulges his secret, to her own therapy, she told an interviewer, "My therapist touched my hand, and I just broke down. I thought at the time, 'This must be what it feels like to be held by your mother.'"[49] Glieberman may have been right that the movie indulged in psychoanalytic overkill. But what was literal in the power of therapy was also metaphoric in the need to find oneself beneath the armor that everyone dons as self-protection. This was the essence of the movie as it was the essence of Streisand.

Janet Maslin, writing in the *New York Times*, spoke for the film's admirers. "Discretion and reserve are not the first qualities that come to mind about Ms. Streisand's work," Maslin wrote, paying her a left-handed compliment, "yet they are very much in evidence this time. So is the frankly emotional style with which she is more often associated, a style perfectly attuned to the film's complex story."[50] The film received seven Oscar nominations, including Best Actor for Nick Nolte as Tom, whose performance was widely praised, and Best Picture. But once again Streisand, unable to escape her image, was stiffed for a directing nomination. "People think she's egomaniacal, demanding, and, frankly, a great big pain in the ass," one director said. "As perverse as it sounds, each success seems to make Hollywood *want* to hate her more and more."[51]

The next backlash—there was always a backlash where Streisand was concerned—came from a quarter heretofore not heard from: the gay community. And it came, ironically, when Streisand announced that she was going to make a film of *The Normal Heart*, based on the 1985 play by AIDS activist Larry Kramer, who was HIV-positive himself, which dealt with the early days of the AIDS crisis in New York City. Streisand had reason to be attracted to the material. First of all, she had a huge gay following. Second, AIDS was a cause about which she had been outspoken, and the Streisand Foundation had raised millions for AIDS research and awareness. And third, there was a personal connection since her son, Jason Gould, was gay. As she later told it, she immediately optioned the rights.

And then began a ten-year struggle. As with her two previous directorial projects, Streisand was diligent, and she was meticulous. She and Kramer wrote draft after draft after draft over several years until Streisand finally hired another writer to, as she put it, "make it more cinematic." It wasn't an easy play to crack. It was polemical, and Streisand, for all her political advocacy, was not a polemical filmmaker. And it was not exactly a big box office prospect, which didn't bother Streisand but which did make it difficult to get financing. After ten years, she finally decided that she wouldn't get financing for a feature film but she could get the film on HBO. The problem, she said, was that HBO was willing to pay Kramer only $250,000 for the rights, and Kramer, who was as difficult as Streisand, demanded $1 million.[52] So Streisand moved on to another film, *The Mirror Has Two Faces*, and Kramer was apoplectic. "She was all set to make 'The Normal Heart,' about a world-wide plague," he raged in *Variety*, "and at the last minute, she switches to a film about a woman who gets a facelift. I didn't think it was decent of her to do to me, her gay fans, and the people with AIDS she talks so movingly about."[53]

The Normal Heart meant a great deal to Streisand; she continued working on the project even after her option lapsed. (It was eventually made by director Ryan Murphy for HBO in 2014.) But *The Mirror Has Two Faces*, which Kramer belittled, meant a great deal to Streisand, too. Like so many of her films, it was the story of her life. "When I first read the script," she told Bernard Weinraub of the *New York Times*, "I said, 'I know this mother. Once I asked my mother, 'Was I pretty as a baby?' and the words out of my mother's mouth were, 'All babies are pretty,' and I said, 'No, I mean me: was I pretty?' and she said, 'What's pretty anyway? Look at what good it did your sister.' I just remember those lines; they were very powerful to me, and we put them in the script because it seemed so very right."[54]

But the attraction to Richard LaGravenese's script, adapted from a French film, was more than just Streisand's identification of the screenplay's mother with her own mother. There was Rose Morgan, the now-aging Jewish woman, no longer a kook, a woman who is intelligent and independent, a college English professor, but who has yet to find romance, and the gentile (of course) math professor (Jeff Bridges), who is drawn to and ditched by beautiful women until he finally decides that the only relationship worth having is a platonic one. "I just want to share my life with someone," he says. "Someone I'm not sexually attracted to." Enter Streisand. There is the poignancy and heartbreak that one usually finds in Streisand romances because the halves, both personal and interpersonal, once again don't mesh. And there is the role of appearance that obscures truth and love. As Streisand herself put it, "I think I am always drawn to films about the mystery of appearances. *The Mirror Has Two Faces* is really a charming love story. But it has serious overtones about vanity and beauty, the external versus the internal."[55]

Mirrors understandably had always been a visual leitmotif in Streisand's films. She had famously begun her film career by looking in one. Later, the cracked mirror in *Yentl* became, as Streisand herself had pointed out, a way to convey the untruthfulness of the image as well as the dueling genders within Yentl. In *The Mirror Has Two Faces*, the mirror is not just a leitmotif; it is the film's dominant metaphor for the primacy (and hollowness) of aesthetics. The two professors begin their platonic relationship, but after they marry, Streisand wants more. When her husband refuses, Streisand, frustrated, eventually takes it upon herself to beautify. No, there isn't a facelift. What there is is a desperate attempt to satisfy the aesthetic demands that most men seem to place on women and that Streisand had both resisted in her films—and her life—and appeased, trying to prove simultaneously the seeming contradiction that appearances don't matter as much as the so-called inner self and that one can will oneself to be beautiful. In her own life, Streisand was an example of both.

By now this is bedrock Streisand. "From the beginning, she had played characters whose appearance is, to say the very least, unconventional," Thomas Mack, a Henry James scholar wrote, comparing *The Mirror Has Two Faces* to James's *Washington Square*, about another alleged ugly duckling. "And this unorthodox beauty proved to be a touchstone by which the truth of other characters might be judged." As Mack delineates the basic Streisand theme, it is a "woman who finds herself only after she frees herself from the expectation of others."[56] This is certainly the case in *The Mirror Has Two Faces*. Though it takes her aesthetic transformation to show her recalcitrant husband who his wife really is—losing Rose, *that* would be a loss!—her transformation is a liberation. As Mack explains the film's primary message, it is the "fact that a mirror can reflect the inner and outer selves," and, he might have added, that in the final analysis, the inner self is what we fall in love with; the outer self is just a wrapping. Again, pure Streisand. And pure Jewish, too, since Jews had had inculcated in them the idea that they had "failed" at aesthetics, that they could be loved only for who they were, not how they looked.

But Streisand herself discussed another aspect of the film— the aspect of the film that was not just about aesthetics generally but about film aesthetics specifically and, even more pointedly, about the distorting illusions within those aesthetics. In a way, Streisand was taking on the very basis of her own industry as well as her own adolescent dreams. As she told interviewer Lawrence Grobel nearly twenty years before she made *Mirror*, "When you kiss in the movies and they score it with violins, people then go around measuring their emotions by hearing violins or not. Our psyches are put in shock. We can't seem to deal with the reality of there's no violins." And she went on: "I'm finding it fascinating now to enter into a second phase of my life and get behind what's really happening in relationships with people and in the awareness of what's going on."[57]

This was bedrock Streisand, too. Barry Dennen recalled a date with Streisand when they took the Staten Island Ferry and tried to re-create the Fred Astaire–Ginger Rogers "They Can't Take That Away from Me" scene in *Shall We Dance* and found the effort supremely unmagical. "The movies are an illusion, honey," Dennen said he told her then. "Magic. That's what we're looking to give them in the theater. The real magic."

To which Streisand lamented, "That's where I'd like to live my life." "In the theater?" he asked. "In the magic of the movies," she answered.[58]

She had, in fact, succeeded in doing so to a remarkable degree. Her life was every adolescent girl's dream—and most adolescent boys' as well. But even though she was a romantic, she was a romantic realist. That had been another lesson of her life, and one that connected with her audience. *It wasn't as easy as the movies made it out to be*, her films said repeatedly in yet another Streisand irony. Virtually every one of them, save junk like *What's Up, Doc?* and even the disasters like *All Night Long*, in which Streisand's character leaves her domineering husband but still is romantically discontented, are not only about romantic failure but about romantic complication that can lead two people who truly and deeply love each other into going their separate ways: Fanny and Nicky, Katie and Hubbell, Yentl and Avigdor, Susan and Tom, to name a few. Streisand, who was fifty-four when she made *Mirror*, was explicit about this, about how *Mirror* addressed "how difficult it is to find people, especially in your middle years."[59] And she laid some of those complications at the feet of our unrealistic movie-induced expectations. At movie's end, Streisand puts a spin on this idea by having the now-chastened husband embrace the wife he realizes he loves, really loves, not because she is beautiful but because she is *beautiful*, as Puccini's "Nessun dorma" swells on the soundtrack. It is a pure movie moment—the kind of overwrought moment Streisand might have watched as a girl at Loew's Kings Theatre in Brooklyn.

With this climax, Streisand isn't reversing herself and suddenly endorsing those fantasies. She is looking at a deeper source that might even be able to sustain them—a dose of romantic realism. The scene is a convergence of the realistic with the illusionary with the message that we *can* find romance, but we find it, not in passion, which is generated largely by the exterior of experience, but in love, which is the interior. Critics didn't much care for the film. Janet Maslin in the *New York Times* found Rose's "cosmetic triumph" to be "gratingly overdone" and thought the film's second half featured a kind of Streisand vanity.[60] But the film said exactly what Streisand wanted it to say, and what it said sounded very much like a summation of and a valedictory to her entire film career—which it almost was.

10

Tsufridnkeit

"WHAT'S YOUR definition of the word 'fame'?" Barbra Streisand was asked. "Not being left alone," she answered.[1] From the time she was in her early twenties, Streisand had not been left alone. Paparazzi followed her. The press hounded her. Fans accosted her as if she were one of them, which had always been part of her pretense and appeal. She would say that when people approached her and asked if she was Barbra Streisand, she would tell them that she *looked* like Streisand. There had always been something recessive about her—a personal counterweight to the professional attention she sought. Her movies became more and more infrequent, and her stage appearances had ceased altogether after her "One Voice" concert at her home in 1986.

Streisand's explanation for her absence was stage fright. She suffered from enormous anxiety—afraid for her safety, afraid of making mistakes (during her Central Park Happening, she had forgotten the words to a song), afraid of what the audience wanted from her (of an appearance at the International Hotel in Las Vegas in 1969, she said, "All I kept thinking about was, What am I supposed to be?").[2] To another interviewer, she said it wasn't stage fright she felt; it was "death."[3] Camille Paglia adduced another fear and another explanation: Streisand's "insecurity about her sexual attractiveness." Paglia said that audiences had begun calling Streisand "cold" on stage, and she surmised that it was probably "psychologically important for Streisand to withdraw in the 1970s and 1980s and become a hausfrau. She wanted to live like a real woman, and to be desired like one." But Paglia called it "embarrassing" to those who worshipped her nonconformity. "She had reverted to convention and become what the 1950s wanted us to be, a housewife and mother. I suffered every time I saw her in that atrocious mop of curls. She looked terrible."[4] In effect, Streisand was living within Betty Freidan's feminine mystique.

Streisand hadn't exactly retreated in those decades; she did make films and albums. But Paglia was right that Streisand didn't desire the limelight and that she preferred a quiet existence now that she had proven her point. "I think I would be much happier if I would chop wood and carry water instead of making movies and being attacked," she told the *Los Angeles Times Magazine*. "I would like that. . . . I have no need to sing, act, direct. I like to nest, design houses, things not for public consumption. The work takes things away from me, it isolates me."[5] She seemed to enjoy a different kind of isolation: privacy. "I hope people enjoy my work—that's what they paid for," she told *Harper's Bazaar*. "But I don't believe they have any claim on my personal life or my personal time."[6] And she talked about how much she liked the idea of spending time with her son, Jason, and being a mother rather than a star.

Of course, she made music, even if she didn't perform it publicly, alternating between the pop style she introduced with

Stoney End and her more traditional ballads, like "The Way We Were," which became a number one hit. Some of these albums were fizzles; she did a water-themed album called *Wet* in 1979, and another called *Emotion* in 1984, neither of which cracked *Billboard*'s top five, and her experiment, *Classical Barbra*, rose only as high as number forty-six. Others were tremendous successes, like her collaboration in 1980 with the Bee Gees' Barry Gibb, which resulted in the number one album, *Guilty*, and its number one title song. Streisand had proven herself in both mainstream and rock, which not even Frank Sinatra could do, though he and Streisand operated from the same musical principles. Sinatra didn't adjust or didn't want to. Streisand changed her style, losing some of her originality in the process.

Streisand was too shrewd not to realize the concession, and after the disaster of *Emotion*, she began pushing for an album of Broadway standards. In yet another meta moment, Streisand begins the album with the Stephen Sondheim song from *Sunday in the Park with George*, about the painter Georges Seurat, "Putting It Together," in which she is hectored about making an album of Broadway songs since no one will want to hear them and the album would have no commercial prospects—which were exactly the warnings she had received from Columbia. (Sondheim, now a Streisand fan, added lyrics especially for her.) *The Broadway Album* (1985) became one of Streisand's most commercially successful records, another number one, and arguably her very best artistically. Stephen Holden in the *New York Times* called it the "album of a lifetime."[7] Not surprisingly, all the songs were written by Jews—Sondheim, Richard Rodgers and Oscar Hammerstein, Leonard Bernstein, George and Ira Gershwin, Frank Loesser. This was because Broadway was an even more Jewish-inflected environment than Hollywood, even more the product of a Jewish sensibility that created fantasy (after all, people generally do not just get up and sing) informed by emotion. By history, Jews had become expert in both—the first by necessity, the second by the tragedy of experience. Streisand's instinct had been impeccable. The creature of fantasy and emotion was the ideal interpreter for these songs.

But that didn't mean that Streisand had softened her attitude toward singing. She professed not to listen to music, save for "classical things, like Mahler or Bartok." She didn't have time. And she said she never listened to her own albums: "I don't like living in the past." Nor did she ever sing for her own amusement. "Not in the shower, even."[8]

Why then did she decide after nearly a decade to return to the concert stage? There were rumors it was about money. In her time with Jon Peters, Streisand had built a house on a twenty-four-acre Malibu ranch and furnished it lavishly. When the relationship ended, the ranch seemed too large (she donated it to the Santa Monica Mountains Conservatory for a tax break), and the house she had bought years earlier, when she arrived in Hollywood, on Carolwood Drive in the tony Holmby Hills section of Los Angeles (Walt Disney lived on the same street) didn't especially excite her, so she was looking for another house to buy. This would require resources, and because she was working so little, Streisand claimed to be less wealthy than she was depicted. In December 1993, she signed a new contract with Sony, which had bought Columbia, for sixty million dollars, covering both albums and films. Then Kirk Kerkorian, who was building the MGM Grand Hotel and Casino in Las Vegas, approached her for a New Year's Eve concert to open it. She was to perform two shows—for thirteen million dollars. By one account, as soon as the engagement was announced, with tickets selling at a thousand dollars apiece, the switchboard was flooded with calls—one million the first day alone.[9]

The concerts were a triumph, which led to the announcement of a six-city tour over the following five months, and more money, though Streisand insisted it was not as much as reported. "They wrote I'm making $100 million from this tour," she grumbled to *Vanity Fair*. "One hundred cities, a million dollars a city! How can they say that? I've done six cities! Six! And do you know what it costs to stage a production like this?"[10] In the end, it was reported that the tour, with twenty-six concerts, grossed sixty-four million dollars, plus merchandise, and a license fee from HBO to broadcast it.[11] This only added to the detractors' criticisms of Streisand as greedy and manipulative—more man-eating Jewish Woman sniping.

But just as her career had been less about money than about psychological satisfaction from personal vindication, so, too, may her concert tour have been about that vindication. She needed to stop hating the audiences who loved her, she needed to stop feeling that they were devouring her, and she needed to believe that she was worth the adulation, that, reversing Groucho Marx's famous quip that he didn't want to be a member of any club that would have him, she could be a star to the audiences who worshipped her. "It worked out," she told *Vanity Fair*, "it was right. It was right for me to gain this confidence, to feel absolutely at ease onstage, to feel I belonged there and deserved to be there, that I could give and receive the love of those audiences. I really am grateful to those people. For too many years I didn't appreciate my own singing." The concert tour, then, was a form of therapy, another step in Streisand's journey of self-acceptance and of bringing her securities back into balance with her insecurities.

In that respect, the tour proved every bit as triumphant as the Las Vegas kickoff. In city after city, she was greeted by adulation. Jon Pareles of the *New York Times*, describing the scene of Streisand's opening at Madison Square Garden, her first concert in the city since 1967, wrote, "Limousines ringed the block; her fans, who had paid $50 and much more for tickets, arrived in tuxedos, suits and evening dresses."[12] David Hinckley in the *New York Daily News*, said the appearance was like "MacArthur returning to the Philippines, De Gaulle to Paris."[13] As Pareles reported, concession stands sold champagne and roses, and fans paid seventy-five dollars apiece for white dress shirts with "Barbra: The Concert" across the front. The audience was dotted with celebrities.

The stakes were high. As ardent Streisand fan Camille Paglia wrote, "Having extorted a river of cash from the crowd, Streisand had set herself up for failed expectations."[14] They weren't. The self-confident Streisand of the earlier concert days was back in evidence, but so was a modest, self-deprecating Streisand. She had had Sondheim revise "I'm Still Here" from *Follies* to include the line, "I kept my nose to spite my face." And she joked at her opening at Madison Square Garden, which happened to coincide with the opening of the Gay Games in the city, that one of the "best things about the games is that I can walk down the street and not be recognized because there are so many impersonators."[15] Paglia said, "It was as if she were resuming a conversation interrupted yesterday."[16]

But if her attitude hadn't changed, her singing, now that she was fifty, had. Orchestra leader and arranger Nelson Riddle had commented that in his later years Sinatra's voice had deepened from violin to viola.[17] That wouldn't happen to Streisand. Her voice was still strong and bright. What did happen is that she didn't attack a lyric quite as fiercely as in her youth. She didn't push as much, which actually made her more effective. Pareles said, "Ms. Streisand chose understatement, holding back syllable-torturing melismas that have been picked up by imitators like Mariah Carey, keeping her tone less brassy than it is on many of her recordings," and thought she brought a "tender restraint to her most romantic sentiments"—restraint not being a quality one would have attributed to the younger Streisand.[18] No longer desperate, she no longer needed to show off. In some ways, she was not just as good as ever, she was better than ever.

Still, this wasn't just a concert, any more than Streisand was just a singer. There was too much history with her audience for it to be that. Virtually every audience member had lived with Streisand for more than thirty years. Everyone could identify with her roots and her rise, and the show included projected photos and film clips from her life and career. "Tears flowed freely in the audience," Paglia wrote of the first Garden appearance.[19] "For New Yorkers," Pareles observed, "Ms. Streisand is the definitive local girl made good, and the concert offered a chance for fans to simultaneously applaud her and share in her success," which had always been her transaction with them.[20] Robert Hilbrun of the *Los Angeles Times* found the same response when she appeared in that city. The audience was not just celebrating the music but showing its "admiration of the independence and determination Streisand has shown over the years in such pursuits as film directing."[21] In short, they were celebrating Streisand's personal victory and, vicariously, theirs.

The one triumph she hadn't won was romance. As feminist writer Letty Cottin Pogrebin described Streisand's Jewish Big Mouth character, "If she wants something, she goes for it. A noncomformist, she won't play her assigned role—either as a Jew or as a Woman." But, continued Pogrebin, she "comes with a curse: she is not allowed to have it all. She has to pay a price for her independence, and the price is love."[22] "Curse" may have been the wrong word. "Penalty" was closer. Strong Jewish women paid a penalty for their strength. Neither in her films nor in her life was Streisand successful in having a sustained relationship—the eternal devotion extolled by the movies—save for in *The Mirror Has Two Faces.* This would have been the final victory: the victory of the *mieskeit* Jewish girl who finds true love without having to compromise her personality.

It didn't begin auspiciously. It was 1996. Christine Peters, Jon Peters's ex-wife, was having a dinner party of about twenty guests at Mr. Chow in Beverly Hills, and asked actor James Brolin's manager, Jerry Wald, if Brolin would like to meet Streisand. Brolin agreed, then contemplated canceling. Streisand, appropriately enough, was editing *Mirror*, and thought it a "real imposition, to have to leave my work and go to a dinner party, which I never like to do anyway." She told the editors she would return in a few hours.[23] Brolin at the time was wearing a severe crew cut for a part, and Streisand's greeting was, "Who screwed up your hair?"[24] When they sat down to dinner, Streisand was flanked by Brolin and ex-heavyweight champion boxer George Foreman, and Streisand anticipated talking to Foreman about the grill he was promoting. But, Streisand recalled of Brolin, "Once we sat down and started to speak, that was it." Brolin said, "After ten minutes I knew we'd be together. After twenty minutes I was a goner, and after two hours, I knew we'd get married some day."[25] "Everyone could see it immediately," Jerry Wald said. "They didn't look up, they didn't talk to anyone else. I don't even think they ate."[26] Brolin insisted on driving her home, and they stayed up until 3:00 a.m. talking.

Brolin even looked like a typical Streisand leading man: tall, broad-shouldered, ruggedly handsome, and conventionally masculine. Of course, he was gentile. And he had the backstory of a Streisand leading man: California-born, the son of a laconic, emotionally distant aerospace engineer; a shy boy who never spoke in class and spent his leisure time surfing; a loner who bought a movie camera when he was fifteen and taught himself how to shoot film. When he was eighteen, a studio representative saw him walking down the street and asked if he had considered acting. Brolin said his response was, "How much does it pay? And how much film can I buy with that?"[27] He eventually signed on as a contract player at Fox and began making films, though his breakthrough was in the television series *Marcus Welby, M.D.* Still, Brolin had difficulty expressing

his emotions in life, if not on the screen. At a friend's sugges-
tion, he enrolled in a love and communication seminar, where
he learned how to hug. When he embraced his frosty father,
Brolin said, "I thought he was going to die. I changed him
completely in just a few months."[28] In effect, Brolin had found
his feminine side. Now he really *was* a Streisand leading man—
a dichotomous male to match her dichotomous female.

Yet in her life as in her films, the course of true love was
torturous. They met again at Streisand's goddaughter's birthday party and "barely had a chance to speak," Streisand said. At
the party's end, Brolin said he would call her. He didn't. Streisand was resigned. "I was into a mode of just being by myself,"
she told *McCall's*, "of staying in bed and reading political jour-
nals and eating coffee ice cream cones. I thought, 'This relationship thing is not for me; it's too difficult.'"[29]

It was a few days after the birthday party that Streisand got
a fax from Brolin: "Respond or I'll start faxing smut." On the
bottom of the page was his phone number and "Tonight, yes?"
They went to a film, discussed the agony of dating, and then
he flew to the Philippines to make a film. When he was gone
their conversations were so long that he said, "I almost spent
my entire salary on the phone bill."[30] And when he returned, he
proposed, though Streisand said she "laughed it off," until she
didn't. He had told her, "I'm here to empower you." To which
Streisand thought, "This is some hell of a guy. You mean to
give me more power? Because I needed to be empowered in
this personal part of me."[31] They were married at her Malibu
estate on July 1, 1998, which was the second anniversary of their
first date. Given the climax of *Mirror*, her life had imitated her
art once again. The Jewess got her *goyisher* guy, but the goy also
got his Jewess. It meant something that Brolin's term of en-
dearment for her was "Beezer," referring to her nose. For
most actresses, the happiness that eludes them in life, they find

on the screen. For Streisand, the happiness that had eluded her on-screen, she had found in life.

Beginning in the late 1990s, Streisand entered a kind of self-imposed exile. She was happily married. There was nothing left to prove in her career. And she had neither the desire nor the need to deal with the press or defend herself from criticisms. She was inured. Even the vicious *South Park* "Mecha-Streisand" episode drew a tepid reaction from her, primarily a concern that young women might come away "feeling that any woman who dares to accomplish something is the incarnation of self-centeredness and greed."[32] She didn't even mention the thinly veiled anti-Semitism.

For a performer who had always worked on her terms and was often vilified for it, she was now living on her own terms. "I turn down movies, television shows, awards, interviews," she said. "Finding love changes your priorities. I don't care about work as much—a lot of my work was a sublimation for love, I think. When I was bored or kind of lonely, I would work. Now, I don't feel very ambitious. I'm content."[33] Basically, she and Brolin would go for long drives through San Bernardino County, eating in the car sandwiches Streisand made, and visit truck stops, which, Brolin said, was an America that Streisand had never seen—goy America.[34] She read avidly, mainly newspapers and news magazines, and watched the news. A friend had introduced her to New Age spiritualism, of which Streisand became a devotee, and her re-Judaization with *Yentl* brought her into contact with Jewish texts and the mystical kabbalah.[35] *New York Times* reporter Bernard Weinraub, after visiting her, wrote, "She seems consumed by a hunger to learn about everything from art to politics," which may have been a vestige of her father's influence.[36]

And the woman who had often been assailed for her business

acumen, another element of the Jewish Woman Syndrome, also became fascinated with finance. She had been investing for years, reading *Barron's* and watching CNBC. She even woke up each morning at 6:30 when the New York exchanges opened to read the tape. She was so successful at playing the market that when she told her friend the fashion designer Donna Karan that she had made $130,000 on eBay stock in a month, Karan insisted on giving her $1 million to invest. After five months of what *Fortune* called "intense trading," Streisand raised Karan's stake to $1.8 million.[37] She would later say, "I've been doing this so long that it feels like another career."[38]

But the things that most occupied Streisand in her exile were her homes. Streisand had long said that if she hadn't become a singer and actress, she would like to have become a designer or architect, and in a very real way, she eventually did. Her New York penthouse was an ongoing project, even though she seldom occupied it, and it was featured in *Architectural Digest*. Her California homes were obsessions. Asked, as early as 1977, how she spent her time when she wasn't working, she said, "Would you believe I sit with contractors for six hours talking about waterproofing vinyl and moisture barriers and who does the caulking, the painter or the roof man?"[39]

The sublimation Streisand had referenced in relation to her work also functioned in her homes. She admitted that she channeled her frustrations at not being able to get *The Normal Heart* off the ground into building a new home.[40] Early in the 1990s, a realtor had shown her an oceanfront home with which she had immediately fallen in love, but she couldn't have afforded it without selling her other properties, and while she dithered, another couple bought it and began renovating. Seven years later, a house just two lots away came onto the market. It was dilapidated and on a single acre, but Streisand bought it with the intention of razing it and building what she had always wanted: a barn house. (A Jewish girl from Brooklyn probably couldn't have gotten any more gentile a domicile than that.) When she became friendly with a nonagenarian couple who owned the house between the one she had bought and the one she had coveted, she bought theirs. And when the couple who had bought the first house divorced, she bought theirs, too. She obtained the building permit in 1999. The project would take nearly ten years—years in which Streisand devoted herself to her homes as devoutly as she had devoted herself to her albums and films.[41] The perfectionist was perfecting life, turning hers into the sort of dreamy fantasies she had had as a girl. Basically, she was living within her movie.

If the homes provided the set, the furnishings provided the set design. Streisand had been a collector from the time she began her career. She collected everything: furniture, china, clothing, dolls, automobiles (in an art deco phase she had a 1933 burgundy Dodge and a 1926 Rolls-Royce Silver Ghost) and later art. And when she tired of a phase, as she did with art deco, she would sell off the items at auction.[42] When she wanted something, she could be dogged. Outbid for a Josef Hoffmann pin at an auction, she eventually traced it to a dealer in Germany, paid four times the auction cost, and then never wore it because, she admitted, it wasn't about the pin. It was about the sense of losing the pin. "Sometimes I think it's all connected to the loss of a parent," she would write, "because you'd do anything to get that mother or father back. But you can't . . . yet with objects there's a possibility."[43]

Others attributed her collecting to compensation for the things she lacked as a girl; her large antique doll collection, which she displayed in the faux doll shop named "Bee's" in the cellar of her new oceanfront home, was the overkill for having to use that hot water bottle as a doll. Still others said the collecting began as a way to keep company. Writer and director Frank Pierson, in his takedown of *A Star Is Born*, said Streisand had told him that when she was starting out in New York she lived alone and was never afraid. "Now she is terrified to ever be alone—especially in the big house, where every antique and precious thing, the Laliques and Klimts and Tiffanys, she says she has pasted a tag so in case it all evaporates some day, she'll know how much she paid for everything. The house is silent."[44] Camille Paglia thought her materialism, her "sharp deals, the acquisition of objects, the compulsive redecorating," was "her ritualistic way of anchoring herself in externals, of rebalancing herself against the buffering emotional vortex from which she draws her knowledge of the psyche."[45]

Streisand would offer two other explanations besides the idea that objects don't die whereas people do. The first had to do with her sense of impermanence, not of other people, but of herself. "I love the movies," she once said. "Life is so short that I want something to remain as proof that I existed. I think that's why I like antiques—because they have proven their immortality. They know something I don't."[46] The second reason was simpler and almost moving in its naïveté from the woman who had always proudly displayed her Jewishness and yet always felt like the Other. "I wanted to be Gentile," she said. "I wanted to have the things that all Gentiles have—like great art. I always thought that having French furniture and art was Gentile."[47] In this case, gentility was, to her, Gentile.

She had become a designer and architect. She spent most of her life now designing the Nantucket barn, and then deciding not to live in it after all because, as she put it, "I don't watch my movies after I make them. I don't listen to my records after I record them. So why would I live in the house that I built?," she built a magnificent main house on the property in which she would live.[48] She did return to the concert stage for a short tour in 2000, during which, in one Los Angeles show, she kicked off her high heels, waved to Elizabeth Taylor in the audience, and said, "I'm tired of putting on high heels, and I don't want to get dressed up anymore. I want to stay home and eat. We're eaters, right, Liz?"[49]

She said that she no longer felt the need to convince her mother of her worth, telling the *New York Times*, "I never liked to sing in front of my mother because it was always so embarrassing: I never knew what she was going to say. I never had that support. I never experienced it." But Brolin's family now provided what her own had not. "They're so accepting of me and so loving and so embracing, it's like this warm bath. I can't explain it. People are actually that way to me. I've never had that."[50] In fact, when Diana Kind was interviewed by Mike Wallace for a *60 Minutes* segment on Streisand and Wallace asked her if she were proud of her daughter, Diana still hedged. "Well, who wouldn't be?" "She was very defensive," Streisand later said. "She couldn't' say, 'I am proud.'"[51]

By this time, Diana Kind had moved to Los Angeles and was living with her other daughter, Roslyn, the pretty one to whom Barbra had been unfavorably compared, in a condominium Barbra had purchased for her. She died on March 27, 2002, after a fall. She was ninety-three, and she had never come to terms with her daughter's success, though in many ways, as Streisand herself would say, her mother's obduracy was central to that success. Streisand spent her life trying to honor the father she never knew and satisfy the mother she couldn't appease.

She had long been an icon, almost from the beginning of her career. She would go on to become a cherished point of identification to some, a caricature of the Jewish woman to others, and a monster to still others. And by the time she had reached her sixties, she would become something that only a handful of entertainers have ever become: a deity. This status might have intimidated her, made her feel as if she had to uphold it. Instead, it seemed to free her. As she told Oprah Winfrey after a 2006 concert tour, she had "said whatever I wanted" and "actually enjoyed myself." The reason? "It's about believing that I am enough."

When she returned to the screen in 2005 after her nearly nine-year absence, she played an oversexed Jewish mother married to an equally oversexed geriatric hippie, played by Dustin Hoffman, in *Meet the Fockers*, the sequel to *Meet the Parents*, which had been an enormous hit comedy for Ben Stiller, who played their son betrothed to a gentile girl whose family didn't fully accept him. Streisand's was a loose, liberated performance, which prompted one reporter to say, "Having taken on the industry and bent it to her will, it was as if finally she'd relaxed and just enjoyed herself on screen."[52] It was also her most Jewish performance in years. As Manohla Dargis observed in the *New York Times*, the film "hinges on the well-traveled idea that there's something comic about being Jewish in America. Not the Philip Roth, take-no-prisoners funny, in which Jewish identity is good, bad, happy, sad, a historical chip on the shoulder, a sign of radical difference. Rather, the post–Borscht Belt funny of the genial sitcom Jews whose difference is amorphous enough to be thoroughly unthreatening; the Jew as an ethnic accessory that non-Jews on both sides of the camera can enjoy without anxiety, like the cut cabala string Madonna likes to wear."[53] But Dargis didn't seem to realize how much of a sea change this was for Streisand. *She* had been the threatening Jew, the one with the "historical chip on her shoulder." *She* had been radically different from gentiles. If she had lost that edge, it wasn't because she had assimilated or been domesticated or even because society's attitude toward Jews generally had changed; it was because she had learned not to take herself so seriously and because she had become so much a part of our consciousness that we accepted her for who she was. The assimilation wasn't hers. It was ours.

To be sure, this was not the way everyone perceived her

performance. Rabbi Daniel Lapin, the Orthodox rabbi who had counseled Streisand on *Yentl* and instructed her in Judaism as he trained Jason for his Bar Mitzvah, had moved to the political right, and he was not amused. Moralistically incensed, he called the movie a "flagrant defamation of Judaism" and a "horrible excrescence," even invoking Adolf Hitler's *Mein Kampf* to illustrate how Jews like Streisand fuel anti-Semites by caricaturing Jews.[54] But his was a minority view—a right-wing Jew's diatribe that only served to demonstrate how much Streisand, no self-hating Jew, had won her point and had been a pioneer in challenging Jewish stereotypes. *Meet the Fockers* would be Barbra Streisand's highest-grossing film and one of the highest-grossing live action comedies to that point.

Over the next decade, she would record three more albums, raise money for countless charities, and perform publicly several more times, though perhaps never so touchingly as when she returned to her roots to open the Barclays Center on Flatbush Avenue in Brooklyn. The two concerts were billed "Back to Brooklyn," and, as Stephen Holden reported in the *New York Times*, they were a "sentimental homecoming and a royal act of noblesse oblige in which a show business monarch regaled the adoring subjects of her native province in a concert that was steeped in Brooklyn lore." Opening with "As If We Never Said Goodbye," from the musical *Sunset Boulevard*, outfitted with new lyrics that referenced Brooklyn's knishes, nova lox, and Erasmus High, Streisand, the woman of gentility, indulged her Brooklynness. One lyric in particular resonated: "Somehow I have always known the past is never past / Now I've waited long enough. I've come home at last." The audience roared. "I love people from Brooklyn because they're real," she told the cheering crowd. "Down to earth. They tell it like it is. That's because they have no manners," which was something she had said of herself when she was starting out.

The voice was different now, different even from when she

returned to the concert stage in 1994. It was darker, fuller, deeper in the lower registers. She didn't climb the scales quite as high as she used to, those Everest heights, though there weren't many notes she couldn't hit. Occasionally the voice frayed slightly at those registers. Nor did she do the *geshreying* the way she had as a young singer. But what she had lost in pyrotechnics and overdramatization, she had gained in emotion. She may be a better singer in her maturity than in her youth—a singer who not only acts her songs but has clearly lived them fully. In song after song, Streisand demonstrates not only the range of her voice but also the range of her emotions. Singing Jule Styne's "Being Good Is Not Good Enough" from *Hallelujah, Baby*, Streisand is obviously telling her own story: "I'll be the best or nothing at all," she concludes. She was.

Stephen Holden found "appetite, curiosity, yearning—whatever you call it—" a quality "embedded in her voice." He ended his review: "Like few singers of any age, she has the gift of conveying a primal human longing in a beautiful sound."[55] All this was true. But everyone also seemed to realize that, as often with Streisand, the concert was not merely a concert. It wasn't even just a homecoming. It was a reminder. Molly Haskell, in analyzing Streisand's popularity in 1975, had written that stars typically become stars through synthesis—by "meaning many things to many people." Not Streisand. "Streisand's way is not synthesis, but alternation. She leaps like a self-propelling pendulum between the raucous Jewish kook and cultured lady, her singing voice WASP [not entirely true], her speaking voice Jewish. It's as if the triumph of Streisand wouldn't taste so sweet without the constant reminder of where she'd been."[56] Now she hadn't just come home. She had come full circle; as she told the crowd, it was the first time she had sung in Brooklyn since she was a little girl on a stoop on Pulaski Street. "Back to Brooklyn" was a reminder to us and to herself of who she was and what remarkable things she had accomplished against nearly impossible odds. It was a reminder of Streisand's conquest.

The miracle of Streisand's career wasn't the way she managed to invade popular culture and enter the national consciousness. Others had done that. The miracle was how deeply she was embedded in that consciousness and how long she managed to stay there—over fifty years. When in 1991 *Saturday Night Live* comedian Mike Myers created his character Linda Richman, the middle-aged Jewish mistress of the kaffeeklatsch, who would get verklempt just thinking of the divine Streisand, whose voice she described as "buttah," part of the joke was how much Streisand had come to mean to women like Richman that they would deify her. At the end of one sketch, Streisand made an appearance herself, sending Richman into paroxysms of ecstasy. She made another surprise appearance in 2001 during the Emmy Award broadcast, which had been rescheduled after 9/11, and sang the finale, "You'll Never Walk Alone"—Streisand as national healer. A fan opened a Streisand museum in the Castro District of San Francisco called "Hello, Gorgeous!" Its proprietor, who had mortgaged his home to finance it, told the *New York Times*, "With my own background, being a gay man, being oppressed, I feel my life is very parallel."[57] Wayne Koestenbaum wrote a poem about her in which he dreams of seeing rare Streisand albums being sold in the rain—Streisand Sings Stravinsky, Schoenberg, Chomsky. The album covers featured Streisand in Cindy Sherman guise. And in the dream she becomes every bit as much a deity as she was for Linda Richman: "on a damask fauteuil I accepted extreme unction / while lip-synching a samizdat, Streisand *Sings* Schiele."[58]

There would be many more honors, including the Kennedy Center Honors in 2008. There would be yet another number one album, *Partners*, a series of duets, in 2014, which would be her eighth at the top of the *Billboard* list, and make her the first performer to have a top album in five different decades. There would be an appearance on *The Tonight Show* with Jimmy Fallon, her first in nearly fifty years since she was banned from the show after getting a case of stage fright and standing up Johnny Carson, where Fallon called her "one of the biggest stars in the history of show business" and treated her reverentially.

There would be another film, *Guilt Trip*, about a Jewish mother who accompanies her son (Seth Rogen) on a cross-country journey—a comic trifle but not piffle. It was a movie that, like nearly all her movies, seemed to be drawn from her own life and played out her own psychic drama, and it was yet another story of reconciliation. One scene, in which the son, Andy, enters his mother's room to find her asleep as a video of him in his childhood runs where she coos, "I love you, Andy. You're my perfect boy," and he lifts the glasses from her, is a nearly exact replication of a scene in *Yentl* where she lifts the glasses off her sleeping father—another role reversal, this time not of gender but of age. There is a scene in which she gobbles m&m's that echoes a scene in *Mirror* where she sneaks contraband Hostess Sno Balls, and she delivers the line "Food is love," which was taken directly from her mother. There is the parody of her diva image when she hits a motor hotel and calls it "absolute heaven." And there is the ending in which she is verklempt over her son's love for her. If *Yentl* was in some ways a means for her to deal with the loss of her father and *Prince of Tides* a means for her to deal with her mother, *Guilt Trip* seems a means for her to express her love to her son. It is surprisingly heartfelt and even moving.

And there was, perhaps above all, the contentment of having come to terms with her accomplishments. At the close of her book, *My Passion for Design*, in which she describes the building of her oceanfront homes, she writes, "I no longer have to document everything I see. All that's left to do now is to be in the moment . . . and enjoy it."[59] She hadn't entirely left us.

But she didn't need us. Her career could end, and it would be complete.

What had it all meant? Of course there was the extraordinary talent—the voice that may have been the greatest of her generation and the art of interpretation that was rivaled possibly only by Sinatra. More, she had changed the way singers sang by creating new ways of approaching a song—speaking it rather than singing it, reinflecting it with her elongations and soaring melismas, making sounds beautiful. And she had revealed a *process* of artistic creation that was itself an inspiration. According to Tennessee Williams, most artists seduced their art, approaching it gingerly, teasing it out. "Barbra Streisand does not do this. There is no need for what I'll call artistic foreplay," he said, "because she has already conquered and organized and recruited all of her talents, and they would not dream of straying from her orbit, so there is no need for gentle steps, remonstrations, bargains: She owns and controls—masters— her talent so the art appears." He called this "exuberating": a "lesson, an example of how it is done."[60]

She always seemed to be an example. She was an example of chutzpah. As one fan would say of Streisand's legacy, "For me, it began with her first revelation: by shoving a Jewish girl's face in front of the cameras she was announcing, beneath all the self-deprecation, I'm here, I'm a bagel, and you're gonna learn to love me."[61] She was an example of how to succeed. "Hers has been a career built on telling herself—telling everyone—that when what you're reaching for is just over the horizon," biographer Tom Santopietro wrote, "the only way you'll get there is to try harder, to keep showing everyone, to keep topping yourself."[62] *Being good is not good enough.* She was an example of power as well as perseverance. Another Streisand biographer, Anne Edwards, said that Streisand did not relate to her audiences the way Judy Garland or Edith Piaf did, singers to whom she had been compared. They displayed their victimhood. They suffered, even in the strain with which they delivered their songs, and their audiences shared their suffering. Streisand experienced her own suffering, but she was no victim. She hit back. As Edwards put it, "Streisand fans are not sharing her pain, they are celebrating her strength to overcome the obstacles that they perceive she has overcome—turning homely into beautiful, making ethnic mainstream, daring to cross over into a man's world as director, producer, business executive."[63] And though Edwards didn't say it, she even overcame the hostility she elicited for the strength she exhibited. Many resented her. Streisand didn't seem to care.

But none of this would have been possible if Streisand hadn't been that homely Jewish girl from Brooklyn. Without those Jewish roots, there would have been no Jewish metaphor. There would have been no sense of otherness, no hostility to her looks and her manner, no harping on her loudness and boldness and bossiness and indomitability and her lack of femininity, and there would have been no loneliness for her audience to feel and with which it could identify, no transformation of the ideal of beauty, no acceptance of women on-screen to be as self-possessed as men had always been allowed to be, no sense that a woman could will herself to be strong and beautiful and desirable, no feeling that, as Pauline Kael had put it so long ago, talent was beauty. None of these things would have been possible without Jewishness, and none of them would likely have been possible without Streisand. Felicia Herman concluded that "Streisand's lasting legacy may be that her characters have provided a bridge between a film world where Jews barely existed and where women were valued only for their looks and their submissiveness, and a world yet to come, where both Jews and women are treated with the respect, complexity, and richness they deserve."[64]

That would be a tremendous legacy—a life-justifying legacy. But what Streisand did is more than provide a bridge with her characters and with her own life. She provided a metaphor—that Jewish metaphor. Barbra Streisand showed us, all of us, how to live in the teeth of rejection and how to surmount any obstacle. Barbra Streisand showed us how to convert the worst of criticisms into the best of results, how to take our insecurities and discover our securities within them. Barbra Streisand showed us, especially the outsiders among us, how to survive. She showed us how to triumph. And, perhaps above all, she showed us how to live on our own terms—just as she always had.

NOTES

An Introduction: Shaynkeit

1. Michael Shnayerson, "The Way She Is," *Vanity Fair*, November 1994.

2. Glenn Gould, "Streisand as Schwarzkopf," *High Fidelity*, May 1976, in *Diva: Barbra Streisand and the Making of a Superstar*, ed. Ethlie Ann Vare (New York: Boulevard Books, 1996), 39; Robert Sandall, "The Price of Fame," *London Times*, April 24, 1994, in Vare, *Diva*, 52.

3. Quoted in James Grissom, "Barbra Streisand: The Ideal Eucharist, Part One," jamesgrissom (blog), November 13, 2012, http://jamesgrissom.blogspot.com/2012/11/barbra-streisand-ideal-eucharist-part.html?q=Streisand.

4. Deborah Kass quoted in David E. Kaufman, *Jewhooing the Sixties: American Celebrity and Jewish Identity* (Waltham, MA: Brandeis University Press, 2008), 262.

5. Barbra Streisand as told to Dixie Dean Harris, "I Was an Ugly Duckling," *Coronet*, March 1964, in Vare, *Diva*, 25.

6. "Interview," *Playboy*, October 1977.

7. Quoted in Kaufman, *Jewhooing the Sixties*, 221.

8. Camille Paglia, "Brooklyn Nefertiti: Barbra Streisand," in *Vamps and Tramps* (New York: Vintage, 1994), 142.

9. Calev Ben-David quoted in Kaufman, *Jewhooing the Sixties*, 248.

10. Leslie and Joyce Field, *Bernard Malamud: A Collection of Critical Essays* (Englewood, NJ: Prentice-Hall, 1975), 11.

11. "Campus Crusader," *Heeb*, December 13, 2007, http://heeb magazine.com/campus-crusader-2/1121.

12. Pauline Kael, *Going Steady* (New York: Bantam, 1971), 161.

13. Grissom, "Barbra Streisand."

14. Arthur Laurents, *Original Story By: A Memoir of Broadway and Hollywood* (New York: Knopf, 2000), 226.

15. Streisand, "I Was an Ugly Duckling," 26.

1. Mieskeit

1. Anne Edwards, *Streisand: A Biography* (Boston: Little, Brown, 1997), 35.

2. Quoted in David McCullough, *Brooklyn and How It Got That Way* (New York: Dial, 1983), frontispiece.

3. Philip Lopate, "Brooklyn the Unknowable," in *The Best American Essays 2010*, ed. Christopher Hitchens (Boston: Houghton Mifflin Harcourt, 2010), 123.

4. Lopate, "Brooklyn the Unknowable," 115.

5. Pete Hamill, "Goodbye Brooklyn, Hello Fame," *Saturday Evening Post*, July 27, 1963.

6. Lopate, "Brooklyn the Unknowable," 116.

7. Peter Evans, "From Barbra Streisand—The Last Word," *Cosmopolitan*, February 1974.

8. James Spada, *Streisand: Her Life* (New York: Crown, 1995), 22.

9. Edwards, *Streisand*, 32–33.

10. Spada, *Streisand*, 9.

11. William Mann, *Hello, Gorgeous: Becoming Barbra Streisand* (New York: Houghton Mifflin Harcourt, 2012), 29.

12. Edwards, *Streisand*, 32–38.

13. Anne Fadiman, "Barbra Puts Her Career on the Line with 'Yentl,'" *Life*, December 1983.

14. Mann, *Hello, Gorgeous*, 10.

15. Paul Rosenfield, "Barbra's New Direction," *Ladies Home Journal*, February 1992.

16. Celia Walden, "Barbra Streisand Interview," *Telegraph*, August 16, 2011.

17. Chaim Potok, "The Barbra Streisand Nobody Knows," *Esquire*, Autumn 1992.

18. Hilary de Vries, "Streisand, the Storyteller," *Los Angeles Times Magazine*, December 8, 1991.

19. Brad Darrach, "Celebration of a Father," *People*, December 12, 1983; Edwards, *Streisand*, 40–41, 43, 46.

20. Darrach, "Celebration of a Father."

21. "Barbra Streisand," *Inside the Actors Studio*, hosted by James Lipton, Bravo, recorded September 8, 2003, broadcast March 21, 2004.

22. Spada, *Streisand*, 17.

23. Edwards, *Streisand*, 47.

24. Spada, *Streisand*, 20.

25. Spada, *Streisand*, 21.

26. Kevin Sessums, "Queen of Tides," *Vanity Fair*, September 1991.

27. Spada, *Streisand*, 28; Edwards, *Streisand*, 52.

28. Mann, *Hello, Gorgeous*, 31.

29. Edwards, *Streisand*, 49.

30. Spada, *Streisand*, 36.

31. Spada, *Streisand*, 22.

32. Nora Ephron, "The Private World of Barbra Streisand," *Good Housekeeping*, April 1969.

33. Spada, *Streisand*, 18.

34. Edwards, *Streisand*, 285.

35. Potok, "The Barbra Streisand Nobody Knows."

36. Mann, *Hello, Gorgeous*, 33.

37. Edwards, *Streisand*, 50.

38. Oprah Winfrey, "Oprah Winfrey Talks to Barbra Streisand," *O, the Oprah Magazine*, October 2006.

39. Gloria Steinem, "Barbra Streisand Talks about Her Million Dollar Baby," *Ladies Home Journal*, August 1966.

40. Edwards, *Streisand*, 54.

41. Mann, *Hello, Gorgeous*, 17.

42. Ephron, "Private World of Barbra Streisand."

43. Edwards, *Streisand*, 45–46.

44. Edwards, *Streisand*, 51.

45. Edwards, *Streisand*, 56.

46. Edwards, *Streisand*, 50–51.

47. Mann, *Hello, Gorgeous*, 33.

48. Edwards, *Streisand*, 28.

49. Darrach, "Celebration of a Father."

50. Anthony Tommasini, "Streisand's Fine Instrument and Classic Instinct," *New York Times*, September 24, 2009.

51. Quoted in Spada, *Streisand*, 24.

52. Tommasini, "Streisand's Fine Instrument and Classic Instinct."

53. Spada, *Streisand*, 19.

54. Spada, *Streisand*, 25.

55. Edwards, *Streisand*, 53.

56. Spada, *Streisand*, 26–27.

57. Christopher Andersen, *Barbra: The Way She Is* (New York: William Morrow, 2006), 38.

58. Spada, *Streisand*, 31.

59. Martin H. Levinson, *Brooklyn Boomer: Growing Up in the Fifties* (Bloomington, IN: iUniverse, 2011), 58.

60. "The Girl," *Time*, April 10, 1964.

61. Barbra Streisand as told to Dixie Dean Harris, "I Was an Ugly Duckling," *Coronet*, March 1964, in *Diva: Barbra Streisand and the Making of a Superstar*, ed. Ethlie Ann Vare (New York: Boulevard Books, 1996), 21.

62. Lawrence Grobel, "Barbra Streisand: 'I'm Just Beginning to Accept Myself,'" *Long Island Newsday*, October 16, 1977.

63. Spada, *Streisand*, 29.

64. Andersen, *Barbra*, 39.

65. Spada, *Streisand*, 37.

66. "The Girl."

67. Steinem, "Barbra Streisand Talks about Her Million Dollar Baby."

68. Shaun Considine, *Barbra Streisand: The Woman, the Myth* (New York: Delacorte, 1985), 45.

69. "Streisand," *Inside the Actors Studio;* Mann, *Hello, Gorgeous*, 53.

70. Spada, *Streisand*, 51.

71. Andersen, *Barbra*, 48.

72. Considine, *Barbra Streisand*, 44.

73. Shana Alexander, "A Born Loser's Success and Precarious Love," *Life*, May 22, 1964.

74. Diana Lurie, "They All Come Thinking I Can't Be That Great," *Life*, March 18, 1966.

75. Polly Devlin, "Instant Barbra," *Vogue*, March 15, 1966.

76. Devlin, "Instant Barbra."

77. "Streisand," *Inside the Actors Studio.*

78. Amy Chua and Jed Rubenfeld, "What Drives Success?" *New York Times*, January 25, 2014.

79. "Streisand," *Inside the Actors Studio.*

80. Spada, *Streisand*, 29.

81. Andersen, *Barbra*, 32.

82. Spada, *Streisand*, 26.

83. Mann, *Hello, Gorgeous*, 30.

84. Spada, *Streisand*, 32.

85. Spada, *Streisand*, 40–41.

86. Spada, *Streisand*, 46–47.

87. Edwards, *Streisand*, 73.

88. Pete Hamill, "Goodbye Brooklyn, Hello Fame," *Saturday Evening Post*, July 27, 1963.

2. Chutzpah

1. "The Girl," *Time*, April 10, 1964.

2. Shaun Considine, *Barbra Streisand: The Woman, the Myth, the Music* (New York: Delacorte, 1985), 78.

3. James Spada, *Streisand: Her Life* (New York: Crown, 1995), 56.

4. Spada, *Streisand*, 56–57.

5. A. J. Waldman, *The Barbra Streisand Scrapbook* (New York: Citadel, 1995), 231.

6. Considine, *Barbra Streisand*, 11.

7. Spada, *Streisand*, 59.

8. Spada, *Streisand*, 59; William Mann, *Hello, Gorgeous: Becoming Barba Streisand* (New York: Houghton Mifflin Harcourt, 2012), 14.

9. Christopher Andersen, *Barbra: The Way She Is* (New York: William Morrow, 2006), 60.

10. Nora Ephron, "The Private World of Barbra Streisand," *Good Housekeeping*, April 1969.

11. Milton Greene, "In Their Tense Demanding World, Alone Is Beautiful," *McCall's*, January 1970.

12. Andersen, *Barbra*, 118.

13. Mann, *Hello, Gorgeous*, 15.

14. Barry Dennen, *My Life with Barbra: A Love Story* (Amherst, NY: Prometheus Books, 1997), 125.

15. Mann, *Hello, Gorgeous*, 17.

16. Spada, *Streisand*, 47–48.

17. "Barbra Streisand," *Inside the Actors Studio*, hosted by James Lipton, Bravo, recorded September 8, 2003, broadcast March 21, 2004.

18. Spada, *Streisand*, 434–435.

19. Mann, *Hello, Gorgeous*, 28.

20. "Interview," *Playboy*, October 1977.

21. Andersen, *Barbra*, 16.

22. Dennen, *My Life with Barbra*, 27–28.

23. Mann, *Hello, Gorgeous*, 17.

24. Lawrence Schiller, "Who Am I Anyway?" *Life*, January 9, 1970.

25. Dennen, *My Life with Barbra*, 26.

26. Anne Edwards, *Streisand: A Biography* (Boston: Little, Brown, 1997), 99.

27. Chaim Potok, "The Barbra Streisand Nobody Knows," *Esquire*, Autumn 1982.

28. Mann, *Hello, Gorgeous*, 35.

29. Spada, *Streisand*, 57.

30. Potok, "The Barbra Streisand Nobody Knows."

31. Kevin Sessums, "Queen of Tides," *Vanity Fair*, September 1991.

32. Edwards, *Streisand*, 79–80.

33. Dennen, *My Life with Barbra*, 71.

34. Edwards, *Streisand*, 87.

35. Spada, *Streisand*, 62–63.

36. "Interview."

37. Dennen, *My Life with Barbra*, 97–98.

38. Mann, *Hello, Gorgeous*, 45.

39. Andersen, *Barbra*, 135.

40. Andersen, *Barbra*, 91.

41. Dennen, *My Life with Barbra*, 238.

42. Spada, *Streisand*, 234.

43. Mann, *Hello, Gorgeous*, 411.

44. Dennen, *My Life with Barbra*, 98.

45. Dennen, *My Life with Barbra*, 47.

46. Mann, *Hello, Gorgeous*, 48–49.

47. Dennen, *My Life with Barbra*, 100–101.

48. Spada, *Streisand*, 64–66.

49. "Streisand," *Inside the Actors Studio*.

50. Edwards, *Streisand*, 99.

51. Considine, *Barbra Streisand*, 12.

52. Mann, *Hello, Gorgeous*, 406.

53. Barbra Streisand, *My Passion for Design* (New York: Viking, 2010), 210.

54. Mann, *Hello, Gorgeous*, 126.

55. Mann, *Hello, Gorgeous*, 84.

56. Andersen, *Barbra*, 61.

57. Edwards, *Streisand*, 106.

58. Mann, *Hello, Gorgeous*, 84–85.

59. Edwards, *Streisand*, 107.

60. Bernard Weinraub, "Barbra Streisand: Still Not Pretty Enough," *New York Times*, November 13, 1996.

61. Dennen, *My Life with Barbra*, 197.

62. Andersen, *Barbra*, 74–75.

63. Spada, *Streisand*, 77.

64. Dennen, *My Life with Barbra*, 64.

65. Camille Paglia, "Brooklyn Nefertiti: Barbra Streisand," in *Vamps and Tramps* (New York: Vintage, 1994), 142.

66. Dennen, *My Life with Barbra*, 63.

67. Spada, *Streisand*, 79, 85.

68. Dennen, *My Life with Barbra*, 172; Edwards, *Streisand*, 114–115.

69. Mann, *Hello, Gorgeous*, 90–91.

70. Barbra Streisand as told to Dixie Dean Harris, "I Was an Ugly Duckling," *Coronet*, March 1964, in *Diva: Barbra Streisand and the Making of a Superstar*, ed. Ethlie Ann Vare (New York: Boulevard Books, 1966), 22.

71. Shana Alexander, "A Born Loser's Success and Precarious Love," *Life*, May 22, 1964.

72. Edwards, *Streisand*, 102.

73. Considine, *Barbra Streisand*, 120.

74. Mann, *Hello, Gorgeous*, 126–127.

75. Joanne Stang, "She Couldn't Be Medium," *New York Times*, April 5, 1964.

76. Spada, *Streisand*, 88.

77. David E. Kaufman, *Jewhooing the Sixties: American Celebrity and Jewish Identity* (Waltham, MA: Brandeis University Press, 2012), 220.

78. Mann, *Hello, Gorgeous*, 123.

79. "Talk of the Town," *New Yorker*, May 19, 1962.

80. Kaufman, *Jewhooing the Sixties*, 224–225.

81. Todd Gold, "Barbra Streisand: The Farewell Interview," *US*, October 9, 2000.

82. Streisand, "I Was an Ugly Duckling."

83. Edwards, *Streisand*, 116.

84. Mann, *Hello, Gorgeous*, 266.

85. Kaufman, *Jewhooing the Sixties*, 226.

86. Ephron, "Private World of Barbra Streisand."

87. Mann, *Hello, Gorgeous*, 98–99.

88. Jerome Weidman, "I Remember Barbra," *Holiday*, November 1963, in Vare, *Diva*, 6.

89. Arthur Laurents, *Original Story By: A Memoir of Broadway and Hollywood* (New York: Knopf, 2000), 222.

90. Weidman, "I Remember Barbra," 10.

91. Spada, *Streisand*, 97.

92. Spada, *Streisand*, 97.

93. Laurents, *Original Story By*, 236.

94. Weidman, "I Remember Barbra," 14–15.

95. Dennen, *My Life with Barbra*, 234–235.

96. Edwards, *Streisand*, 128.

97. Considine, *Barbra Streisand*, 20.

98. Mann, *Hello, Gorgeous*, 217.

3. Tsezingen Zikh

1. *Variety*, May 30, 1962.

2. "New Face," *Time*, January 25, 1963.

3. Robert Ruark, "She'll Cry You a River," [Sarasota] *Herald-Tribune*, January 20, 1963.

4. Anne Edwards, *Streisand: A Biography* (Boston: Little, Brown, 1997), 145.

5. William Mann, *Hello, Gorgeous: Becoming Barbra Streisand* (New York: Houghton Mifflin Harcourt, 2012), 108, 111.

6. Chaim Potok, "The Barbra Streisand Nobody Knows," *Esquire*, Autumn 1962.

7. Shaun Considine, *Barbra Streisand: The Woman, the Myth, the Music* (New York: Delacorte, 1985), 15.

8. Arthur Laurents, *Original Story By: A Memoir of Broadway and Hollywood* (New York: Knopf, 2000), 222.

9. Considine, *Barbra Streisand*, 17.

10. Laurents, *Original Story By*, 223.

11. Considine, *Barbra Streisand*, 17.

12. Considine, *Barbra Streisand*, 22–23.

13. Mann, *Hello, Gorgeous*, 259.

14. Edwards, *Streisand*, 134.

15. Mann, *Hello, Gorgeous*, 282–283.

16. James Spada, *Streisand: Her Life* (New York: Crown, 1995), 113.

17. Considine, *Barbra Streisand*, 26.

18. Spada, *Streisand*, 118; Mann, *Hello, Gorgeous*, 300.

19. Spada, *Streisand*, 118.

20. Considine, *Barbra Streisand*, 156.

21. Christopher Andersen, *Barbra: The Way She Is* (New York: William Morrow, 2006), 98.

22. Joseph Morgenstern, "Superstar: The Streisand Story," *Newsweek*, January 5, 1970.

23. Tom Santopietro, *The Importance of Being Barbra* (New York: St. Martin's, 2006), 15.

24. "Interview," *Playboy*, October 1977.

25. Spada, *Streisand*, 125–126. Another source says 101 weeks.

26. Mann, *Hello, Gorgeous*, 342.

27. Mann, *Hello, Gorgeous*, 334, 338.

28. Andersen, *Barbra*, 103.

29. Rick Du Brow, "Song Stylist Streisand Saves Keefe Brasselle TV Opener," June 26, 1963, available at *Barbra Streisand Archives*, http://barbra-archives.com/tv/60s/keefe_brasselle_show _streisand.html.

30. Considine, *Barbra Streisand*, 51.

31. Andersen, *Barbra*, 108.

32. Considine, *Barbra Streisand*, 56.

33. "The Girl," *Time*, April 10, 1964.

34. Laurents, *Original Story By*, 226.

35. Barbra Streisand as told to Dixie Dean Harris, "I Was an Ugly Duckling," *Coronet*, March 1964, in *Diva: Barbra Streisand and the Making of a Superstar*, ed. Ethlie Ann Vare (New York: Boulevard Books, 1996), 21–26.

36. Considine, *Barbra Streisand*, 97.

37. Pete Hamill, "Goodbye Brooklyn, Hello Fame," *Saturday Evening Post*, July 27, 1963.

38. Maureen Dowd, "Barbra the Speech Plays to a Packed House at Harvard," *New York Times*, February 4, 1994.

39. Considine, *Barbra Streisand*, 26.

40. Mann, *Hello, Gorgeous*, 341.

41. Considine, *Barbra Streisand*, 73.

42. "Bea, Billie and Barbra," *Newsweek*, June 3, 1963n in Vare, *Diva*, 28.

43. June Sochen, "From Sophie Tucker to Barbra Streisand," in *Talking Back: Images of Jewish Women in American Popular Culture*, ed. Joyce Antler (Hanover, NH: Brandeis University Press, 1998), 78.

44. Felicia Herman, "The Way She Really Is: Images of Jews and Women in the Films of Barbra Streisand," in Antler, *Talking Back*, 172.

45. Janet Jakobsen, "Queers Are Like Jews, Aren't They? Analogy and Alliance Politics," in *Queer Theory and the Jewish Question*, ed. Daniel Boyarin, Daniel Itzkovitz, and Ann Pellegrini (New York: Columbia University Press, 2003), 83.

46. "Barbra Streisand," *Inside the Actors Studio*, hosted by James Lipton, Bravo, recorded September 8, 2003, broadcast March 21, 2004.

47. Todd Gold, "Barbra Streisand: The Farewell Interview," *US*, October 9, 2000.

48. Andre Agassi, *Open: An Autobiography* (New York: Knopf, 2009), 173–174.

49. Gold, "Barbra Streisand."

50. Anthony Tommasini, "Streisand's Fine Instrument and Classic Instinct," *New York Times*, September 24, 2009.

51. Mann, *Hello, Gorgeous*, 68.

52. Lawrence Schiller, "Who Am I Anyway?" *Life*, January 9, 1970.

53. Emory Lewis, "Bravos for Barbra," *Cue*, December 26, 1963.

54. Tommasini, "Streisand's Fine Instrument and Classic Instinct."

55. Roger Ames, interview by author, July 31, 2014.

56. Laurents, *Original Story By*, 222.

57. Streisand, "I Was an Ugly Duckling."

58. Pete Hamill, *Why Sinatra Matters* (Boston: Little, Brown, 1998), 115–116.

59. Gay Talese, "Frank Sinatra Has a Cold," *Esquire*, April 1966.

60. Hamill, *Why Sinatra Matters*, 69–70.

61. Santopietro, *Importance of Being Barbra*, 48.

62. Hamill, "Goodbye Brooklyn, Hello Fame."

63. Gene Lees, *Singers and the Song* (New York: Oxford University Press, 1987), 103.

64. Hamill, "Goodbye Brooklyn, Hello Fame."

65. Kevin Sessums, "Queen of Tides," *Vanity Fair*, September 1991.

66. Herb Michaelson, "Interview with Judy Davis, Vocal Coach," April 3, 1964, available at *Barbra Streisand Archives*, http://barbra-archives.com/bjs_library/60s/judy_davis_story_1964.html.

67. Hilary de Vries, "Streisand, the Storyteller," *Los Angeles Times Magazine*, December 8, 1991.

68. Diana Lurie, "They All Come Thinking I Can't Be That Great," *Life*, March 18, 1966.

69. Schiller, "Who Am I Anyway?"

70. Edwards, *Streisand*, 273.

71. Lees, *Singers and the Song*, 106.

72. Glenn Gould, "Streisand as Schwartzkopf," *High Fidelity*, May 1976, in Vare, *Diva*, 40.

73. Hamill, *Why Sinatra Matters*, 42.

74. Lees, *Singers and the Song*, 112.

75. Hamill, *Why Sinatra Matters*, 94.

76. For a fuller discussion of schwa, see Alicia Okrent, "The Schwa Is the Laziest Sound in All of Human Speech," *Slate.com*, June 5, 2014, http://www.slate.com/blogs/lexicon_valley/2014/06/05/schwa_the_word_for_the_most_common_vowel_sound_in _english_comes_from_hebrew.html.

77. Roger Ames interview.

78. Emory Lewis, "Bravos for Barbra," *Cue*, December 26, 1963.

79. Jerome Robbins, "Barbra Streisand," *McCall's*, October 1966.

4. Bine Aktrise

1. Eric A. Goldman, *The American Jewish Story through Cinema* (Austin: University of Texas Press, 2013), 126.

2. William Mann, *Hello, Gorgeous: Becoming Barbra Streisand* (New York: Houghton Mifflin Harcourt, 2012), 423.

3. Mann, *Hello, Gorgeous*, 206.

4. "Interview," *Playboy*, October 1977.

5. James Spada, *Streisand: Her Life* (New York: Crown, 1995), 139.

6. Mann, *Hello, Gorgeous*, 265.

7. Mann, *Hello, Gorgeous*, 278–279.

8. Anne Edwards, *Streisand: A Biographer* (Boston: Little, Brown, 1997), 164–165.

9. Mann, *Hello, Gorgeous*, 414.

10. Mann, *Hello, Gorgeous*, 416.

11. Mann, *Hello, Gorgeous*, 18.

12. Spada, *Streisand*, 142.

13. Chris Andersen, *Barbra: The Way It Was* (New York: William Morrow, 2006), 117.

14. Jerome Robbins, "Barbra Streisand," *McCall's*, October 1966.

15. Mann, *Hello, Gorgeous*, 422.

16. Mann, *Hello, Gorgeous*, 403.

17. Joanne Stang, "She Couldn't Be Medium," *New York Times*, April 5, 1964.

18. Shaun Considine, *Barbra Streisand: The Woman, the Myth, the Music* (New York: Delacorte, 1985), 65; "Interview."

19. Mann, *Hello, Gorgeous*, 458–459.

20. "The Girl," *Time*, April 10, 1964.

21. "The Girl."

22. Andersen, *Barbra*, 123.

23. Barbra Streisand Archives, http://barbra-archives.com/live/60s/hollywood_bowl_67_streisand.html.

24. Shana Alexander, "A Born Loser's Success and Precarious Love," *Life*, May 22, 1964.

25. Considine, *Barbra Streisand*, 65.

26. Howard Taubman, "Funny Girl," *New York Times*, March 27, 1964.

27. Spada, *Streisand*, 152.

28. Spada, *Streisand*, 150.

29. Stang, "She Couldn't Be Medium."

30. Stang, "She Couldn't Be Medium."

31. Alexander, "Born Loser's Success and Precarious Love."

32. Spada, *Streisand*, 164.

33. Alexander, "Born Loser's Success and Precarious Love."

34. Polly Devlin, "Instant Barbra," *Vogue*, March 15, 1966.

35. Alexander, "Born Loser's Success and Precarious Love."

36. Rick Du Brow quoted in Spada, *Streisand*, 165.

37. Rick Du Brow quoted in Spada, *Streisand*, 156–157.

38. Mann, *Hello, Gorgeous*, 482.

39. Arthur Laurents, *Original Story By: A Memoir of Broadway and Hollywood* (New York: Knopf, 2000), 244.

40. Considine, *Barbra Streisand*, 83.

41. Spada, *Streisand*, 152.

42. Andersen, *Barbra*, 85.

43. Edwards, *Streisand*, 182.

44. Diana Lurie, "They All Come Thinking I Can't Be That Great," *Life*, March 18, 1966.

45. Spada, *Streisand*, 151.

46. Lurie, "They All Come Thinking."

47. Lurie, "They All Come Thinking."

48. "Flip-Side Streisand," *Time*, April 8, 1966.

49. Rex Reed, "Color Barbra Very Bright," *New York Times*, March 27, 1966.

50. Spada, *Streisand*, 169.

51. Celia Walden, "The Barbra Streisand Interview," *Telegraph*, August 16, 2011.

52. Laurents, *Original Story By*, 244.

5. Holivaud

1. See my book *An Empire of Their Own: How the Jews Invented Hollywood* (New York: Crown, 1988).

2. Paul Rosenfield,"Barbra's New Direction," *Ladies Home Journal*, February 1992.

3. Anne Edwards, *Streisand: A Biography* (Boston: Little, Brown, 1997), 242–243.

4. James Spada, *Streisand: Her Life* (New York: Crown, 1995), 207.

5. Spada, *Streisand*, 203.

6. Spada, *Streisand*, 201–202.

7. Chris Andersen, *Barbra: The Way She Is* (New York: William Morrow, 2006), 163.

8. Joseph Morgenstern, "Superstar: The Streisand Story," *Newsweek*, January 5, 1970.

9. Pete Hamill, "Barbra the Great: Talented Girl on a Triumphal March," *Cosmopolitan*, February 1968.

10. Hamill, "Barbra the Great."

11. John S. Wilson, "Barbra Streisand's Free Sing-In Jams Sheep Meadow in the Park," *New York Times*, June 18, 1967.

12. The movies as a percentage of US spectator recreational spending had steadily fallen throughout the 1950s and 1960s from 77 percent in 1950 to 48 percent in 1969, when *Funny Girl* had the bulk of its grosses. In the same period, the movies had fallen nearly two-thirds as a percentage of personal spending. See Cobbett Steinberg, *Reel Facts* (New York: Vintage, 1978), 373.

13. Morgenstern, "Superstar."

14. Stanley Kauffmann, "Funny Girl," in *Figures of Light* (New York: Harper Colophon, 1971), 114–115.

15. Renata Adler, "Funny Girl," *New York Times*, September 20, 1968.

16. Pauline Kael, "Bravo," in *Going Steady* (New York: Bantam, 1971), 161–166.

17. Pauline Kael, "Teamwork," in *Deeper into Movies* (Boston: Atlantic Monthly Press, 1973), 185.

18. Morgenstern, "Superstar."

19. Edwards, *Streisand*, 262.

20. Andersen, *Barbra*, 173.

21. Spada, *Streisand*, 212–213.

22. Nora Ephron, "The Private World of Barbra Streisand," *Good Housekeeping*, April 1969.

23. Spada, *Streisand*, 217.

24. Kael, "Keep Going," in *Deeper into Movies*, 80–85.

25. Morgenstern, "Superstar."

26. Arthur Laurents, *Original Story By: A Memoir of Broadway and Hollywood* (New York: Knopf, 2000), 226.

27. Jerome Robbins, "Barbra Streisand," *McCall's*, October 1966.

28. John Halowell, "Funny Girl Goes West," *Life*, September 20, 1967.

29. Sander Gilman, *The Jew's Body* (New York: Routledge, 1991), 180.

30. Gilman, *Jew's Body*, 180.

31. "Barbra Streisand: The Girl Who Catches the Light," *Vogue*, April 1966.

32. David E. Kaufman, *Jewhooing the Sixties: American Celebrity and Jewish Identity*. Waltham, MA: Brandeis University Press, 2012), 221.

33. Gloria Steinem, "Barbra Streisand Talks about Her Million Dollar Baby," *Ladies Home Journal*, August 1966.

34. Kaufman, *Jewhooing the Sixties*, 214.

35. Henry Bial, *Acting Jewish: Negotiating Ethnicity on the American Stage and Screen* (Ann Arbor: University of Michigan Press, 2005), 91.

36. "Interview," *Playboy*, October 1977.

37. "Interview."

38. Shaun Considine, *Barbra Streisand: The Woman, the Myth* (New York: Delacorte, 1985), 150.

39. Spada, *Streisand*, 229.

40. "Interview."

41. For a fuller examination, see Sander L. Gilman, "Happi-

ness and Unhappiness as a 'Jewish Question,'" *Social Research* 77 (2010): 545–568. The "pessimism" quotation is on 547.

42. Barry Dennen, *My Life with Barbra: A Love Story* (Amherst, NY: Prometheus Books, 1997), 191.

43. Spada, *Streisand*, 200.

44. Barbra Streisand as told to Dixie Dean Harris, "I Was an Ugly Duckling," *Coronet*, March 1964, in *Diva: Barbra Streisand and the Making of a Superstar*, ed. Ethlie Ann Vare (New York: Boulevard Books, 1996), 24–25.

45. Ephron, "Private World of Barbra Streisand."

46. Rex Reed, "Color Barbra Very Bright," *New York Times*, March 27, 1966.

47. Ephron, "Private World of Barbra Streisand."

48. Polly Devlin, "Instant Barbra," *Vogue*, March 15, 1966.

49. "Barbra Bemoans Her Bad Press," September 29, 1968, available at *Barbra Streisand Archives*, http://barbra-archives.com/bjs_library/60s/bemoans_bad_press.html.

50. Chaim Potok, "The Barbra Streisand Nobody Knows," *Esquire*, Autumn 1982.

51. Edwards, *Streisand*, 223.

52. Kevin Sessums, "Queen of Tides," *Vanity Fair*, September 1991.

53. John Hallowell, "The Truth Game," *New York*, Sept. 9, 1968.

54. Considine, *Barbra Streisand*, 117–118.

55. Ettore Scola quoted in Considine, *Barbra Streisand*, 109.

56. Grover Lewis, "The Jeaning of Barbra Streisand," *Rolling Stone*, July 24, 1971.

57. Kael, "Teamwork," 183.

58. Celia Walden, "Barbra Streisand Interview," *Telegraph*, August 16, 2011.

59. Camille Paglia, "Brooklyn Nefertiti: Barbra Streisand," in *Vamps and Tramps* (New York: Vintage, 1994), 144.

60. Vincent Canby, "On a Clear Day," *New York Times*, June 18, 1970.

61. Spada, *Streisand*, 265.

62. John Simon, "Kid Stuff," *The Critic John Simon*, February 5, 1973, http://thecriticjohnsimon.com/reverse-angle/kid-stuff/.

63. Felicia Herman, "The Way She Really Is: Images of Jews and Women in the Films of Barbra Streisand," in *Talking Back: Images of Jewish Women in American Popular Culture*, ed. Joyce Antler (Hanover, NH: Brandeis University Press, 1998), 173.

6. Supervuman

1. Quoted in Jack Newfield, "Diva Democracy," *George*, November 1996.

2. William Norwich, "Barbra Streisand: Truth Has a Golden Voice," *Interview*, April 1993.

3. David E. Kaufman, *Jewhooing the Sixties: American Celebrity and Jewish Identity* (Waltham, MA: Brandeis University Press, 2012), 250–251.

4. Newfield, "Diva Democracy."

5. Camille Paglia, "Brooklyn Nefertiti: Barbra Streisand," in *Vamps and Tramps* (New York: Vintage, 1994), 142.

6. Michael Shnayerson, "The Way She Is," *Vanity Fair*, November 1994.

7. James Spada, *Streisand: Her Life* (New York: Crown, 1995), 75.

8. William Mann, *Hello, Gorgeous: Becoming Barbra Streisand* (New York: Houghton Mifflin Harcourt, 2012), 165.

9. Todd Gold, "Barbra Streisand: The Farewell Interview," *US*, October 9, 2000.

10. Anne Edwards, *Streisand: A Biography* (Boston: Little, Brown, 1997), 327.

11. Andy Tiemann, "The Barbra Streisand Litmus Test," in *Diva: Barbra Streisand and the Making of a Superstar*, ed. Ethlie Ann Vare (New York: Boulevard Books, 1996), 195–197.

12. Kaufman, *Jewhooing the Sixties*, 249.

13. Quoted in Howard M. Sachar, *A History of the Jews in America*. New York: Knopf, 1992, 835.

14. Quoted in Joyce Antler, *The Journey Home: Jewish Women and the American Century* (New York: Free Press, 1997), 260.

15. "Interview," *Playboy*, Oct. 1977.

16. Quoted in Harry Brod, *Superman Is Jewish? How Comic Book Superheroes Came to Serve Truth, Justice, and the Jewish-American Way* (New York: Free Press, 2012), 8.

17. Brod, *Superman Is Jewish?* 10.

18. Barbra Streisand, "Insight," *Elle*, November 1992.

19. Arthur Laurents, *Original Story By: A Memoir of Broadway and Hollywood* (New York: Knopf, 2000), 247–248.

20. Michael F. Callan, *Robert Redford: The Biography* (New York: Knopf, 2011), 190–192.

21. Edwards, *Streisand*, 334–335.

22. Callan, *Robert Redford*, 192.

23. Laurents, *Original Story By*, 272–273.

24. Callan, *Robert Redford*, 94.

25. Callan, *Robert Redford*, 195.

26. Christopher Andersen, *Barbra: The Way She Is* (New York: Morrow, 2006), 212.

27. Laurents, *Original Story By*, 278.

28. Kaufman, *Jewhooing the Sixties*, 241.

29. Manohla Dargis, "Barbra Streisand, at a Gala and in Memory," *New York Times*, April 23, 2013.

30. Pauline Kael, "Three," in *Deeper into Movies*, 246–247.

31. Vincent Canby, "The Way We Were," *New York Times*, October 18, 1973.

32. Andersen, *Barbra*, 221.

33. Newfield, "Diva Democracy."

34. Norwich, "Barbra Streisand."

35. Andersen, *Barbra*, 303.

36. Newfield, "Diva Democracy."

37. Michael Spector, "Anger and Regret in Aspen as Boycott Grows," *New York Times*, December 30, 1992.

38. Newfield, "Diva Democracy."

39. Tom Santopietro, *The Importance of Being Barbra* (New York: St. Martin's, 2006), 166.

40. Edwards, *Streisand*, 475–476.

41. Anne Taylor Fleming, "Peekaboo Power Suits," *New York Times*, January 28, 1993.

42. Paglia, "Brooklyn Nefertiti," 141.

43. Laurents, *Original Story By*, 246.

44. Michael Shnayerson, "The Way She Is," *Vanity Fair*, November 1994.

45. Barbra Streisand, "The Artist as Citizen," speech delivered at John F. Kennedy School of Government, Harvard University, February 3, 1995, available at http://www.barbrastreisand.com/us/statement/artist-citizen. See also Maureen Dowd, "Barbra the Speech Plays to a Packed House at Harvard," *New York Times*, February 4, 1995.

46. Frank Rich, "Barbra at Harvard," *New York Times*, February 9, 1995.

7. Shaygetz

1. James Spada, *Streisand: Her Life* (New York: Crown, 1995), 83.

2. Anne Edwards, *Streisand: A Biography* (Boston: Little, Brown, 1997), 461.

3. "Interview," *Playboy*, October 1977.

4. Spada, *Streisand*, 49–50.

5. William Mann, *Hello, Gorgeous: Becoming Barbra Streisand* (New York: Houghton Mifflin Harcourt, 2012), 88.

6. Barry Dennen, *My Life with Barbra: A Love Story* (Amherst, NY: Prometheus Books, 1997), 261.

7. Christopher Andersen, *Barbra: The Way She Is* (New York: Morrow, 2006), 73.

8. Shana Alexander, "A Born Loser's Success and Precarious Love," *Life*, May 22, 1964.

9. Alexander, "A Born Loser's Success and Precarious Love."

10. Barbra Streisand as told to Dixie Dean Harris, "I Was an Ugly Duckling," *Coronet*, March 1964, in *Diva: Barbra Streisand and the Making of a Superstar*, ed. Ethlie Ann Vare (New York: Boulevard Books, 1996), 24.

11. Bernard Weinraub, "Barbra Streisand, Still Not Pretty Enough," *New York Times*, November 13, 1996.

12. John Simon, "What's Up, Doc?," *Chris Tookey's Movie Film*

Review, http://www.movie-film-review.com/devfilm.asp?rtype=3& id=11802; Stanley Kauffmann, "Funny Girl," in *Figures of Light* (New York: Harper Colophon, 1971), 115.

13. Kauffmann, "Funny Girl," 115.

14. Evans, "From Barbra Streisand—The Last Word," *Cosmopolitan*, February 1974.

15. Henry Bial, *Acting Jewish: Negotiating Ethnicity on the American Stage and Screen* (Ann Arbor: University of Michigan Press, 2005), 86–87.

16. Manohla Dargis, "Barbra Streisand, at a Gala and in Memory," *New York Times*, April 23, 2013.

17. Ira Mothner, "Barbra," *Look*, October 15, 1968.

18. John Hallowell, "Funny Girl Goes West," *Life*, September 20, 1967.

19. Spada, *Streisand*, 396.

20. Spada, *Streisand*, 278.

21. Felicia Herman, "The Way She Really Is: Images of Jews and Women in the Films of Barbra Streisand," in *Talking Back: Images of Jewish Women in American Popular Culture*, ed. Joyce Antler (Hanover, NH: Brandeis University Press, 1998), 173.

22. Molly Haskell, "What Makes Streisand Queen of the Box Office?" *New York Times*, March 9, 1975.

23. Spada, *Streisand*, 84.

24. Edwards, *Streisand*, 518.

25. Camille Paglia, "Brooklyn Nefertiti: Barbra Streisand," in *Vamps and Tramps* (New York: Vintage, 1994), 143.

26. Andersen, *Barbra*, 178–179.

27. Andersen, *Barbra*, 144.

28. Edwards, *Streisand*, 142.

29. Spada, *Streisand*, 227.

30. Barbra Streisand, *My Passion for Design* (New York: Viking, 2010), 21.

31. Spada, *Streisand*, 196.

32. Andre Agassi, *Open: An Autobiography* (New York: Knopf, 2009), 174.

33. Spada, *Streisand*, 390.

34. Letty Cottin Pogrebin. *Deborah, Golda, and Me: Being Female and Jewish in America* (New York: Crown, 1991), 260.

35. Andersen, *Barbra*, 214.

8. Rediskovering Iugnt

1. Paul Grein, "Streisand's 20-Year Blitz," *Billboard*, April 16, 1983.

2. Shaun Considine, *Barbra Streisand: The Woman, the Myth, the Music* (New York: Delacorte, 1985), 63.

3. Gene Lees, *Singers and the Song* (New York: Oxford University Press, 1987), 115.

4. Grover Lewis, "The Jeaning of Barbra Streisand," *Rolling Stone*, June 24, 1971.

5. "Interview," *Playboy*, October 1977.

6. Considine, *Barbra Streisand*, 100.

7. Glenn Gould, "Streisand as Schwartzkopf," *High Fidelity*, May 1976, in *Diva: Barbra Streisand and the Making of a Superstar*, ed. Ethlie Ann Vare (New York: Boulevard Books, 1996), 41.

8. Considine, *Barbra Streisand*, 154–155.

9. Roger Ames, interview by author, July 31, 2014.

10. Ann Fadiman, "Barbra Puts Her Career on the Line with 'Yentl,'" *Life*, December 1983.

11. Nancy Griffin and Kim Masters, *Hit and Run: How Jon Peters and Peter Guber Took Sony for a Ride in Hollywood* (New York: Touchstone, 1996), 11–28.

12. Anne Edwards, *Streisand: A Biography* (Boston: Little, Brown, 1997), 353; James Spada, *Streisand: Her Life* (New York: Crown, 1995), 314.

13. Andrew Smith quoted in Considine, *Barbra Streisand*, 275.

14. Judy Wieder, "Barbra Streisand Lets It All Hang Out," 1974, available at the Barbra Streisand Archives, http://barbra-archives.com/bjs_library/70s/lets-it-all-hang-out.html.

15. Christopher Andersen, *Barbra: The Way She Was* (New York: Morrow, 2006), 233.

16. Andersen, *Barbra*, 258–259.

17. Edwards, *Streisand*, 359.

18. Alison J. Waldman, *The Barbra Streisand Scrapbook* (New York: Citadel Press, 1995), 230.

19. Considine, *Barbra Streisand*, 221–222.

20. Marie Brenner, "Collision on the Rainbow Road," *New Times*, January 24, 1975.

21. Considine, *Barbra Streisand*, 232.

22. "Interview."

23. Spada, *Streisand*, 369.

24. "Barbra Streisand: For the First Time She Talks about Her Lover, Her Power, Her Future," *People*, April 26, 1976.

25. Lawrence Grobel, "Barbra Streisand: 'I'm Just Beginning to Accept Myself,'" *Long Island Newsday*, October 16, 1977.

26. Brenner, "Collision on the Rainbow Road."

27. Frank Pierson, "My Battles with Barbra and Jon," *New York Magazine*, November 15, 1976.

28. "Interview."

29. Considine, *Barbra Streisand*, 250.

30. John Simon, "A Star Is Born," *Chris Tookey's Movie Film Review*, http://www.movie-film-review.com/devharsh.asp?act=2&param=887

31. Spada, *Streisand*, 366.

32. Andersen, *Barbra*, 252.

33. Pauline Kael, "Contempt for the Audience," in *When the Lights Go Down* (New York: Holt, Rinehart and Winston, 1980), 240–244.

34. Spada, *Streisand*, 367.

35. Waldman, *Barbra Streisand Scrapbook*, 228.

36. Molly Haskell, "What Makes Streisand Queen of the Box Office?" *New York Times*, March 9, 1975.

37. Spada, *Streisand*, 323–324.

38. Tom Santopietro, *The Importance of Being Barbra* (New York: St. Martin's, 2006), 92.

39. Considine, *Barbra Streisand*, 215.

40. Grobel, "Barbra Streisand."

41. Spada, *Streisand*, 332.

42. Grobel, "Barbra Streisand."

43. "Interview."

44. Haskell, "What Makes Streisand Queen of the Box Office?"

45. Oprah Winfrey, "Oprah Talks to Barbra Streisand," *O, the Oprah Magazine*, October 2006.

46. Jacob Bernstein, "Barbra Streisand, A Voice to Be Reckoned With," *New York Times*, September 12, 2014.

9. Macher

1. Jacob Bernstein, "Barbra Streisand: A Voice to Be Reckoned With," *New York Times*, September 12, 2014.

2. Sander Gilman, *The Jew's Body* (New York: Routledge, 1991), 192.

3. Chris Andersen, *The Way She Is* (New York: William Morrow, 2006), 194–196.

4. Camille Paglia, "My Night with Streisand," *New Republic*, July 18, 1994.

5. Allison J. Waldman, *The Barbra Streisand Scrapbook* (New York: Citadel, 1995), 230.

6. Anne Edwards, *Streisand: A Biography* (Boston: Little, Brown, 1997), 137.

7. Kevin Sessums, "Queen of Tides," *Vanity Fair*, September 1991.

8. Chaim Potok, "The Barbra Streisand Nobody Knows," *Esquire*, Autumn 1982.

9. "Interview," *Playboy*, October 1977.

10. Pauline Kael, "Collaboration and Resistance," in *Deeper into Movies* (Boston: Atlantic Monthly Press, 1973), 432.

11. Michael Shnayerson, "The Way She Is," *Vanity Fair*, November 1994.

12. J. Curtis Sandburn, "Conversation with a Superstar," *Harper's Bazaar*, November 1983.

13. Stephen Holden, "Barbra Streisand: 'Don't Get Me Wrong,'" *New York Times*, December 22, 1991.

14. Michael F. Callan, *Robert Redford: The Biography* (New York: Knopf, 2011), 195.

15. "Interview," *Playboy*.

16. James Spada, *Streisand: Her Life* (New York: Crown, 1995), 332.

17. Pauline Kael, "Talent Isn't Enough," in *Reeling* (New York: Warner Books, 1976), 605–613.

18. Potok, "The Barbra Streisand Nobody Knows."

19. Edwards, *Streisand*, 302.

20. Shaun Considine, *Barbra Streisand: The Women, the Myth, the Music* (New York: Delacorte, 1985), 298.

21. Spada, *Streisand*, 401.

22. Anne Fadiman, "Barbra Puts Her Career on the Line with 'Yentl,'" *Life*, December 1983.

23. Potok, "The Barbra Streisand Nobody Knows."

24. Andersen, *Barbra*, 282.

25. "Interview," *Playboy.*

26. Rabbi Daniel Lapin, "Why the Streisand I Once Knew Was Never Obscene," *The Barbra Streisand Forum*, posted October 13, 2006, by Valin, thebarbrastreisandforum89123.yuku.com/topic/1185#.VRnhouGZOJ8.

27. Fadiman, "Barbra Puts Her Career on the Line with 'Yentl.'"

28. Fadiman, "Barbra Puts Her Career on the Line with 'Yentl.'"

29. Andersen, *Barbra*, 281.

30. Pauline Kael, "The Perfectionist," in *The Age of Movies: Selected Writings of Pauline Kael*, ed. Sanford Schwartz (New York: New Library of America, 2011), 735–736.

31. Edwards, *Streisand*, 414.

32. Arthur Laurents, *Original Story By: A Memoir of Broadway and Hollywood* (New York: Knopf, 2000), 234.

33. Kael, "Perfectionist," 731.

34. Jeanette Kupfermann, "Streisand's New Direction," *Sunday Times Magazine* [London], March 4, 1984.

35. Holden, "Streisand."

36. See Mark Spilka, "Empathy with the Devil: Isaac Bashevis Singer and the Deadly Pleasures of Misogyny," *NOVEL: A Forum on Fiction* 31 (1998): 430–444.

37. Isaac Bashevis Singer, "I. B. Singer Talks to I. B. Singer about the Movie 'Yentl,'" *New York Times*, January 29, 1984.

38. Considine, *Barbra Streisand*, 314.

39. Jeff Jarvis, "Yentl Shmentl Says Hollywood," *People*, March 12, 1984.

40. Jarvis, "Yentl Shmentl Says Hollywood."

41. Andersen, *Barbra*, 287.

42. Hilary de Vries, "Streisand, the Storyteller," *Los Angeles Times Magazine*, December 8, 1991.

43. Kevin Sessums, "Queen of Tides," *Vanity Fair*, September 1991.

44. Edwards, *Streisand*, 445.

45. Sessums, "Queen of Tides."

46. Eric A. Goldman, *The American Jewish Story through Cinema* (Austin: University of Texas Press, 2013), 149.

47. Owen Glieberman, "Prince of Tides," *Entertainment Weekly*, December 20, 1991.

48. "Interview," *Playboy*.

49. Spada, *Streisand*, 465.

50. Janet Maslin, "Prince of Tides," *New York Times*, December 25, 1991.

51. Andersen, *Barbra*, 322.

52. Barbra Streisand as told to Gregg Kilday, "Barbra Streisand on 'The Normal Heart': 'I Tried Very Hard to Get It Made,'" *Hollywood Reporter*, April 9, 2014.

53. Edwards, *Streisand*, 516.

54. Bernard Weinraub, "Barbra Streisand, Still Not Pretty Enough," *New York Times*, November 13, 1996.

55. Edwards, *Streisand*, 19.

56. Tom Mack, "Henry James and Barbra Streisand: The Permutation of Beauty," unpublished paper available online at http://www.usca.edu/english/pdf/HenryJames_%20BarbraStreisand.pdf.

57. Lawrence Grobel, "Barbra Streisand: 'I'm Just Beginning to Accept Myself,'" *Long Island Newsday*, October 16, 1977.

58. Barry Dennen, *My Life with Barbra: A Love Story* (Amherst, NY: Prometheus Books, 1997), 193.

59. Weinraub, "Barbra Streisand, Still Not Pretty Enough."

60. Janet Maslin, "The Mirror Has Two Faces," *New York Times*, November 15, 1996.

10. Tsufridnkeit

1. "Interview," *Playboy*, October 1977.

2. James Spada, *Streisand: Her Life* (New York: Crown, 1995), 237–238.

3. Shaun Considine, *Barbra Streisand: The Woman, the Myth, the Music* (New York: Delacorte, 1985), 159.

4. Camille Paglia, "Brooklyn Nefertiti: Barbra Streisand," in *Vamps and Tramps* (New York: Vintage, 1994), 143.

5. Hilary de Vries, "Streisand, the Storyteller," *Los Angeles Times Magazine*, December 8, 1991.

6. J. Curtis Sandburn, "Conversation with a Superstar," *Harper's Bazaar*, November 1983.

7. Stephen Holden, "Barbra Streisand: 'This Is the Music I Love," *New York Times*, November 10, 1985.

8. Alan Jackson, "Queen B," *Sunday Times Magazine* [London], November 19, 2005.

9. Tom Santopietro, *The Importance of Being Barbra* (New York: St. Martin's, 2006), 139.

10. Michael Shnayerson, "The Way She Is," *Vanity Fair*, November 1994.

11. Anne Edwards, *Streisand: A Biography* (Boston: Little, Brown, 1997), 501.

12. Jon Pareles, "Local Girl Makes Good," *New York Times*, June 22, 1994.

13. Quoted in Chris Andersen, *Barbra: The Way She Is* (New York: Morrow, 2006), 359.

14. Camille Paglia, "My Night with Streisand," *New Republic*, July 18, 1994.

15. Edwards, *Streisand*, 499.

16. Paglia, "My Night with Streisand."

17. Quoted in Gene Lees, *Singers and the Song* (New York: Oxford University Press, 1987), 112.

18. Pareles, "Local Girl Makes Good."

19. Paglia, "My Night with Barbra."

20. Pareles, "Local Girl Makes Good."

21. Edwards, *Streisand*, 499.

22. Letty Cottin Pogrebin, *Deborah, Golda, and Me: Being Female and Jewish in America* (New York: Crown, 1991), 260.

23. Holly Sorensen, "The Way They Are," *McCall's*, March 1998; Sheryl Berk, "The Luckiest People in the World," *McCall's*, December 1999.

24. Andersen, *Barbra*, 375.

25. Berk, "Luckiest People in the World."

26. Sorensen, "The Way They Are."

27. Sorensen, "The Way They Are."

28. Sorensen, "The Way They Are."

29. Berk, "Luckiest People in the World."

30. Berk, "Luckiest People in the World."

31. Claudia Dreifus, "At Home: With Barbra Streisand," *New York Times*, November 11, 1997.

32. Claudia Dreifus, "The Way She Is," *Mirabella*, May 1998.

33. Berk, "Luckiest People in the World."

34. Sorensen, "The Way They Are."

35. Shnayerson, "The Way She Is."

36. Bernard Weinraub, "Barbra Streisand, Still Not Pretty Enough," *New York Times*, November 13, 1996.

37. Jeanne Lee, "If I See Red, I Sell Quickly," *Fortune*, June 21, 1999.

38. Barbra Streisand, *My Passion for Design* (New York: Viking, 2010), 286.

39. Lawrence Grobel, "Barbra Streisand: 'I'm Just Beginning to Accept Myself,'" *Long Island Newsday*, October 16, 1977.

40. Barbra Streisand, *My Passion for Design*, 26.

41. Streisand, *My Passion for Design*, 30–31.

42. Andersen, *Barbra*, 352–353.

43. Streisand, *My Passion for Design*, 24.

44. Frank Pierson, "My Battles with Barbra and Jon," *New York*, November 15, 1976.

45. Paglia, "My Night with Streisand."

46. Edwards, *Streisand*, 286.

47. Andersen, *Barbra*, 127.

48. Streisand, *My Passion for Design*, 30–31.

49. Todd Gold, "Barbra Streisand: The Farewell Interview," *US*, October 9, 2000.

50. Weinraub, "Barbra Streisand, Still Not Pretty Enough."

51. Stephen Holden, "Barbra Streisand: 'Don't Get Me Wrong,'" *New York Times*, December 22, 1991.

52. Alan Jackson, "Queen B.," *Sunday Times Magazine* [London], November 19, 2005.

53. Manohla Dargis, "Opposites Detract: Jews vs. Bluebloods, *New York Times*, December 22, 2005.

54. Rabbi Daniel Lapin, "Jews Have Debased Jewish and American Culture," rense.com, January 24, 2005, http://www.rense .com/general62/deb.htm.

55. Stephen Holden, "A Sentimental Journey," *New York Times*, October 12, 2012.

56. Molly Haskell, "What Makes Streisand Queen of the Box Office?" *New York Times*, March 9, 1975.

57. Carey Goldberg, "Barbra, Gorgeous, You Have a Shrine," *New York Times*, May 21, 1996.

58. Wayne Koestenbaum, "Streisand Sings Stravinsky," in *Blue Stranger with Mosaic Background* (New York: Turtle Press, 2012), 53–54.

59. Streisand, *My Passion for Design*, 292.

60. Quoted by Jim Grissom in "Barbra Streisand: The Ideal Eucharist, Part One," jamesgrissom (blog), November 13, 2012, james grissom.blogspot.com/2012/11/barbra-streisand-ideal-eucharist -part.html.

61. Marcy Sheiner, "Maybe I Could Be—Like Barbra— Gawjus!" *Lilith*, Spring 1996.

62. Santopietro, 147–148.

63. Edwards, *Streisand*, 500.

64. Felicia Herman, "The Way She Really Is: Images of Jews and Women in the Films of Barbra Streisand," in *Talking Back: Images of Jewish Women in Popular Culture*, ed. Joyce Antler (Hanover, NH: Brandeis University Press, 1998), 190.

SELECTED BIBLIOGRAPHY

Adler, Renata. "Screen: Funny Girl." *New York Times*, September 20, 1968.

Agassi, Andre. *Open: An Autobiography.* New York: Alfred A. Knopf, 2009.

Alexander, Shana. "A Born Loser's Success and Precarious Love." *Life*, May 22, 1964.

Andersen, Christopher. *Barbra: The Way She Is.* New York: William Morrow, 2006.

"Barbra Bemoans Her Bad Press." September 29, 1968. Available at *Barbra Streisand Archives*, http://barbra-archives.com/bjs_library/60s/bemoans_bad_press.html.

"Barbra Streisand." *Inside the Actors Studio.* Hosted by James Lipton. Bravo. Recorded September 8, 2003; broadcast March 21, 2004.

"Barbra Streisand: For the First Time She Talks about Her Lover, Her Power, Her Future." *People*, April 26, 1976.

"Barbra Streisand: The Girl Who Catches the Light." *Vogue*, April 1966.

"Barbra Streisand Couldn't Have Posted a More Perfect 1st Instagram Photo." Aol.com, Lifestyle, August 8, 2014. http://www.stylelist.com/read/barbra-streisand-couldnt-have-posted-a-more-perfect-1st-instagr/.

Berger, Joseph. "A Streisand Encore, 5 Decades Overdue." *New York Times*, May 9, 2012.

Berk, Sheryl. "The Luckiest People in the World." *McCall's*. December 1999.

Bernstein, Jacob. "Barbra Streisand, a Voice to Be Reckoned With." *New York Times*, September 12, 2014.

Brenner, Marie. "Collision on the Rainbow Road." *New Times*, January 24, 1975.

Callan, Michael F. *Robert Redford: The Biography*. New York: Alfred A. Knopf, 2011.

Canby, Vincent. "Screen: The Way We Were." *New York Times*. October 18, 1973.

Carlson, Peter. "*Architectural Digest* Visits Barbra Streisand." *Architectural Digest*, May 1978.

Considine, Shaun. *Barbra Streisand: The Woman, the Myth, the Music*. New York: Delacorte, 1985.

Dargis, Manohla. "Barbra Streisand, at a Gala and in Memory." *New York Times*, April 23, 2013.

———. "Opposites Detract: Jews vs. Bluebloods." Review of *Meet the Fockers*. *New York Times*, December 22, 2004.

Darrach, Brad. "Celebration of a Father." *People*, December 12, 1983.

Dennen, Barry. *My Life with Barbra: A Love Story*. Amherst, New York: Prometheus Books, 1997.

Devlin, Polly. "Instant Barbra." *Vogue*, March 15, 1966.

de Vries, Hilary. "Streisand, the Storyteller." *Los Angeles Times Magazine*, December 8, 1991.

Dowd, Maureen. "Barbra the Speech Plays to a Packed House at Harvard." *New York Times*, February 4, 1994.

Dreifus, Claudia. "At Home: With Barbra Streisand." *New York Times*, November 11, 1997.

———. "The Way She Is." *Mirabella*, May 1998.

Du Brow, Rick. "Song Stylist Streisand Saves Keefe Brasselle TV Opener." Column, June 26, 1963. Reprinted at *Barbra Streisand Archives*, http://barbra-archives.com/tv/60s/keefe_brasselle_show _streisand.html.

Edwards, Anne. *Streisand: A Biography.* Boston: Little, Brown, 1997.

Ephron, Nora. "The Private World of Barbra Streisand." *Good Housekeeping*, April 1969.

Erens, Patricia. *The Jew in American Cinema.* Bloomington: Indiana University Press, 1984.

Evans, Peter. "From Barbra Streisand—The Last Word." *Cosmopolitan*, February 1974.

Fadiman, Anne. "Barbra Puts Her Career on the Line with 'Yentl.'" *Life*, December 1983.

Fleming, Ann Taylor. "Peekaboo Power Suits." *New York Times*, January 28, 1993.

Gilman, Sander. *The Jew's Body.* New York: Routledge, 1991.

"The Girl." *Time*, April 10, 1964.

Gold, Todd. "Barbra Streisand: The Farewell Interview." *US*, October 9, 2000.

Goldberg, Carey. "Barbra, Gorgeous, You Have a Shrine." *New York Times*, May 21, 1996.

Goldman, Eric A. *The American Jewish Story through Cinema.* Austin: University of Texas Press, 2013.

Greene, Milton. "In Their Tense, Demanding World, Alone Is Beautiful." *McCall's*, January 1970.

Grein, Paul. "Streisand's 20-Year Blitz." *Billboard*, April 16, 1983.

Grobel, Lawrence. "Barbra Streisand: 'I'm Just Beginning to Accept Myself.'" *Long Island Newsday*, October 16, 1977.

Hamill, Pete. "Barbra the Great: Talented Girl on a Triumphal March." *Cosmopolitan*, February 1968.

———. "Goodbye Brooklyn, Hello Fame." *Saturday Evening Post*, July 27, 1963.

———. *Why Sinatra Matters.* Boston: Little, Brown, 1998.

Herman, Felicia. "The Way She Really Is: Images of Jews and Women in the Films of Barbra Streisand." In *Talking Back: Images of Jewish Women in American Popular Culture*, ed. Joyce Antler, 171–190. Hanover, MA: Brandeis University Press, 1998.

Hallowell, John. "Funny Girl Goes West." *Life*, September 20, 1967.

———. "The Truth Game." *New York Magazine*, September 9, 1968.

Haskell, Molly. "What Makes Streisand Queen of the Box Office?" *New York Times*, March 9, 1975.

Holden, Stephen. "Barbra Streisand: 'Don't Get Me Wrong.'" *New York Times*, December 22, 1991.

———. "A Sentimental Journey." *New York Times*, October 12, 2012.

"Interview." Interview by Lawrence Grobel. *Playboy*, October 1977.

Jackson, Alan. "Queen B." *Sunday Times Magazine* [London], November 19, 2005.

Jaffe, Rona. "Barbra Streisand: 'Sadie, Sadie, Married Lady . . . .'" *Cosmopolitan*, April 1969.

Kael, Pauline. "A Bagel with a Bite Out of It." In *Deeper into Movies*, 327–333. Boston: Atlantic Monthly Press, 1973.

———. "Bravo." In *Going Steady*, 161–166. New York: Bantam, 1971.

———. "Collaboration and Resistance." In *Deeper into Movies*, 426–433. Boston: Atlantic Monthly Press, 1973.

———."Contempt for the Audience." In *When the Lights Go Down*, 240–244. New York: Holt, Rinehart and Winston, 1980.

———. "Keep Going." In *Deeper into Movies*, 80–85. Atlantic Monthly Press, 1973.

———. "The Perfectionist." In *The Age of Movies: Selected Writings of Pauline Kael*, ed. Sanford Schwartz, 730–736. New Library of America, 2011.

———. "Talent Isn't Enough." In *Reeling*, 605–613. New York: Warner Books, 1976.

———. "Teamwork." In *Deeper into Movies*, 183–185. Boston: Atlantic Monthly Press, 1973.

———. "Three." In *Reeling*, 243–247. New York: Warner Books, 1976.

Kauffmann, Stanley. "Funny Girl." In *Figures of Light*, 114–115. New York: Harper Colophon, 1971.

Kaufman, David E. *Jewhooing the Sixties: American Celebrity and Jewish Identity*. Waltham, MA: Brandeis University Press, 2012.

Koestenbaum, Wayne. *Blue Stranger with Mosaic Background*. New York: Turtle Point, 2012.

Kupfermann, Jeanette. "Streisand's New Direction." *Sunday Times Magazine* [London], March 4, 1984.

Laurents, Arthur. *Original Story By: A Memoir of Broadway and Hollywood*. New York: Alfred A. Knopf, 2000.

Lee, Jeanne. "If I See Red, I Sell Quickly." *Fortune*, June 21, 1999.

Lewis, Emory. "Bravos for Barbra." *Cue Magazine*, December 26, 1963.

Lewis, Grover. "The Jeaning of Barbra Streisand." *Rolling Stone*, June 24, 1971.

Lurie, Diana. "'They All Come Thinking I Can't Be That Great.'" *Life*, March 18, 1966.

Mack, Tom. "Henry James and Barbra Streisand: The Permutation of Beauty." Unpublished paper available at http://www.usca.edu/english/pdf/HenryJames_%20BarbraStreisand.pdf.

Mann, William. *Hello, Gorgeous: Becoming Barbra Streisand*. New York: Houghton Mifflin Harcourt, 2012.

Michaelson, Herb. "Interview with Judy Davis, Vocal Coach." April 4, 1964. Available at *Barbra Streisand Archives*, http://barbra-archives.com/bjs_library/60s/judy_davis_story_1964.html.

Miller, Cheryl. "Six Artists Are Honored at Kennedy Center." *New York Times*, December 7, 2008.

Morgenstern, Joseph. "Superstar: The Streisand Story." *Newsweek*, January 5, 1970.

Newfield, Jack. "Diva Democracy." *George*, November 1996.

Norwich, William. "Barbra Streisand: Truth Has a Golden Voice." *Interview*, April 1993.

Paglia, Camille. "Brooklyn Nefertiti: Barbra Streisand." In *Vamps and Tramps*, 141–145. New York: Vintage, 1994.

———. "My Night with Streisand." *New Republic*, July 18, 1994.

Pareles, Jon. "Local Girl Makes Good, Sings. *New York Times*, June 22, 1994.

Pierson, Frank. "My Battles with Barbra and Jon." *New York Magazine*, November 15, 1976.

Pogrebin, Letty Cottin. *Deborah, Golda, and Me: Being Female and Jewish in America*. New York: Crown, 1991.

Potok, Chaim. "The Barbra Streisand Nobody Knows." *Esquire*, Autumn 1982.

Reed, Rex. "Color Barbra Very Bright." *New York Times*, March 27, 1966.

Rich, Frank. "Barbra at Harvard." *New York Times*, February 9, 1995.

Robbins, Jerome. "Barbara Streisand." *McCall's*, October 1966.

Rosenfield, Paul. "Barbra's New Direction." *Ladies Home Journal*, February 1992.

Sandburn, J. Curtis. "Conversation with a Superstar." *Harper's Bazaar*, November 1983.

Santopietro, Tom. *The Importance of Being Barbra*. New York: St. Martin's, 2006.

Schiller, Lawrence. "Who Am I Anyway?" *Life*, January 9, 1970.

Sessums, Kevin. "Queen of Tides." *Vanity Fair*, September 1991.

Sheiner, Marcy. "Maybe I Could Be—Like Barbra—Gawjus!" *Lilith*, Spring 1996.

Shnayerson, Michael. "The Way She Is." *Vanity Fair*, November 1994.

Simon, John. "Kid Stuff." *The Critic John Simon*. February 5, 1973. http://thecriticjohnsimon.com/reverse-angle/kid-stuff/.

———. "Review: A Star Is Born." *Chris Tookey's Movie Film Review*. http://www.movie-film-review.com/devharsh.asp?act=2&param=887.

———. "Review: On a Clear Day." *Chris Tookey's Movie Film Review*. http://www.movie-film-review.com/devharsh.asp?act=2&param=887.

———. "Review: What's Up Doc?" *Chris Tookey's Movie Film Review*. http://www.movie-film-review.com/devharsh.asp?act=2&param=887.

Singer, Isaac Bashevis. "I. B. Singer Talks to I. B. Singer about the Movie 'Yentl.'" *New York Times*, January 29, 1984.

Sochen, June. "From Sophie Tucker to Barbra Streisand." In *Talking Back: Images of Jewish Women in American Popular Culture*, ed. Joyce Antler, 68–84. Hanover, NH: Brandeis University Press, 1998.

Sorensen, Holly. "The Way They Are." *McCall's*, March 1998.

Spada, James. *Streisand: Her Life*. New York: Crown, 1995.

Spector, Michael. "Anger and Regret in Aspen as Boycott Grows." *New York Times*, December 30, 1992.

Stang, Joanne. "She Couldn't Be Medium." *New York Times*, April 5, 1964.

Steinem, Gloria. "Barbra Streisand Talks about Her Million Dollar Baby." *Ladies Home Journal*, August 1966.

Streisand, Barbra. "Insight." *Elle*, November 1992.

———. *My Passion for Design*. New York: Viking, 2010.

Talese, Gay. "Frank Sinatra Has a Cold." *Esquire*, April 1966.

"Talk of the Town." *New Yorker*, May 19, 1962.

Tommasini, Anthony. "Streisand's Fine Instrument and Classic Instinct." *New York Times*, September 24, 2009.

Vare, Ethlie Ann, ed. *Diva: Barbra Streisand and the Making of a Superstar*. New York: Boulevard Books, 1996.

Viladas, Pilar. "*Architectural Digest* Visits Barbra Streisand." *Architectural Digest*, December 1993.

Walden, Celia. "Barbra Streisand Interview." *Telegraph*, August 16, 2011.

Waldman, Alison J. *The Barbra Streisand Scrapbook*. New York: Citadel, 1995.

Weinraub, Bernard. "Barbra Streisand, Still Not Pretty Enough." *New York Times*, November 13, 1996.

Wieder, Judy. "Barbra Streisand Lets It All Hang Out." 1974. Available at *Barbra Streisand Archives*, http://barbra-archives.com/bjs_library/70s/lets-it-all-hang-out.html.

Wilson, John S. "Barbra Streisand's Free Sing-In Jams Sheep Meadow in the Park." *New York Times*, June 18, 1967.

Winfrey, Oprah. "Oprah Talks to Barbra Streisand." *O, the Oprah Magazine*, October 2006.

ACKNOWLEDGMENTS

Did you talk with Barbra Streisand? That is the question I am always asked immediately when people hear I have written a book about Streisand. The answer is "No." There are reasons for that. For one thing, this is not a full-scale biography of Streisand. It is a biography of the metaphor of Streisand and a personal interpretation of her life and work. I didn't feel an interview was necessary. For another, Streisand is, as a reader can see from the text, a notoriously prickly individual whom one approaches with caution, and I was gun-shy. Marcy Sheiner, a Streisand fanatic, wrote in the Jewish woman's magazine *Lilith* about a chance encounter with her heroine in, of all places, a Howard Johnson's restaurant in Tarrytown, New York. As she gently touched Streisand's arm (a grave mistake) with both trepidation and numb awe, and burbled, "I don't want to bother you, but . . . ," Streisand wheeled on her and "spat out," "Why don't you just cool it?" Sheiner says she cried for eight hours. No one wants to be in front of that bazooka, even if one can appreciate that having given us her life, Streisand doesn't

269

feel she owes us her autograph or pleasantries. On the other hand, the critic Pauline Kael, a longtime booster who reluctantly excoriated Streisand in a review of *Funny Lady*, said she received a warm and considerate phone call from Streisand commiserating with Kael for feeling the necessity to deliver that lashing. Streisand can be complicated that way. Last, it is highly unlikely Streisand would have consented to an interview.

Not having spoken to Streisand, then, I must acknowledge the interviewers who did, especially Lawrence Grobel, whose *Playboy* interview is a trove; the biographers who researched her life, particularly Christopher Andersen, Shaun Considine, Anne Edwards, William Mann, Tom Santopietro, and James Spada; and the journalists who provided an ongoing chronicle of her life. Any Streisand scholar must acknowledge the Barbra Streisand Archives website and its proprietor, Matt Howe, without whom Streisand work would be vastly more difficult. It and he are inestimable.

I also owe an enormous debt of gratitude to Steve Zipperstein, an exceptional scholar and friend, who recruited me for this project and didn't flinch when I proposed Streisand as my subject, and substantial debts to my friends Elizabeth Bassine, who read and commented on the manuscript, and Roger Ames, an extraordinary composer and music teacher, who explained the vicissitudes of music to me and helped me appreciate Streisand's gift; to another beloved friend, Craig Hoffman, who also read the manuscript and who has always been unstinting in his enthusiasm and his concern over too many years for either of us to want to remember; to the librarians, Francine Lane, Corrine Page, and Meghan Pease, at the Amagansett Free Library, in my little village, who filled without complaint my many, many requests for books; to my agent, Joy Harris, who takes care of the things I cannot; to Lawrence Schiller for generously giving me permission to use his beautiful photograph as the frontispiece; and, once again, to my daughters, Laurel and Tänne, and my son-in-law, Braden, for their encouragement, support, belief, and love. And to Christina.

All the errors are mine. All the blessings are theirs.

INDEX

JEWISH LIVES is a major series of interpretive
biography designed to illuminate the imprint of Jewish
figures upon literature, religion, philosophy, politics, cultural and
economic life, and the arts and sciences. Subjects are paired with
authors to elicit lively, deeply informed books that explore the
range and depth of Jewish experience
from antiquity through the present.

Jewish Lives is a partnership of Yale University Press
and the Leon D. Black Foundation.

Ileene Smith is editorial director. Anita Shapira and
Steven J. Zipperstein are series editors.

PUBLISHED TITLES INCLUDE:

Ben-Gurion: Father of Modern Israel, by Anita Shapira
Bernard Berenson: A Life in the Picture Trade, by Rachel Cohen
Sarah: The Life of Sarah Bernhardt, by Robert Gottlieb
Leonard Bernstein: An American Musician, by Allen Shawn
Léon Blum: Prime Minister, Socialist, Zionist, by Pierre Birnbaum
Louis D. Brandeis: American Prophet, by Jeffrey Rosen
David: The Divided Heart, by David Wolpe
Moshe Dayan: Israel's Controversial Hero, by Mordechai Bar-On
Benjamin Disraeli: The Novel Politician, by David Cesarani
Einstein: His Space and Times, by Steven Gimbel
Becoming Freud: The Making of a Psychoanalyst, by Adam Phillips
Emma Goldman: Revolution as a Way of Life, by Vivian Gornick
Hank Greenberg: The Hero Who Didn't Want to Be One,
    by Mark Kurlansky
Peggy Guggenheim: The Shock of the Modern, by Francine Prose
Lillian Hellman: An Imperious Life, by Dorothy Gallagher
Jabotinsky: A Life, by Hillel Halkin
Jacob: Unexpected Patriarch, by Yair Zakovitch
Franz Kafka: The Poet of Shame and Guilt, by Saul Friedländer
Rav Kook: Mystic in a Time of Revolution, by Yehudah Mirsky
Primo Levi: The Matter of a Life, by Berel Lang
Groucho Marx: The Comedy of Existence, by Lee Siegel
Moses Mendelssohn: Sage of Modernity, by Shmuel Feiner
Proust: The Search, by Benjamin Taylor
Walter Rathenau: Weimar's Fallen Statesman, by Shulamit Volkov
Mark Rothko: Toward the Light in the Chapel, by Annie Cohen-Solal
Solomon: The Lure of Wisdom, by Steven Weitzman
Barbra Streisand: Redefining Beauty, Femininity, and Power,
    by Neal Gabler
Leon Trotsky: A Revolutionary's Life, by Joshua Rubenstein

FORTHCOMING TITLES INCLUDE: